The Galleys at Lepanto

THE
GALLEYS
—AT—
LEPANTO

Jack Beeching

Charles Scribner's Sons
New York

Library of Congress Cataloging in Publication Data
Beeching, Jack.
  The galleys at Lepanto.

  Bibliography: p.
  Includes index.
  1. Lepanto, Battle of, 1571.   I. Title.
DR 516.B43   1983   909'.5   83-3201
ISBN 0-684-17918-0

Printed in the United States of America.

Contents

Illustrations

EUROPE AND THE MEDITERRANEAN IN 1571

Spanish Habsburg possessions

Austrian Habsburg possessions

Venetian territory

Ottoman Empire and Protectorates

(Figures in brackets: year conquered or acquired)

Vienna

TRANSYLVANIA
(1541)

HUNGARY
(1528)

MOLDAVIA
(1504)

OTTOMAN

BLACK SEA

PLES

(1459)

ALBANIA

(1478)

CORFU

Constantinople
(1458)

(1461)

EMPIRE

Bursa
(1326)

Lepanto NEGROPONT

CEPHALONIA

CHIOS
(1566)

ANATOLIA

ZANTE MOREA
(1540)

STRAITS OF
MESSINA

Modon

NAXOS
(1566)

RHODES
(1522)

(1514-17)

CYPRUS
(1571)

Famagusta

SYRIA

CRETE

EGYPT
(1517)

Alexandria

RED SEA

1
Gerónimo

The battle of Actium decided the empire of the world. The battle
of Lepanto arrested the greatness of the Turk.
FRANCIS BACON: *Of True Greatness of Kingdoms and States*

When asked to describe the private life of the Emperor Charles V, the
Venetian ambassador wrote home, confidentially, 'Charles is by
nature sensual, but never guilty of a violent or a dishonourable act.'
When a bachelor he had kept a mistress – a Flemish girl called Johanna
van der Gheest, who was the daughter of a tapestry weaver. But once
married, Charles stayed faithful to his Empress, Isabella. Once or
twice since her death he might have lapsed from grace, but any affairs
had been managed with such discretion that even busybodies at the
court could never be quite sure.

Charles V ruled an immense jigsaw of possessions, extending from
Tunis to Patagonia – the largest empire of modern times. He had
readily acknowledged Margaret – his daughter by Johanna van der
Gheest. Margaret became like another son to him: deep-voiced,
coarse-featured, large of limb, and popular in Flanders, where eventually she acted as Regent. Charles V's legitimate heir, Prince Philip –
the future King Philip II of Spain – was all that could be hoped for in a
son: industrious, intelligent, conscientious, but perhaps a little too
much in earnest.

'There is more at the back of his head,' a papal legate once observed
of Charles V, 'than appears in his face.' Portraits of the Emperor
sometimes make him look grandiose, but in fact he was small and
ugly, with the protuberant chin of his family, the Habsburgs, and a
mouth always half-open; blemishes that he hid under a short beard.
He was fond of flowers, particularly carnations – after capturing Tunis
he sent back to Europe the first root of an Indian pink. Charles V was

passionately fond of music, and took the imperial choir with him, even on campaign.

A resolute Christian as well as a brave soldier, Charles tried to engage only in defensive wars – an Italian general once said that the presence on the battlefield of the Emperor himself was worth 25,000 infantry. He was essentially a simple and a good man. His favourite reading was romances of chivalry, and he liked to think of himself as a knight errant, chosen by God to defend Catholic Europe against her chief enemies – the acquisitive Lutheran princes to the north, the ever present Turkish threat from the east.

And yet, *by nature sensual*?

Charles V's besetting weakness was greed. 'Surely kings must think their stomachs not made like other men's!' exclaimed his closest friend, an old soldier called Luis Quixada, at the dinner table one day, when Charles was swallowing oysters by the dozen. The Emperor began his day's intake at five in the morning, by reaching through his window for a huge pot of beer, placed outside on the sill to cool. Then he heard a Mass for the repose of the soul of the Empress Isabella – but only after having gulped down a bowl of chicken broth, the Pope having dispensed him from fasting before communion. His dinner was mutton, hare, beef, chicken and a mountain of pastry, all gobbled down in lumps, for he had long ago lost his teeth. He suffered from both piles and gout, so beer was bad for him. But when his Italian doctor advised him to give up beer, Charles refused. With such a crushing political responsibility upon his shoulders Charles V no doubt needed to break out somewhere, and gluttony may have appeared to be a sin which harmed nobody but himself. But by 1546 – at a time when the Lutheran and Catholic princes were taking sides and threatening war – the Emperor could hardly sit astride a horse, much less lead his troops in battle. He was persuaded to take a cure, and it did him a great deal of good.

The Emperor Charles V led his men through Liège and Saarbrucken, and on 10 April 1546, a fortnight before Easter, they entered the fortress city of Regensburg, on the Danube. When the Turks had surged up the Danube valley, a generation before, Regensburg was the place deepest into Europe that their cavalry ever managed to reach. In the hope of a last-minute accommodation with the insurgent Protestant princes, the Diet was to meet there. Charles V was a reasonable man, willing to compromise if his enemies would meet him halfway. But this time there was no chance of it; the Lutheran challenge must be met in battle. At forty-seven, Charles V found himself enjoying a new lease of life. At last he had relief from his ailments. He could ride a horse; he enjoyed himself out hunting; he almost felt young again.

Among suitors coming to court that Easter to importune the Emperor was the widow of an officer living nearby called Blomberg. She had three children to launch into life, and when she handed Charles V her petition, the widow made sure that he caught sight of her daughter, Barbara – a white-skinned, silky-haired and large-eyed blonde of about twenty-two. Barbara Blomberg sang for Charles that night in her alluring voice when he sat down to supper. Not long after she was sharing his bed.

An Emperor's mistress, if prudent and discreet, could be a power behind the scenes. But Barbara was pleasure-loving and wildly self-centred, moreover, she had an unlucky gift for making enemies. The courtiers showed their dislike of her – perhaps their envy of her sudden rise to celebrity – by putting it about that Barbara's mother had once been a washerwoman and that the Emperor's new mistress used to sing in taverns. Untrue, but it showed what they thought of her.

When Charles V rode out at last, to do battle with the ludicrously fat Elector of Saxony and his alliance of Lutheran princes, Barbara broke the rules and followed the camp. When they told her that Charles was sick of a fever, she borrowed a trooper's charger and his jacket, to make her way through the line of sentries and surprise the Emperor in his tent. She chased out his attendants and nursed him herself. She could afford by this time to shrug off what others might be saying of her. She was pregnant. The Emperor had only one son, she might bear him another.

From the Danube, Charles V marched his men to the Elbe opposite Mühlberg. John Frederick of Saxony had burned the wooden bridge across the river, but assembled a bridge of boats on the far bank for his own use. Sword between teeth, a dozen of the Emperor's Spanish veterans – the best troops in Europe – swam the river under cover of their comrades' arquebus fire. Seizing the bridge of boats they dragged it back, for their own infantry to march over. The Emperor crossed by a ford, on horseback, 'white as a ghost with fever.'

John Frederick himself fought to the last, but his Lutheran allies let him down, so that the victory of Charles V at Mühlberg was dazzling and complete. He captured all their guns and baggage, and took more than a third of the Lutheran army prisoner. Charles V arrived back at his tent that night in high spirits – the day's exertions had cured his fever. 'Get my supper ready,' he shouted gaily, turning John Frederick's notorious corpulence into a joke, 'for I have been hunting all day long, and have caught the pig, and very fat he is!' Next morning Charles came out with a more considered utterance, which from then on he took as his motto: 'I came, I saw, God conquered.' His favourite painter, Titian, portrayed the victor of Mühlberg in full armour, astride his charger, chin up, aiming his lance, and wearing across his breastplate the Order of the Golden Fleece – emblem of an aristocratic brotherhood sworn to defend Europe against the Turk: Charles V's entire character is there.

Barbara Blomberg's child was born on 24 February 1547 – a blue-eyed, fair-haired boy. But Charles V appeared to be in no hurry to grant this love child the same recognition as he had accorded years ago to Margaret. Courtiers wondered if that great victory at Mühlberg might have stirred up the Emperor's religious feeling. Or was he sensing remorse for his infidelity to the memory of his dead Empress? Or was it simply that his gout was much worse?

The little boy was to be disposed of somehow, out of sight – and Charles V left the management of this awkward business to his trusted friend, Luis Quixada. The child had been taken away from Barbara and put out to nurse. She herself was married off to a court chamberlain called Jerome Pyramus Kegel – by whom she had other children, Kegel having been given a profitable job as army commissary in Brussels.

Luis Quixada discovered that one of the Emperor's musicians, a Fleming called Francisco Massi, a viol player, wanted to retire to a village in Castile with his wife, Ana, who had inherited a house there. Quixada as it happened knew the priest in that village. After swearing Ana and Francisco to secrecy, Luis Quixada offered them 50 ducats a year – enough to live on in comfort – if they would adopt a little boy called Gerónimo, now three years of age. He let them suppose that Gerónimo's father was a groom of the imperial chamber called Adrian Buès, a notorious womanizer. He arranged for them to travel back to Spain in the suite of Prince Philip, and gave them another 100 ducats for travelling expenses. Gerónimo was in good hands. The parish priest would keep an eye on him. He would grow up speaking Spanish and more than a smattering of Flemish. But he would have vanished.

★   ★   ★

On 25 May 1550, word reached Prince Philip in Augsburg that the snow in the Brenner Pass had melted. He ordered his cavalcade of soldiers and courtiers to proceed southward over the Alps towards Italy. The Prince's suite rode downhill at last to a small city where the sun shone more brightly and the streets were full of priests: Trent, on the Italian side. The Council set up years before to reform abuses in the Catholic church was once again sitting in Trent. Prince Philip though only twenty-three was a serious-minded young man. While his courtiers amused themselves with masques and jousting, much of his own time at Trent was passed in religious conversation with bishops and cardinals. Too dangerous for a game, yet not quite war, was how the Emperor's most persistent enemies, the Turks, had once described jousting: men in armour rode full tilt at one another, lance in rest, each trying to knock the other out of the saddle. Although he must have caught glimpses of the little fair-haired boy, being held up by the old musician to watch these excitements, Philip to every appearance was not yet aware that Gerónimo was his own half-brother. His true identity had been buried deep.

The royal party travelled across northern Italy, much of it then in Charles V's possession, and reached Genoa, a city of palaces on the curved slope of a rising hill, overlooking a bay full of ships. The merchants of Genoa were bankers to the kingdom of Spain. A squadron of Genoese war galleys had been hired from the republic's admiral, Prince Andrea Doria, to convey Prince Philip and his party along the coast to Barcelona, and these galleys must have been the strangest sight that Gerónimo had yet encountered.

War galleys were two-masted, long and narrow, rowed by oars and helped along when the wind was favourable by a pair of large, three cornered sails. Ship's officers and passengers lived aft, crowded into cabins in the gilded poop. A metal ram like a bird beak jutted from the galley's prow, and underneath, on a platform, were three large guns. But for most of its length a galley was open, like a huge rowing boat. Chained by the ankle, the rowers sat five abreast along broad benches on each side of a narrow catwalk – one huge oar to a bench. As the blade went backward with the current, the rowers all half stood. The boatswain on the poop blew his silver whistle, and they fell back in unison to the bench, using their bodily weight to create the leverage which shifted the galley's bulk through the water. Up and down the catwalk went a petty officer, whip in hand, to lash out at any rower not pulling his weight. The courtiers on the poop might feign not to

notice the naked men working the huge oars, but there was no
ignoring the stink which came up from them, since they could never
leave the bench where they worked at the oar, night or day.

A rower's status could be told by the way his head had been shaved.
A man smooth all over had been enslaved – he was very likely a North
African corsair taken prisoner. A man allowed a small tuft of hair was
a convict, sentenced to a term of years in the galleys. A handful of the
rowers – those allowed to grow moustaches – were not chained all the
time by the ankle, except in harbour. They were volunteers – men
who at some time or other had found themselves in such a plight that a
galley slave's rations were better than starvation. They all sat in their
own filth, and if the wind dropped, the cabin passengers could hardly
breathe. Most doused themselves with scent, a few stuffed their
nostrils with spices. The habit that in the Mediterranean is still acceptable, of men using strong perfume, has come down to us from the
heroic days of galley warfare, when the approach of another galley
from half a mile to windward was first made evident by its smell.

By mid-July the first sea voyage of Gerónimo's life was over, and
the smell of a galley was imprinted in his memory. They had scarcely
ever gone out of sight of land. At Barcelona the Genoese galley
squadron dropped anchor offshore, under the guns of the fortress on
the hill of Montjuich. The rest of the journey to Ana's house was made
on horseback, jogging endlessly across a mountainous terrain where
cultivated fields were flashes of green amid dry hills.

Leganes was a corn growing village, midway between Madrid and
Toledo, baking hot in summer, bitterly cold in winter. Gerónimo was
sent to learn his letters from the parish priest, who lazily handed over
the job to his sacristan – Luis Quixada was not pleased when he got to
hear. Once he could read, Gerónimo went to a day school, three miles
distant, walking both ways. The man who later collected tales of his
boyhood was told by schoolfellows – then old men – that Gerónimo
was their ringleader in all boyish mischief. They spoke of his skill at
bringing down sparrows with a toy crossbow.

A youngster at the imperial court in whom Charles V then placed
great hopes was William Prince of Orange – fourteen in the year
Gerónimo was born. William since the age of eleven had held not only
the title of Prince but one of the greatest landed estates in Europe.
Before that he had lived in the tumbledown castle of Nassau-

Dillenburg, the eldest son in a large and penny-pinching family of impoverished German aristocrats. What had made the difference was the unexpected death on active service of his cousin, Réné, which left William heir both to the princely title and the vast estates – but only on condition that he became a Roman Catholic.

William had in fact been christened according to the Catholic rite. But his father a year later turned Lutheran – and no doubt, as men sneered at the time, from conviction, since 'the Catholic church owned little of value in Nassau-Dillenburg.' But Count Nassau was hardly a man to allow one more change of religion to stand in the way of his son's worldly prosperity.

Thus the auburn-haired and brilliantly intelligent little boy entered upon his life at court as Prince of Orange and a Catholic. Charles V was always on the lookout for youngsters of promise, who could be trained up in the imperial service. He liked William very much, and fixed on him, perhaps mistakenly, as someone who one day might administer the Netherlands on behalf of Prince Philip, his own son and heir.

The Emperor would for instance let young William stay in the conference chamber for an audience with an ambassador when all the courtiers were expected to leave the room. While he thus learned politics at the very source, the lad was also being trained as a soldier. When he was sixteen, William gave an elaborate entertainment – feasting and fireworks – to Prince Philip in his own great mansion at Breda, a year before Philip left for Spain with an entourage which included little Gerónimo. The two young men were expected to get to know and like one another, but this they never did, then or later. There was no basis for mutual confidence. William of Orange was to all appearance easy-going in life as in religion – he hid his native obstinacy behind a convivial good humour. Philip was tongue-tied, neurasthenic, deadly serious. Above all, he detested heretics. William was known to have changed his religion as easily as he might shift his shirt – suppose he did it again? The two of them – rivals in their youth for the Emperor's affection – from then on watched each other with mistrust. William disliked intensely the plans Philip was known to have in mind for governing the Netherlands more efficiently. So far from serving Philip all his life as a high official, William soon became leader of the long revolt of the Dutch against him.

The hopes placed in William of Orange by Charles V were thus to be disappointed. Margaret though illegitimate was a good and useful daughter to him, but not very bright. Prince Philip was a model son, who took his future responsibility as monarch very seriously – but he was always conscious of standing in his famous father's shadow. And it looked as if the Emperor proposed to ignore and forget Gerónimo.

Luis Quixada was doing service at the court in Brussels when word reached him that the old viol player, Francisco Massi, Gerónimo's foster father, had died. Though intensely loyal to Charles V, Luis Quixada was also a man of tender conscience. He had evidently by this time made his mind up that the Emperor must not be allowed to overlook his obligations towards the little boy. Gerónimo had better be trained to cope with a recognition that might one day change his life.

Quixada sent a groom of the imperial chamber called Charles Prévost to manage matters for him in Leganes. On the roads of Spain in those days, a coach was hardly ever seen. Men went on horseback, women sometimes used riding mules, the infirm were carried in a litter. But Prévost insisted on travelling to Leganes in his own coach. As the preposterous vehicle went rumbling down the village street, all the small boys of Leganes ran out hooting and clung on behind. Prévost showed Ana his letter from Luis Quixada, authorizing him to take the boy away. Ana cried, but all Gerónimo's village friends ran alongside the coach, to cheer him on his way.

Prévost reported back to Luis Quixada that though he was ready-witted, the mysterious Gerónimo had the manners of a village lad. (To the end of his life he was never to lose the knack of expressing himself pungently in common speech.) But Prévost had brought with him in the coach an outfit of the expensive clothes which so visibly in those days marked distinctions of class: at least something could be done about the boy's appearance. Thus fitted out, Gerónimo was delivered to a country house called Villagarcia, a dozen miles beyond the city of Valladolid.

The estate of Villagarcia belonged to Magdalena de Ulloa, now twenty-nine, whom Luis Quixada had married by proxy five years before. There was a twenty-year difference in age between man and wife, and Quixada's duties kept him away from home. Magdalena was childless.

Her husband had written telling her that Gerónimo, now eight, was 'the son of a great man, the writer's dear friend'. Not unnaturally, Magdalena began to plague herself with the surmise that Gerónimo might be the son of some woman her husband had once kept as his mistress. But Gerónimo was luckily a charming boy, a child of grace, and he overcame her mistrust; he had been told to call her aunt.

He started Latin with Magdalena, and learned to ride. She worked hard to polish his manners. Best of all she liked reading to him, for hours on end, from the books of full-blown chivalry which Cervantes a few years later was to laugh out of existence. Magdalena had a devotion to the Blessed Virgin fervent even for a Spanish Catholic. Gerónimo by this impressionable age had already lost his real mother, Barbara, and his foster mother, Ana, so he took to Magdalena's cult with a fervour like her own – his devotion to Our Lady met a lack in his own lonely childhood, and tinctured his entire life. He grew up in this remote country house, believing implicitly not only in the values of Magdalena's religious faith, but with no less conviction in the principles of knight errantry. Knighthood was the way in which a gentleman who did not actually enter religion was required to live. When he came out into the real world, Gerónimo had not surprisingly a poignant sense of being different.

Prince Philip too had been brought up as a boy in Spain, and under the influence of the Empress Isabella's religious fervour – it was the country where he felt most at home. At sixteen, Philip had been married off to his cousin, Mary of Portugal, who gave him an heir, Don Carlos, but she died at eighteen. A second marriage was then arranged for the young Prince with Mary Tudor, Queen of England – a woman eleven years older than himself.

Though in cordial agreement with Mary's policy of forcibly restoring England to Catholicism, Philip did not like her very much personally, and cared even less for her countrymen. Though not many were as yet outright heretics, the English on their cloudy island were uncomfortably independent-minded.

When Philip's second wife, the English Queen Mary, died prematurely, flooding back from Geneva to London came the Calvinist exiles, to help establish her half-sister, Elizabeth, on the throne. Philip was glad to go elsewhere. Larger things were coming his way.

On 16 January 1556, Charles V resigned his own regal functions as King of Spain to his son, Prince Philip, who was also to rule his father's possessions in Italy, the Netherlands and America. His uncle Ferdinand took over the Habsburg inheritance in central Europe, ruled from Vienna – the land frontier with the Turks – and was elected Emperor. Charles V had voluntarily renounced and divided his vast empire partly because gout was by this time making a cripple of him. But he also craved peace of mind.

Charles V's two great political ambitions – to hold back the Lutherans and to drive the Turks out of Catholic Europe – had never quite been attained, because they were too much to accomplish both at once. His decisive victory over them at Mühlberg, in the year Gerónimo was conceived, had not daunted the Lutherans for long. A more uncompromising breed of Protestant – the Calvinists of Geneva – were coming to the fore, and initiating social change not only in Elizabeth's England and John Knox's Scotland, but in the Netherlands and France.

The impetuous advance of the Turks up the Danube a generation before had certainly been checked – the imperial frontier was by now established in Hungary. But Charles V was well aware that if his lifelong antagonist, Soleiman the Magnificent, were to set his mind once again on subduing Christendom, he could attack just as well by sea as by land. The Sultan could send his great fleet of war galleys into the Western Mediterranean, well aware that his vassals, the North African corsairs, would act as his skirmishers.

By 1557, Charles had virtually lost the use of his hands. Spain was the most intensely Catholic of his dominions – a very long way from the troublesome heretics of the north. The sun there would do him good. As his place of retirement Charles hit on a locality a hundred miles west of Madrid and right off the map: the Hieronymite monastery of Yuste in Extremadura. Almond, orange and lemon trees grew there, breezes from the Sierra de Gredos would mitigate the baking heat of summer. He sent Luis Quixada off to Yuste, to arrange for that most uncommon of historical events: the voluntary retirement of an immensely powerful man.

Against the monastery's outer wall, Quixada built his friend a four-room villa, so that through an opening in his room Charles without stirring would have a view of the high altar. Under his window there would be a pool full of trout – Charles could amuse himself with rod and line without going out of doors. The garden was planted with all his favourite flowers, and Quixada furnished the villa with tapestries, statues, paintings. On the Emperor's wall hung Titian's *Gloria*. There were clocks, maps and globes to play with. Charles with so much of the world at his personal disposal had always

been intrigued by geography. He would have a court of fifty attendants, a yearly pension of 20,000 ducats, the consolations of religion.

Once the job was done, Luis Quixada was allowed to go home to
Villagarcia, there to enjoy his own retirement in the company of
Magdalena de Ulloa and Gerónimo. He found that the boy was all he
might have hoped for in a son of his own – charming, willing,
courageous. But unless Gerónimo were formally acknowledged by
the Emperor, his future would be precarious.

The peace of mind Charles V had so much hoped to find at Yuste
was no longer within his grasp. The future of the dynasty was an
anxiety to him, since Philip's only son, Don Carlos, had turned out to
be a deformed and neurotic boy who made everyone uncomfortable.
('His manner and humour please me very little,' reported Charles V
disparagingly, 'and I do not know what he will be capable of, in the
future.') Since coming to Yuste, Charles had felt not better but worse.
The neighbourhood was in fact malarial, and mosquitoes from the
ex-Emperor's fishpond had already infected him.

While thus irritably tormented in mind and body, rumours reached
Charles V of irregular thinking among churchmen on matters of faith,
even here in Spain. A rudimentary kind of Spanish Protestantism was
emerging. In his exasperation, Charles gave his son, Philip, now King
of Spain, a piece of his mind: 'exterminate heresy, lest it take root and
overthrow the state and social order.' Philip was not sorry to hear this,
since it sanctioned what he had in mind to do anyway, and with the
greatest possible efficiency and force.

Everyday life at Yuste began to get on Charles V's nerves; even the
monks were making a nuisance of themselves. So the indispensable
Luis Quixada was told to leave his own retirement at Villagarcia,
come back posthaste to Yuste, and put things right. Grumbling at yet
again being expected 'to go and eat truffles and asparagus in
Extremadura' the shrewd old soldier-courtier made up his mind that
this time he would take with him both Doña Magdalena and
Gerónimo. The boy, now eleven, had been hidden out of sight for
long enough. The Emperor should at least have the chance to set eyes
on him.

2
Rule Half the World with a Slip of Paper

I am the King's vassal and servant. I would give my life and estate
for his service. But what has the King to do with my soul? If
I choose to give it to the devil, what is that to him?
FRAY LORENZO DE VILLAVICENCIO to Philip II, 1565

Luis Quixada settled Magdalena and Gerónimo in a house a mile from
the Emperor's little court, on a hill, amid a wood of sweet chestnut
trees. What with gout, incipient diabetes, and the malaria which was
the unseen peril of the neighbourhood, Charles V was evidently near
the end of his life. Gerónimo began by getting into a scrape – he led the
local boys to raid an orchard, and when they were all up in the trees,
the peasants converged and threw stones at them. Then he redeemed
himself in the Emperor's eyes by his serious demeanour in church, and
the frankness of his face.

As he lay dying, Charles V sent privately for Luis Quixada, and
arranged to have him buy Barbara Kegel an annuity of 200 crowns.
Charles wrote to his son Philip, to ask him to be kind to his father's old
servants, and particularly to take the barber, Gila, into his own employ. While all this was going on, Luis Quixada must have felt sure that
the Emperor would do the right thing by Gerónimo in his will.

The Emperor Charles V's elaborate funeral ceremonies took three
days. Gerónimo was inconspicuously present throughout, dressed in
deep mourning. Whispers as to the boy's identity began to spread
among the courtiers. As executor of his will, Charles had picked upon
a trusted friend from his own youth, Father Francisco, the former
Duke of Gandía, who had given up his dukedom to become a Jesuit.
He was a close friend of Doña Magdalena's, too, and a man quite
incorruptible. But in the Emperor's will, no mention whatever was
made of Gerónimo.

King Philip himself was by this time well aware that the fair-haired boy glimpsed at his father's funeral was his own half-brother. But he too did nothing, except to tell Quixada to take the boy back with him to Villagarcia and keep him out of sight. Luis Quixada, however, made sure that the King was continually reminded of his ultimate responsibility, writing for example on 13 December 1558, 'I do nothing likely to excite observation, or beyond what was done in the life of the Emperor; but I take great care that the lad should learn and be taught all that is necessary, and belonging to his age and quality.' What most interested Gerónimo himself, with a veteran soldier in the house to instruct him, were horsemanship and the use of arms, but he was also kept hard at his book. Eventually, King Philip's hand was forced. A letter came to sight, written by Charles V four years earlier, in Brussels, which was 'to be observed and executed like a clause of my will.'

'Being a widower,' Charles confessed to his son, 'I had by an unmarried woman a natural son, who is called Gerónimo.' He went on to suggest that the best arrangement might be for the boy 'of his free and spontaneous will' to 'take the habit of some order of reformed friars, without any pressure or force being employed towards him.' If, however, Gerónimo 'prefers to lead a secular life, it is my pleasure and command that he should receive each year from 20,000 to 30,000 ducats from the revenues of the kingdom of Naples. I charge the Prince my son to do him honour, and cause him to be honoured, and that they show him fitting respect.'

Yet still Philip hesitated. Though a highly intelligent and conscientious man he was by nature cautious and dilatory, and sometimes morbidly suspicious. Under Charles V the kingdom of Spain had been governed in a way that Philip considered too easy-going. He proposed to change all that. And a brave and charming bastard half-brother might perhaps make trouble for him – even become a focus of discontent. With a wrong-headed and disagreeable heir like Don Carlos, King Philip already had trouble enough.

Spain had been liberated from the last of her Islamic conquerors only about sixty years before. The Moorish kings had not stopped those of their subjects, Christian or Jewish, who rejected Islam from practising their own religion instead – a policy of toleration for which they have been much admired. But Jew and Christian alike paid double taxes for this privilege. The great irrigated estates of southern Spain were

worked for the Moors by Christian slaves. Sharecroppers had to give
the Moslem overlord a third of their crop. The only way to avoid
double taxation, or to escape from slavery, was to turn Moslem. Over
the centuries some did, but many, Jew and Christian alike, bravely
held out.

To Old Christians in Granada whose forbears had clung obstinately
to their faith, the change in their lives when the Moorish kings were
defeated must have felt like a social revolution. They had in fact only
exchanged one master for another. Sharecroppers would go on being
sharecroppers; they would go on being poor. But the Old Christians –
the peasants, and the poor of the towns – saw it differently. They were
now top dogs. Men better off financially and better educated than
themselves had suffered defeat. All those who in the past had been
willing renegades to Islam were now their social inferiors. What really
counted was not worldly success, but the Faith. The Moors in
Granada might own land but they were also conspicuous as craftsmen,
shopkeepers and manufacturers. A Jew was likely to be a dealer, a
physician, a pawnbroker, perhaps an *almojarife* or tax collector. The
people of whom the Old Christians now had such a low opinion were
predominantly middle-class.

In 1492, the year when Granada was conquered, all practising Jews
in Spain had been given four months to quit the country. Perhaps as
many as 150,000 fled; the rest simulated a conversion to Christianity
in which nobody quite believed. Talavera, Archbishop of Granada, had
hopes, however, of winning the Moors over by slow degrees, until
they assimilated: 'we must adopt their works of charity, and they our
Faith.' Patience and kindness had been advocated in his day by Saint
Francis of Assisi as the right course with conquered Moslems. But in
1499 the Catholic Kings were stampeded by Ximenes, Archbishop of
Toledo and later Inquisitor-General, who urged compulsory mass
conversions. The Moors rose in revolt, so in 1502 a brutal sim-
plification was imposed upon them. Let every adult in Spain not
already Christian either accept baptism or get out. When King Philip
came to the throne there might be a public pretence that all Spaniards
were Catholic, but everyone knew that Moors and Jews alike, after a
masquerade of baptism, went on practising their own religion in
secret.

King Philip had from the very start of his reign a clear idea of what
would be needed. His father's wars in defence of Christendom had
been costly, and the abdicating Emperor had cheerfully left the bills,

amounting to twenty million ducats, for the next generation to honour. Philip urgently needed more authority and more revenue, since only if everyone deferred to the King's justice and paid his taxes in full would Spain be governable. Most of his subjects were Christian peasants, who would much rather have royal justice than the arbitrary rule of some local tyrant living in his private castle. Once a peasant saw that law and order were to his advantage, though he might grumble at the King's taxes he would pay them.

Philip needed also to impose his will upon those classes in society who might disagree with him. He proposed to keep the upper hand by means of the Spanish Inquisition. In Spain – though not elsewhere – high officials of the Inquisition were appointed by the King himself, and would do what he indicated: this put into Philip's hand a powerful weapon for controlling all dissent. Charles V had chosen not to use the Inquisition as a political instrument, except against violent revolutionaries in Germany and the Low Countries. For years it had done little in Spain except weed out such social misfits as bigamists, sodomites, sorcerers and vendors of contraband printed matter. But King Philip's Inquisition was to serve him as a moral police force, competent to extinguish dangerous thoughts.

The mass of poor people who had held unwaveringly to their faith under Moslem rule were hardly likely to quarrel with King Philip's new policy of imposing religious conformity by fear. A peasant sharecropper had no reason to dread the Inquisition – on the contrary. He might very likely have to buy his next year's seed corn with money borrowed at rates of interest rising from 25 per cent to 40 per cent. Men richer and cleverer than himself were a burden upon him. The educated moneylender was an everyday reality to him, and usury a sin. Former Moslems and Jews who had opted to stay in Spain because they had property there might well go round these days pretending to be Catholic. But so far as any Christian peasant could see, the well-to-do had not changed their role in society: moneyed men were likely to live off the food producer by means of usury. Thus the poor were inclined to look upon the Spanish Inquisition as an organization which defended them in the name of church and King against their social oppressors: the Inquisition was popular. Even if few Inquisition victims were in fact usurers, a sufficient number of dissenters both in politics and religion came from the moneyed classes for them all to be tarred with the same brush.

A good Catholic was in the nature of things a good subject of King

Philip's. Anyone who disagreed was a potential traitor. A priest who might have the bright idea of appealing over the King's head to the Pope was suspect. Grandees who liked to lord it on their estates needed bringing to heel. Devotees with notions of reforming the church from within had better be frightened a little, or they might lay hands on important vested interests. This was the programme.

King Philip's change of policy came in the nick of time for Hernando de Valdés, the Inquisitor-General. Valdés was no reformer of church abuses. In fact he was in bad odour just then himself, for not paying his rightful share of a forced loan imposed on the clergy for war expenses. But the King needed his Inquisitor, so Valdés's neck was saved. With the self-publicizing vigour of a man seeking to distract attention from his own misdeeds, he began to smoke out heretics.

Though Spain in those days had a population of about eight million, Valdés's informers were able to lay hands on only about 400 suspected Protestants. Groups inclining to such novelties in religion had been meeting in Seville and in Valladolid, and were often recruited from the families of converted Jews. With its emphasis on Bible reading, its respect for the teachings of the Old Testament and the value it placed on private judgement, Protestantism had attractive resemblances to Judaism. But the 'Protestantism' of most of those arrested had been little more than a daring intellectual fashion, not very deeply held. Under the cruel and clever pressures that the familiars of the Inquisition knew how to bring to bear on body and mind, all but twenty of those caught in Valladolid recanted. Two escaped, but were caught again in Pampeluna, when trying to cross the Pyrenees into France. They were given a large escort of soldiers back to Valladolid – not so much to prevent their escaping once again, as to stop the angry crowds gathered in every town along their way from tearing them into pieces as traitors to God and the King.

The Inquisition in theory judged but did not punish. The guilty were handed over to be dealt with by the civil power. They became figures in an auto-da-fé – a dramatic spectacle acted out in public, which culminated with the guiltier victims being burned alive, and all the others publicly humiliated. An auto-da-fé was designed to strike the imagination of onlookers, rich and poor alike, with the need for single-mindedness in religion and obedience to the throne. Anyone who came along to watch was granted an indulgence for sins. Anyone who fed the pile of faggots with his own billet of wood was granted yet another. This was revolutionary justice. Since the crime of thinking differently is always private and individual, the punishment for it was to be collective, and approved by the people at large.

Doña Magdalena was well aware that for Gerónimo not to show himself as publicly as possible at the auto-da-fé announced for Trinity Sunday, 21 May 1559 in Valladolid would be imprudent. His loyalty to throne and altar should remain above suspicion. But she herself must have taken him to Valladolid with mixed feelings, since many of the victims sent by Valdés to parade the streets before execution would be of her own social class, some were people she knew well, and one was her unlucky brother.

King Philip had not yet arrived in Spain from Flanders – where he was trying to set the same system going. His sister, Doña Juana, was acting as Regent of the realm, and today would represent the royal power. The streets all the way from the prison of the Inquisition to the Plaza Mayor had been lined with high wooden stands – the onlooking crowds were enormous. Doña Magdalena's place was in the plaza itself, chosen to be conspicuous. The hooded victims began to move towards her in a long procession from the prison to the plaza, down a narrow gap between rank upon rank of human heads, all shouting in chorus 'A muerte – to death! to death!'

Hernando de Valdés had skilfully provoked a mood of hysterical popular anger in Valladolid. Everyone was sure by now that these men were traitors. The prison of the Inquisition had been guarded all last night by 100 volunteers. There was a plot – so people had been told – to rescue the guilty by blowing a hole in the prison wall with gunpowder.

The outstanding personality among the fifty or so Protestant sympathizers caught in Valladolid had been Dr Agustín de Cazalla, a priest from a distinguished family of converted Jews, and at one time Charles V's favourite preacher. The house of his mother, Doña Leonor de Vivero, had been the headquarters of the group. Six of Doña Leonor's ten children had been arrested by the Inquisition; the rest got away, and Doña Leonor herself had died before she could be condemned. But today, wearing a painted foolscap and widow's weeds, she led the procession in effigy. Behind Doña Leonor's stuffed dummy as it approached the plaza where Magdalena and Gerónimo were watching came the coffin with her mortal remains. Her corpse was to be burned at the stake.

Carrying a lighted candle and wearing a hooded *sanbenito* painted with both flames and devils, to signify that he too was for the bonfire, her son, Dr Agustín de Cazalla, walked after his mother's coffin. At Yuste, Magdalena had known him well. He had recanted his theological errors, so mercy was to be shown him: he would be strangled before they lit the flames under him. His brother and sister were also to be burned. Of the thirty walking in procession, fourteen were to be burned.

At the rear walked the sixteen whose lives had been granted to them on terms. One was an English Protestant called Anthony Baker, caught up in the net more or less by accident: he would have to do penance. Another was a friend of Magdalena's called María Henriquez. In a plain black robe she walked the street barefoot, with a lighted candle in her hand. Her arrest for 'heresy' – for mild intellectual curiosity – had been a shrewd piece of policy by Valdés, since it struck a blow at both the grandees and the Jesuits simultaneously. María's brother, the marqués de Alcañices, was brother-in-law to Father Francisco, once Duke of Gandía, later Charles V's executor, and now Commissary-General of the Jesuits in Spain, Portugal and the Indies. The Dominicans who ran the Inquisition regarded the Jesuits – a new order growing in influence – as their rivals.

The saddest sight that day for Magdalena must have been of the man entering the great square with his head erect, like a soldier on the march, but hidden inside a *sanbenito* painted with flames: her brother, Don Juan de Ulloa, a Knight of Malta who had fought for Charles V at Tunis and Algiers. The Knights of Malta were an aristocratic military order – 'the chivalry of the faith' – outside the King of Spain's control, and owing allegiance directly to their Grand Master, and to the Pope. Don Juan's presence there, among the condemned, was to serve as warning that no one was to consider himself so highly placed as to escape the Inquisition. Don Juan had been sentenced to disgrace, perpetual imprisonment and the confiscation of all his goods (because of such confiscations, the Inquisition usually managed to work at a profit). But this time Valdés had gone a little too far. The family brought influence to bear in Rome, and Don Juan de Ulloa was eventually set free, and given back his rank in the Order.

Both the grotesquely garbed victims and the vast audience had then to listen to a sermon lasting an hour given by a Dominican called Father Melchior Cano – Valdés's right-hand man, and regarded as the best preacher in Spain. Melchior Cano had made a name for himself by his bold assertion that in matters concerning the church, King Philip had no need to defer to the Pope. This was just what the King wanted to hear. Philip's Regent, Doña Juana, and his heir apparent, Don Carlos, then took oath on the King's behalf that they would help extirpate heresy without respect of persons. To the cheers of the tens of thousands of spectators, those doomed to die were mounted on donkeys, and led to the place near the city wall where the faggots had been piled. For Gerónimo, the show was over.

What effect this ugly performance may have had on him can only be surmised. He was certainly not intimidated by what he saw: in later life in matters concerning king or church he always spoke his mind. The auto-da-fé may even have had on the boy who watched it that day an effect opposite from that intended. Later when he had power he tried whenever he could to behave in a way that by the standards of his time was tolerant and even merciful.

Notice had already been taken of Gerónimo's presence here at the auto-da-fé, and a minor scandal was imminent. A lady of the highest rank was coming towards him, lifting up her veil as she came near: the Regent herself. Gerónimo caught a glimpse of eyebrows sloping up to the bridge of a huge hooked nose, a voluptuous mouth, a receding chin. Before he could be hidden inside the cloak flung over his head by Doña Magdalena's companion, the Regent had embraced him. So great had been her curiosity to see this fascinating half-brother, obstinately kept hidden by King Philip, whom courtiers were beginning to nickname the Unknown, that she had broken through the strict rules of Spanish court etiquette. The young and always envious heir apparent, Don Carlos, was disgusted.

Luis Quixada managed to nudge the King's elbow yet again, writing to him on 8 July – six weeks later – about the boy's education. 'Though of excellent disposition,' reported Quixada of Gerónimo, 'he proceeds with his studies with much difficulty, and there is nothing he does with so much dislike.' What French he knew 'he pronounces very well' but 'riding on horseback in the military manner is his chief delight, and when your Majesty sees him you will think he tilts in great style.'

This hardly sounded like a promising candidate for a reformed order of friars.

The meeting between King Philip and Gerónimo was stage-managed so as to look like a happy accident. On St Luke's Day in 1559, Luis

Quixada took Gerónimo out hunting in the wood near Valladolid. Once out of sight he dismounted, begging leave to kiss Gerónimo's hand, and assuring him solemnly, 'You will soon learn from the King himself why I do this.'

Near the rocky pass of Torozos, they met as if by chance a party of huntsmen, led by a short, spare man wearing black, with a pale face, a sandy beard, cold grey red-rimmed eyes and the pouting underlip of the Habsburgs. This was King Philip. On his doctor's advice he sometimes went hunting – it was good for his asthma – but he could never drive from his mind the thought that not long ago a King of France had been accidentally killed when out hunting. To a volley of cheers from a crowd of peasants standing by, who perhaps had been given a hint what to expect, the King got down from his horse to embrace Gerónimo, declaring loudly as he did so, 'King Charles the Fifth my lord and father was also yours. You could not have had a more illustrious sire. I am bound to acknowledge you as my brother.' Then, to the applause of both peasants and courtiers, Philip added (conscientiously, and in strict accordance with what his father had written), 'Know and honour this youth as the natural son of the Emperor and as brother to the King.'

Gerónimo was to be known henceforth as Don Juan de Austria – Englishmen then and since have always called him Don John. With King Philip's usual clever if pedantic attention to ceremonial detail, the youngster's exact position at court was soon made clear to everyone. By sticking his half-brother on a lonely eminence above the heads of the grandees King Philip gained a political advantage, since it kept them at an even greater distance from the royal family than before. But Don John too must be kept at a proper distance. In most ways he was to be treated as an Infante – a royal offspring – yet without holding the actual rank or sharing some of the more evident privileges. He was for instance to be called Excellency, rather than by the royal title of Highness. Nor might he live in any royal palace. Nor during church services was he to stand under the canopy where the royal family foregathered. None of this contradicted what Charles V had said must be done for Don John – yet it kept him in his place.

At Villagarcia Don John had been carefully trained in both fidelity and good manners. This upbringing stood him now in good stead. The courtiers found that he carried off the little awkwardnesses of his position surprisingly well. To King Philip himself – the brother whom hitherto he had never known, the monarch who had so suddenly created him a personage of importance – Don John was to show a loyalty which Philip's cold temperament seldom allowed him to return. It was at times as if King Philip felt it was only prudent to mistrust Don John, even though there might never be any evidence or any need.

King Philip's only son, Don Carlos, was by this time behaving so oddly that even staunch royalists had begun to shudder at the prospect of having to put up with him one day as their King. Don Carlos was deformed in mind as well as body. When his new shoes were a tight fit his idea of a joke was to stew them and make the bootmaker eat them. He would swallow some disgusting object, then oblige everyone nearby, servants and courtiers too, to swallow one as well. He had done his best to throw one servant who displeased him out of a high window, and another he had threatened to castrate. Dr Mann, the English ambassador, wrote home to say that he had 'never dealt with a more dissolute, desperate and unconvertible person'. Don John never let himself be bullied by Don Carlos, and by patience managed to stay on good terms with him, until the day arrived when he was almost the only person the unhappy young man would still confide in.

There was however another youngster at court with whom Don John made fast friends: Alexander Farnese, the son of Charles V's deep-voiced illegitimate daughter, Margaret of Parma. Alexander was dark where Don John was fair, he was small, thin, intense, vigorous, a boy of high intelligence, and with a passion for the life of a soldier.

In 1561, when Don Carlos had reached the age of seventeen, he was sent with Alexander Farnese and Don John as his companions to the University of Alcalá a recent foundation, and vivid with the new knowledge of the Renaissance. Don John's tutor was Honorato Juan, now a scholarly cleric, though in earlier life he had served Charles V in the Tunis campaign. All three young undergraduates were lodged in the Archbishop's palace, and Don Carlos promptly fell in love with the girl in the porter's lodge. She agreed to meet him after dark in the garden, but on his way downstairs Don Carlos fell and cracked his skull. He was vigorously prayed over and expertly trepanned. On recovering he fulfilled a vow to give four times his body weight in gold and seven times in silver to the religious houses which had prayed so heartily for his recovery. But after that blow on the head his behaviour, previously never very wholesome, became impossible.

When he was with his children, King Philip showed an affectionate side to his nature. As monarch he might need to be ruthless, but as a father he had the chance to be tenderhearted. But after hurting his head, Don Carlos began to display a crazy hatred for his own father. No one was convinced by the reasons he began to give. There had once, for example, been talk of betrothing him to Elizabeth de Valois, then only fifteen, but King Philip though much older had married her instead – royal marriages were not love matches, but arranged for reasons of state. Don Carlos seized on this as yet another motive for hating his father. Melodramatically he pretended to be in love with his own stepmother, though nobody believed him. He did everything he could think of to exasperate King Philip politically – from boasting that he had read heretical books to letting it be supposed that his sympathies were with William of Orange and the rebels in the Netherlands.

All this came to a head at last on Christmas Eve 1567, when Don Carlos tried to enmesh Don John – the only friend he had not quarrelled with utterly – in a pantomime of a plot to assassinate King Philip. In exchange for help in killing the King, Don Carlos let it be supposed that he might be prepared to give Don John one or other of Spain's outlying possessions: the Kingdom of Naples, perhaps, or the Dukedom of Milan.

Don John had the good sense not to take all this as a macabre joke, but to go at once and warn his half-brother the King. This was just as well, as the King already knew. Wearing armour and taking with him a handful of men he could trust completely – among them, Luis Quixada – King Philip surprised Don Carlos that night in his bedroom. He was disarmed and made prisoner. 'Henceforth I am going to treat you, not as a father,' said Philip coldly, 'but as a King.'

In his strict confinement, the crazy young fellow's mental sickness ebbed and flowed, but evidently he was beyond cure. There was a strain of madness in the family – Charles V's mother, Juana la Loca, had been hopelessly insane for years. Don Carlos went on behaving in captivity as if he were a mirror image of the King himself, giving open expression to everything wild and evil, absurd and heretical, which King Philip himself, with his rigid sense of duty and his immense self-control, thought it right to repress, both in himself and in the world at large.

All over Europe, gossip about Don Carlos was rampant. Those in Italy, England or the Low Countries who had reason to hate Philip of Spain said he was being monstrous towards his own son. Romantics from Schiller to Verdi have been tempted to portray Don Carlos as onc who secretly shared their revoluntionary impulse, and so was maltreated. But as King Philip wrote with curt accuracy to inform the Pope, his son and heir was 'wholly devoid of aptitude for government; there was no hope of his amendment.' Spain, with the largest empire in the world, could simply not afford a mad king. Don Carlos died in prison – the malicious said of poison. But there is every reason to suppose that the nauseous substances the young prince took such a delight in swallowing did for him at last.

Don John was still intended for the church. Behind the scenes, negoti-ations were going on with Rome to make sure that once he entered religion, his promotion to cardinal would be rapid. But in 1565, when he was eighteen, Don John got into a scrape which made King Philip wonder.

The imagination of gallant young men everywhere had been set on fire that year by the resistance made by the Knights of Malta to the immense fleet and army despatched by Sultan Soleiman the Magnifi-cent to capture their island fortress. Small though it was, Malta barred the great Sultan's sea route into the Western Mediterranean, thus holding up his plans of further conquest.

From all over Christendom, grey-haired veterans and young volun-teers were hurrying to Malta. Some reached the island in time to join in the fighting against the Turks. Latecomers waited with the fleet which King Philip's viceroy in Sicily, Don García de Toledo, was preparing, so that Malta could be relieved as soon as King Philip gave him the word. The slowness with which Philip of Spain made up his mind scandalized all Europe. When Don John impulsively asked if he might go and join the fleet in Sicily, the King's answer was a cold no. He was too young; he was intended for the church. Instead he sent the young man off with Alexander Farnese to escort his Queen, Elizabeth de Valois, on a journey northwards to meet her mother, Catherine de' Medici, at Bayonne.

With Alexander's connivance, Don John slipped away quietly from the cavalcade and rode for Barcelona, where a squadron of royal galleys was fitting out for Sicily. But as bad luck would have it, near Saragossa he went down with fever. The Archbishop of Saragossa, visiting Don John on his sickbed, told him that the galleys for Sicily had already sailed. A letter arrived for him from Luis Quixada, imploring Don John to come back or he would risk losing the King's favour.

Once his fever went down, Don John decided to press on. He made a new plan – to ride breakneck through France, and pick up the royal galleys when they put into Genoa. But a blunt order reached him from King Philip. He must go back to court at once, on pain of disgrace and arrest. Even if he did reach Genoa in time, the galley commander had orders from the King not to let him come aboard. Don John arrived back crestfallen, to face Philip's frowns and beg his pardon, and to be teasingly asked by the young Queen if he had found that the Moors and Turks were brave soldiers.

No coast anywhere in the Western Mediterranean was safe just then from corsair raids. From North African ports like Algiers, which owed fealty to Sultan Soleiman, the corsairs sent out their fleets every summer to rob, kidnap and rape along the Christian coasts until human life there became a nightmare of uncertainty. Now that the Turks were planning to assert themselves from one end of the Mediterranean to the other, these raids were rising to a crescendo.

Even inland Spain was no longer safe. According to the French ambassador, in the year Malta was besieged 30,000 forcibly Christianized Moors – or Moriscos as they were commonly called – had been ready to rise in armed insurrection at a signal from the Grand Turk. The Moriscos certainly had arms hidden away. From 16,377 Morisco houses rummaged in 1563 as a precaution, 14,930 swords and 3854 crossbows had been impounded.

No less serious was the fact, of which King Philip was always painfully aware, that Spain hardly grew enough corn for her daily bread. Large merchant ships were in use every year to bring grain from Sicily to Spanish ports – and the sea route from Sicily to Spain, parallel to the North African coast, was the corsairs' happy hunting ground.

There would evidently be more glory to be gained in years to come by fighting on sea than on land. In October 1567, having sized up the young man's character, King Philip invested Don John as General of the Sea. He was twenty. Don John found himself back again amid the smell so vividly reminiscent of his earliest childhood – of the mass of unclad, shaven-headed galley slaves, toiling and stinking in the belly of a narrow ship of war. The Knights of Malta – who had a sense of hygiene acute for those days – would clean out their galleys at every chance that came their way, by sinking them in shallow water. Spanish captains tended to ignore the perpetual stench more stoically.

In Spain not long before there had been a repugnance to forcing men into the galleys. The Catholic Kings, Ferdinand and Isabella, had accepted at one time the argument put forward by the Dominicans, who disapproved of galley slavery on principle as creating 'a new hell'. But those who try to impose their will arbitrarily on others by means of the state are never averse, even when they are atheist, to frightening their opponents with an artificial secular hell: for veteran Jacobins or Communards, Devil's Island; for Irish rebels, Botany Bay; for old Bolsheviks, the Gulag. A government like Philip's, busily imposing royal law and always short of money, found that galley slavery came cheaper than building new prisons. In corsair galleys, most of the rowers had been kidnapped, but Don John's galley slaves were nearly all convicts.

A few had volunteered from hunger; some, from sheer mad recklessness. The poet Thomas Nashe, well acquainted with the European underworld of his time, describes a kind of Russian roulette, in which a soldier who had plenty of money would put up a stake. Two of his comrades who happened to be penniless would roll dice. The winner took the money; the loser volunteered for the galleys.

The unluckiest floating inhabitants of 'the new hell' were victims of the Spanish Inquisition, most of whom both in their social origins and in their 'crimes' resembled disturbingly the German concentration camp victims of our own day: Judaizers, heretics, homosexuals, priests who had misbehaved or spoken out of turn, sorcerers, forgers. For blasphemy – a few words thoughtlessly uttered and accidentally overheard – the maximum penalty was the same as for bigamy: ten years at the oar. In practice any man's sentence might last out his lifetime, since even after a convict had served his full stretch, a captain hard-pressed for men might well not let him go.

To keep an eye on Don John aboard his flagship, the Prudent King had appointed as Vice-Admiral a Catalan aristocrat and trusted royal servant called Don Luis de Requeséns. He was there to save the young man from possible blunders on his first cruise – which was to lead a powerful squadron of thirty-three galleys south and east of Gibraltar against the North African corsairs. Requeséns reported favourably of Don John. He had behaved well under stress; he had an evident gift for this kind of warfare.

King Philip decided to build a tomb for his father which might also serve as a mausoleum for members of the royal family in centuries to come. He found a site that pleased him, on high grey rock at a place

called Escorial, under the snowy ridge of Guadarrama, a long day's
march out of Madrid. The air was keen, the water pure, and the
bareness of the place chimed in with Philip's mood. After the death of
Don Carlos – so courtiers said of him – his smile was like a stab.

King Philip also decided that at Escorial he would build a Hieronymite monastery, where monks could say Mass in perpetuity for the
souls both of Charles V and of all his descendants. He himself decided
to live simply when up there in the mountains, as much like a monk as
possible – except for the occasional mistress he might cause to be
smuggled in. The ground plan of the Escorial was to be a copy of the
gridiron upon which St Lawrence met his martyr's death: the saint had
been born in Spain, and upon St Lawrence's Day was fought the battle
at St Quentin which had settled matters between Spain and France to
Philip's satisfaction.

From then on nothing pleased Philip more than to turn his back on
the court, with its wearisomely elaborated ceremonial, and go off to
his cell in the mountains. He declared that he could do four times more
work in the Escorial than in Madrid. He tolerated wandering friars
there, and groups of beggars, and was more affable with his workmen
than with any grandee who might intrude upon him. To build and
furnish the great edifice to his satisfaction took twenty years. When
there was a hitch, Philip would put the blame on alien heretic spies.

The movement for reform inside the Roman Catholic church had
given an impulse to church building all round the world, from the
Philippines to Peru. New churches and cathedrals with stunning
façades and dramatic interiors were going up everywhere. Most were
derived architecturally from the Gesù – the original Jesuit church in
Rome – which had initiated a style meant to be at once sublime and
astonishing: the baroque. There were occasional reminiscences of this
new style in the Escorial – the dome, for instance, is an echo of
Michelangelo's cupola for St Peter's. But King Philip's monastery
and mausoleum stand in austere contrast to the gaiety of the baroque –
less exuberant, more severe and neurotically overwhelming. Philip
had drawn his own portrait in stone.

In art and letters, Philip of Spain had excellent judgement. He sent
agents all over Europe to buy up books and manuscripts for the library
of the Escorial – whenever possible at bargain prices. He negotiated
for masterpieces by Titian, Tintoretto, Raphael, El Greco – he
revelled in Hieronymus Bosch. He took pains to acquire holy relics –
authenticated bones of St Peter, St James, St Bartholomew and an

entire arm which had once belonged to St Lawrence himself. There was a school in the Escorial, a workshop, a hospital – but Philip himself lived and eventually died there in a cell twelve feet square. The humblest monk, men were fond of saying, 'had a better room, and better furnished, than the King of Spain'. But Philip found there in the mountains what in the royal court of those days were unprocurable luxuries: privacy, and quiet of mind.

When King Philip was away at the Escorial, a flood of despatches arrived for him every day from viceroys, generals, judges and ambassadors all over the world. These papers were receipted and deciphered, then organized in tidy heaps on a long table in the cheerless little room where King Philip sat for hours, alone, pen in hand. His industry was unremitting. The sheer quantity of these state papers almost overwhelmed him at times, yet upon most of them he managed to fasten his mind, and to grope his way conscientiously towards the right decision.

In his nervous, mannered handwriting, Philip would sometimes make a marginal note which would change the destiny of some distant people. But he was just as likely to correct a spelling, or relieve his feelings by scribbling a pedantic little joke. Philip was always deeply conscious that as King he must carry out God's will on earth. Fleets and armies might be kept waiting, and the royal council sit nerve-wracked, but the King of Spain alone would decide, after brooding and praying and scrupulously weighing alternatives, since God expected more of kings than of other men.

The task of administering the Spanish Empire was gigantic, and King Philip's dilatoriness became notorious. 'If death came from Madrid,' said the sarcastic South American proverb, 'we should all live for ever.' But this rigorous personal control by a man of high intelligence at the very heart of things had one advantage. King Philip as he sat like a hermit in his bare, bleak room in the mountains could keep alive in his mind's eye a picture of his entire empire. No minister was ever allowed to become familiar with more than a fragment of that picture. Thus no sectional interest or personal ambition could ever dominate what King Philip considered to be the good of the whole. Ministers and proconsuls might rage with frustration – all essential decisions were for the King, and for him alone. Here in the Escorial – his own monument in grey granite, chilly and baking by turns – King Philip as God's regent 'ruled half the world with a slip of paper from a cell in a monastery in Spain.'

3

The Great Antagonist

The conquered are slaves of the conquerors, to whom their goods,
their women and their children belong, as lawful possessions; in
converting the children to Islam by force one is enrolling them as
soldiers in the service of the faith, one is working for their
happiness in this world, and for their eternal salvation.

KARA KHALIL CHANDERELI, by tradition
the founder of the janissaries

In the Mediterranean of those days, only the Ottoman Empire with
Soleiman the Magnificent as its supreme ruler was large enough to
menace King Philip's Spain. Soleiman – an only son – had become
Sultan when he was twenty-six, and was to die, on active service, in
1566, as an old man of seventy-two. Like King Philip he had a passion
for justice – his nickname among the Turks was the Lawgiver – and
like Philip he, too, had great trouble with his heirs.

In a letter sent to the Emperor Ferdinand on 27 November 1562,
Sultan Soleiman introduced himself, hyperbolically, as 'I, Lord of the
Orient from the land of Tsin [China] to the extremity of Africa . . .'
The Ottoman Empire did not in fact reach as far as China – or even to
the Atlantic coast of Africa – but it did stretch from Yemen at the
mouth of the Red Sea almost to the Straits of Gibraltar. Soleiman
during his long reign led the Turkish army personally on thirteen
successive campaigns, and added Aden, Algiers, Baghdad, Budapest
and Rhodes to the Empire.

As well as being Sultan, Soleiman was Caliph – the divinely sanctioned Defender of the Faith acting on behalf of all Islam, with the
duty of spreading the True Faith at the point of his sword. Yet in his
lifetime of conquest there were occasional failures. He never managed
to impose his will on those he regarded as Islamic heretics – the Shia
sect who ruled Persia then as now – any more than Charles V had been
able to subdue the Lutherans. A Russian army – Orthodox Christians,
submissive to their czar, Ivan the Terrible – was to foil Soleiman's
plan of establishing Turkish overlordship between the Don and the

Volga, so as to tap the caravan routes to China and enter Persia by the back door, across the Caspian Sea. And though his cavalry had ridden as deep into Europe as Regensburg – where little Barbara Blomberg, at the age of five, might well have seen them galloping past, with their turbans and yataghans and huge moustaches – yet in 1529 the Emperor Charles V had managed to roll them back from the gates of Vienna. Turkish aggressiveness – that is to say – petered out only when they came up against people of a different religious belief who were solidly united against them.

The Christian Balkans, split as they were from top to bottom, had fallen to the Turks like a row of dominoes. Greek and Slav though living there side by side could hardly abide one another. All their neighbours despised the heretic Bogomils – forbears of our present-day Baptists. Islam, with its emphasis on personal cleanliness, the sanctity of contracts and the brotherhood of man, attracted the Bogomils by its Protestant flavour   and in Bosnia they went over wholesale to the Faith of the Prophet, though some of the more strait-laced villages, while embracing Islam, declined to give up monogamy.

But what chiefly softened up the Balkans for the advance of Soleiman's armies was the ever present social conflict there between grasping landowners and their peasants. So much unpaid work and such heavy dues were extorted from the serfs in the Balkans that often they welcomed Turkish soldiers as liberators – even though they might live to regret it.

In 1514, for example, Cardinal Bakocz collected together thousands of Hungarian peasants for a crusade against Turkish aggression. But their leader, Gyorgy Dozsa, chose instead to lead his men in rebellion against the Hungarian nobility. They defeated Dozsa, and he died under torture. At a session of the Diet, the victorious nobles then condemned all their peasants to 'a real and perpetual servitude'. When in 1526 the Turks arrived under Sultan Soleiman, those condemned to 'perpetual servitude' showed little relish for the fight. By ranging his field artillery wheel by wheel, Soleiman on the field of Mohacs smashed the Hungarian army to bits in two hours, killing King Louis and making sure of Budapest. On the night after Mohacs, Sultan Soleiman slept with 2000 Hungarian heads ranged around his tent, impaled on spikes. He took back to Constantinople 105,000 captives, and left behind him a wilderness.

★   ★   ★

The Turks needed foreigners for their skills. A Jew who had left Spain rather than betray his religion is said to have passed on to Soleiman the pattern of the lightweight French gun carriage which enabled him to mass his field guns at Mohacs. The Sultan's war galleys were designed and built by shipwrights many of whom had learned their trade in the Arsenal of Venice. The best Turkish cannon were cast by immigrant gun founders; yew wood for Turkish composite bows came through Venice from southern Germany; long oars to propel corsair galleys were smuggled across from Marseilles to Algiers. Leaving behind them a Europe rigid with class distinctions, craftsmen looking for higher wages, religious tolerance or more scope for their private ambition found that in the underpopulated Turkish empire they were made welcome, whether or not they were prepared to change their religion and accept Islam.

Ever since, centuries before, they had started raiding out of their barren little homeland in northern Anatolia, and gone on to besiege and capture the great city of Constantinople, the Ottoman Turks had been a people organized for war. The government and even the judges followed the army on the march. A Turkish cabinet – or divan – might well meet and confer on horseback. Ministers doubled as generals; the sultan himself was both monarch and commander in chief. War had become the Ottoman way of life, and until now it had paid off handsomely.

In all his long reign, Soleiman asked for only one new tax – a very light poll tax to meet the cost of his third Hungarian campaign. Taxation remained low because plunder and tribute went on arriving. Though the Turks might be notorious for their policy of ruthlessness, yet they saw themselves not as mere conquerors, but as armed missionaries. In their own eyes they were inspired by the same high motives as had prompted the militant followers of Mahomet seven hundred years before. By extending the bounds of Islam they were bringing others more benighted to a knowledge of the True Faith.

What held the Ottoman Empire together day by day – what gave it cohesion – was the moral ascendancy of Koranic law, conservative yet extraordinarily flexible, which brought the utterances of the Prophet to bear on every new social or political problem as it arose. To all appearance, Sultan Soleiman wielded absolute power. Yet the Mufti – the Empire's most eminent authority on Koranic law – often stood up to the Sultan, and was prepared if necessary to contradict him. A sultan who defied the Koran could lawfully be deposed. The Mufti –

not the sultan – had the right to define any particular campaign as a holy war against the infidel. After victory, the mosque had a right to its share in the plunder. The consequence – after such a long run of profitable victories – was that a large part of the Turkish economy had become socialized.

Estates set apart in the past as religious endowments – which were never taxed and could never be confiscated – amounted by this time to a third of Sultan Soleiman's empire. These estates paid for necessary social services – they financed schools and hospitals, built bridges, founded libraries, provided fountains and caravanserais and public baths. A city mosque with a large endowment might well run a hospital, an insane asylum, a secondary school, a soup kitchen for the destitute. All Moslems were brothers, and for poor people the enlightened way in which the mosque spent its income made life bearable.

Moslem subjects of Sultan Soleiman were on the whole better educated than Christian subjects of King Philip. They were certainly more tolerant. In the Sultan's dominions, Jews and Moors who had quit Spain rather than submit to baptism were allowed to live in their own self-governing religious communities. Mahomet had acknowledged both Moses and Jesus as his prophetical forbears. Their followers, too, were 'people of the Book' – misguided, but worthy of respect.

Thousands of Venetians did business with the Ottoman Empire. In their quarter of Constantinople, in Galata, across the Golden Horn, they had been allowed to build their own Roman Catholic church. On Corpus Christi, the Italian Catholics would pay janissaries to clear the streets for them while the Sacrament was carried in procession and all knelt as it went by. Meanwhile, on the far side of the Horn, in the four hundred splendid mosques around the Bazaar, a vast crowd of white-turbanned faithful were prostrating themselves in prayers to Allah.

Soleiman the Magnificent was a tall, thin and severe man, with a habitually gloomy expression. He had schooled himself to meet changes of fortune imperturbably. News of a great victory would not betray him into a smile, nor would he frown at defeat. During his lifetime the continual flow of war plunder had begun to incite a taste for luxury among the once frugal Turks: the time would soon arrive when 'the slipper of a Turkish woman would cost more than the entire costume of a Christian princess.' Yet Soleiman himself was all for simplicity. He wore cotton garments and forbade the use of cloth of gold. He would not allow silver plate at table, and towards the end of his life – in 1562 – he made an effort to stamp out the winebibbing that, though contrary to Koranic law, had become fashionable in Constantinople. To one of his sons – Selim, a toper who was setting everyone a bad example – he wrote earnestly, telling him that he should abstain from wine, pay more regard to the precepts of the Koran, and, incidentally, put to death Murat, his companion in debauch. Murat paid the price. Prince Selim, however, went on with his potations, though more discreetly.

Soleiman's own harem was a modest little establishment for an Ottoman sultan – 100 females, young and old, guarded by forty black eunuchs. For as long as she lived, the most important woman in the harem was the Valide-sultan, or mother of the reigning sultan. She kept the place in order. She oversaw the training of the beautiful and intelligent girls who, as new recruits, were shipped into Constantinople from all over the Empire. She taught them all they would need to know as concubines, from sewing a fine seam and behaving politely to the refinements of sexual deportment. A girl once trained would be given her chance to catch the sultan's eye until she reached the age of twenty-five. If he went on ignoring her, she would then be married off to some officer or other in his horse guards.

Since all harem women were slaves, any reigning sultan was bound on his mother's side to be the son of a slave, and this was what those of his subordinates who were slaves themselves bore in mind: they had something important in common with their master. The janissaries, for example – the crack regulars of the sultan's army – were also his slaves, and they were proud of it. The sultan's overwhelming supremacy, psychological as well as physical, came therefore from an acceptance both of the brute fact of slavery, and of the moral authority of Koranic law. But powerful though he was, it was never easy for a sultan to control his own family. Sometimes his sons were obliged to rebel to save their own necks.

The ambition of every female slave in the harem was to become the mother of a son by the sultan. If this son of hers should in course of time also become sultan, then she herself would then be Valide-sultan and rule the roost. But any son of the sultan's ran a terrible risk. Since the time of Mahomet II who had captured Constantinople a hundred years before, and thus made the Ottoman Turks a world power, once a sultan was chosen, to clear the scene of potential rivals all his brothers must be killed, so as to avoid a civil war. One son born in the harem could become sultan. The rest would be put to death.

Koranic law made no distinction between the son of a harem concubine and the son of any harem slave the sultan might lawfully have married. All alike were legitimate, and eligible for the throne. The mother of Sultan Soleiman's eldest son, Mustafa, was a Circassian beauty known as Gul-bahar – the Rose of Spring. At first everyone took it for granted that Mustafa would be the next sultan, and in 1533 Soleiman sanctioned this choice.

But meanwhile he had had two younger sons, Selim and Bayezid, and a daughter, Mirhmah, by Khurrem, a favourite harem slave, nicknamed the Cheerful One, and known in literature as Roxelana. Khurrem was the captive daughter of a Russian Orthodox priest. As he got older and more religious, Sultan Soleiman married Khurrem, and lived with her monogamously. Khurrem had married her daughter Mirhmah off to Rustem the Grand Vizier – a man of whom the Turkish poets complain that he never smiled. Khurrem behind her own ever smiling face – her mask – was well aware that when Soleiman died, both her own sons must by law be killed, so as to make the throne safe for Mustafa. With infinite subtlety Khurrem went to work to get the heir apparent out of the way.

Mustafa had all the old-fashioned Turkish virtues – courage, piety, respect for tradition. He was handsome and intelligent, and wrote well-intentioned if not very astonishing poetry under a pen name signifying the Sincere. Old-fashioned Turkish country gentlemen were looking to Mustafa to stamp out the money influence, spreading outwards of late from Constantinople and Cairo, which in their opinion had begun to contaminate the austere qualities of character which had made the Ottoman Turks great. The janissaries, too, found in Mustafa a man after their own heart. But he was altogether too straightforward and confident to evade such an intrigue as Khurrem was mounting against him. From now on in Ottoman history the harem becomes an important focus of power, as the women imprisoned there, though slaves, use all their fascination and all their wits to lead their lord and master and his high officials by the nose.

Khurrem began by making the harem so disagreeable for Mustafa's mother, Gul-bahar, that she went off to join her son in Magnesia, the province which since 1534 he had been governing in Soleiman's name. That left no one in the harem to watch jealously over Mustafa's interests. Hint by gentle smiling hint, Khurrem implanted in

Soleiman's mind a number of plausible suspicions. Since Magnesia was obviously a centre of sedition – and she found clever ways of proving it – might not Mustafa's popularity with the janissaries and the country gentry be a political risk? At the same time as arousing these suspicions of Mustafa, she used her son-in-law, Rustem the Grand Vizier, as a source of inside information, so that on all other important matters she could give Soleiman advice which he was bound to recognize as true and in his own best interests. She told clever lies only about Mustafa – and by telling the shining truth about all else, she gave those lies weight.

As he grew aware that for some inexplicable reason he was losing his father's confidence, Mustafa began to act rashly, as Khurrem knew he would. Mustafa's greatest political resource was his popularity among the janissaries – yet the moment he took advantage of it, he was a rebel. But the risk was too tempting – and Khurrem's chance arrived. The Mufti, when asked for his judgement in a hypothetical case of a sultan's son rebelling, turned up a text – 'sedition is worse than execution' – which could be wrenched to serve Khurrem's turn. By 'sedition' in the context, the Prophet was more likely to have meant lapsing from the True Faith, but the text served to satisfy Soleiman that the death of a potentially rebellious son like Mustafa was morally justified.

In 1553, Sultan Soleiman was out on campaign against the Persians, in the company of Selim, the elder and more dissipated of his two sons by Khurrem. Mustafa – then nearly forty years old – was ordered to join them, and on the evening of 12 September he arrived in their bleak camp at Eregli, between a salt marsh and the Taurus mountains. Rustem and the other viziers came to Mustafa's tent next morning, to kiss hands and offer him magnificent presents. They then rode with him amid an escort of admiring janissaries to his father's tent. Expecting a private audience, Mustafa entered alone.

Soleiman was inside the tent all right, but hidden behind a silk curtain. Mustafa was confronted with seven mutes, each holding a bowstring. They closed in on him, and he was overpowered and strangled, while from behind his transparent curtain Sultan Soleiman looked on without saying a word. The last scene was played elsewhere. Mustafa had one small son. That same morning a eunuch of his harem called Ibrahim took the little boy by a trick from his mother's arms, and strangled him as she looked on, helpless and horrified.

The great Turkish poet Yahya, a man of Albanian origin and

himself a former janissary, wrote a funeral elegy for Mustafa. Rustem – Khurrem's son-in-law – was all for having Yahya killed, but the Sultan would have none of it, and indeed after Rustem's death he gave Yahya a pension. He was suffering from remorse. He had begun to wonder if he might have misjudged Mustafa.

The question of the next sultan still had to be settled – by now there were but two contenders. The accomplished intriguers of the Ottoman court knew that if only they backed the right man, their future careers would be assured. Might not a tipsy sultan like Selim be easier to manage? The intrigue was no longer in Khurrem's control – however the dice fell, she would lose a son. And the cleverest men at court were already looking for ways to direct Sultan Soleiman's misgivings against her favourite son, Bayezid.

In the armies of Christendom, nearly all the higher commands in those days were held by aristocrats. Yet though the Turkish janissary was a slave, he knew that there was almost no upper limit to his promotion. His pay was regular – given him on a ceremonial parade every three months, when the sultan himself stood in the ranks and symbolically drew the pay of a private soldier. The janissary's training was thorough, his weapons were good. Most other Turkish troops were still using the bow and arrow, but janissaries had begun to master that newfangled firearm, the arquebus, the lead bullet from which flew straight, hit hard, and could knock a hole through armour. Almost everywhere else in the world, worn-out soldiers were left at the roadside to beg. Janissaries were given paid leave, and at the end of their time were generously pensioned. Yet the janissaries of the Ottoman sultan – his *yeni çeri* or new troops – as well as being slaves were not even Turkish.

Some had been adolescents made captive in war – a third of all prisoners was the sultan's share, and he preferred to take boys of fourteen and upwards who might be suitable for training as janissaries. But most were sons of Christian families in the conquered Balkans – Albania, Serb, Croat, Bulgarian, Greek – taken away from their parents by force. Every year the sultan took as an ongoing 'blood tribute' from the conquered Christians, thousands of their sons, often 10,000, and in years when losses had been heavy, as many as 40,000.

An official would come to a Christian village with a quota of slave boys to fill, and there conduct the *devşirme* –the four-yearly official inspection for suitable adolescents to take away as slaves. The official was an expert in boy flesh as another man might be in horseflesh. Until the 1570s both Armenians and Jews were exempt, but in Christian villages the official would use the baptismal register of the parish church to make sure that no boy of suitable age had slipped through the net.

Parents anxious to save a son might marry him off, however young he was, or pay a heavy bribe. Some, more ambitious on their son's behalf, were not sorry to see him go, since in Constantinople he might well better himself. This diabolically ingenious Turkish policy turned the family – the living heart of a Christian community – into a cattle farm. Parents were bringing up their brightest and strongest merely for the use of the sultan, and since year by year the best were sent away, the breeding stock as time went on became inferior, and the Christians themselves more demoralized and less likely to revolt.

The *devşirme* made slaves of Christian boys at puberty, the time in their lives when they might well feel like shaking off parental control and having adventure – the age when religious sanctions had least hold over them, and their sexual preferences had not yet been confirmed. The Turks themselves looked upon the *devşirme* as a missionary activity: they were claiming the flower of the flock for Islam.

A boy would be shipped from his village and carefully examined when he got to Constantinople. Poverty-stricken though his origins might have been, an exceptionally good-looking and gifted boy – only 200 were chosen in any year, from the thousands who arrived – might become an imperial page, and eventually join the spahis of the Porte, the sultan's horse guards. This was the corps which served as nursery for the high officials chosen to govern the Ottoman Empire.

An imperial page was given the same upbringing as a royal prince. He received a literary education in Arabic and Persian – the Latin and Greek of Turkish culture – together with instruction in mathematics, rhetoric and music. Masters trained him in arms – and following a tradition both Islamic and Jewish, he was also taught a handicraft, so that in misfortune he could earn his own living. Good manners were drummed into him, he was given pocket money and soon named to some small responsibility in court. One page looked after the parrots, another the nightingales, another the diamond brooch on the sultan's turban. Thus by imperceptible degrees the peasant boy from nowhere became a courtier and a soldier.

Boys taken away from their village by the *devşirme* were forcibly circumcised, but no pressure was put on them afterwards to repeat the sacred verbal formula which would have made Moslems of them. But a page, living in a society where religion and the state were one, was under a subtle impulsion to act like everyone else. Inevitably he would be brought to reject his parents' religion of his own free will. When this occurred he was congratulated and rewarded – in changing his deepest loyalties voluntarily he had shown the power of Islam.

The training of an imperial page went on until he was twenty-five. He was then given an embroidered coat, and a bloodstock horse from the sultan's own stables, and drafted to fill a vacancy in the horse guards. He was immune from taxation. The highest positions in the land were open to him. His social status might only be that of a *köle* – a slave – yet the sultan's eye was upon him: he might even become grand vizier. From 1453 to 1623, only five out of forty-eight grand viziers were of Turkish birth. But efficiency was maintained by fear. The higher such a *köle* rose in the Turkish service, the likelier that he would be made to pay for any error of judgement with his head. As they were training in the palace, pages often saw death warrants being sent out all over the empire – and on some days forty or fifty decapitated heads might arrive, as vouchers that the sentence of death for incompetence or failure had been properly carried out.

Most of the Christian boys enslaved by the *devşirme* had been chosen for their muscular development, and so they became not pages but janissaries – fighting soldiers. A boy would be dressed in red uniform and sent away to the estate of some provincial gentleman, where for the next three years he would learn Turkish and be taught manners, and the use of weapons, as well as developing his physique by unpaid work on the land. He would then go back to Constantinople for another examination. Some were then drafted to war galleys, as marines, or given work in the sultan's shipyards. Others went to one of the sultan's three palaces, to work as gardeners, woodcutters or scullions. Their weapon training meanwhile continued. At twenty-five – or earlier if there had been heavy wartime losses – they would at last join the corps of janissaries.

A janissary must be clean-shaven, and was not allowed to marry – though the rule against marriage was increasingly evaded. They lived together in messes of ten men, each company of ten messes being commanded by an officer promoted from the ranks. Janissaries were exempt from civil courts and could be punished only by their officers. There was no limit to their promotion – but the higher a janissary rose in rank, the heavier his punishment for failure. Half the corps served overseas, on garrison duty or as police. They had nothing whatever in common with the people they had to control, and so were the less likely to join in rebellious plots. A man who had shown conspicuous bravery earned the right to wear an ostrich feather in a gold tube on the front of his turban.

Though janissaries seldom numbered more than a quarter of the men a sultan could put into the field, they were the backbone of his army. Good infantry were rare in the east, where cavalry was the dominating arm, and his janissaries gave the sultan's armies their exceptional striking power. On the battlefield they were expected to show by example how belief in Islam could turn a timid Christian youth into a Moslem hero, capable of giving his comrades a lesson in self-sacrifice. The bulk of the Ottoman armies were feudal levies, raised by the Turkish country gentry who had first licked the janissaries into shape – men who held land from the sultan in return for military service. Such feudal levies were brave and willing soldiers – but they lacked the regular pay, the chances of promotion, the long training and the discipline of the janissaries. Foreign eyewitnesses in Soleiman's reign speak of their good order, their silence in camp, their frugality and cleanliness, their instant obedience. They were loyal only to the reigning sultan; they were his slaves.

But to whom should the janissaries be loyal when the identity of the next sultan was still in doubt? Bitterly disappointed at seeing their favourite, Mustafa, deprived of his right to the throne, the janissaries in the last years of Soleiman's reign made the dangerous discovery that they might be kingmakers. With that heady piece of knowledge began their slow demoralization.

Soleiman the Magnificent was never addicted to unnatural vice – the Koran no less than the Bible condemns it. But there were other sultans before and after him who made use of the handsome boys brought every year to Constantinople as a trouble-free parallel harem. Thus the bizarre method by which janissaries were recruited not only humiliated and debased the Christian villages from which they came, but in the long run implanted yet another corruption in the sultan's court. But so long as Soleiman lived and exerted his power, the decadence slowly burgeoning in his harem and among his janissaries was hardly apparent. Few as yet supposed that a sultan might be browbeaten, manipulated or corrupted. When Soleiman even as an old man went out to war amid his loyal and fearless corps of janissaries, marching in their iron studded shoes, with the Sultan himself perhaps carrying his jewel studded scimitar in their ranks, the élite of the Ottoman army was still to all appearances invincible.

Khurrem died in 1558, aware that one or other of her sons was bound to be the next sultan. She expected the choice to fall upon her younger son, Bayezid – her favourite. He was tall and thin like his father. Selim, the elder son, was short and plump like his mother. Selim was fonder of wine, women and song than of warfare – his nickname was Selim the Sot. Except when his father the Sultan was keeping a close eye on him, he would stay up into the small hours with a tipsy entourage of poets, wits and beautiful girls, and let official business slide – a way of life that, though reprehensible, at least directed political suspicion away from him. Bayezid, father of five sons, was more soldierly but less adroit, and apt to do the wrong thing on impulse.

The doubt as to which of them would succeed Soleiman was resolved by a complicated and exceptionally treacherous intrigue, entrusted to Lala Mustafa, who knew the characters of the two princes inside out since they were boys: he had been their tutor. Lala Mustafa began by convincing Bayezid that he was profoundly loyal to the younger and more soldierly of his former pupils, whatever dissimulation might be forced upon him. This private declaration of loyalty did not come as a surprise to Bayezid, who for his own part was perfectly sure that what the Ottoman Empire needed was a man like himself, not a tippler like his brother. He agreed to follow Lala Mustafa's secret advice; from then on he was doomed.

Lala Mustafa took up an appointment at Prince Selim's court, one of his prearranged duties being to keep the Sultan informed confidentially of how Selim behaved. Thus whatever happened Lala Mustafa had the Sultan's ear. While continuing to inform Soleiman about his son Selim's life of dissipation, Lala Mustafa began subtly to discredit Bayezid in the Sultan's eyes, by prompting him to actions which looked all right to Bayezid himself, but on which a cleverer man could place a discreditable interpretation. Outwitted from the start, Bayezid followed Mustafa's prompting and played his game. For example, he sent his brother Selim an insulting joke gift of a set of women's clothes – a skirt, blouse and bonnet. But did not this clearly imply that no one would want an unwarlike, womanish sultan? Did it not suggest – Lala

Mustafa hinted to Soleiman – that Bayezid had become cocksure of inheriting his father's throne? Soldierly Bayezid was the obvious threat – no one feared Selim.

An unconvincing manoeuvre by Selim provoked Bayezid into raising an army of 20,000 scratch levies, Kurds, Turcomans and Syrians. He was in open rebellion. He had shot his bolt. This was when the shrewdest man among Soleiman's viziers – Mahomet Sokolli – declared for Selim. On 8 May 1559 Sokolli marched against Bayezid's large but ramshackle army with a much smaller force – but it included 1000 janissaries, a corps of spahis, and an artillery train of forty guns. They were highly trained men, and Sokolli – who in the past had served Soleiman as general, judge, governor and even admiral – handled them superbly. In a two-day battle at Konya, lasting through 29 and 30 May, Sokolli broke up the rebel army. With only twenty-one camels, sixty horses and twenty mules to mount his closest followers, Bayezid went hotfoot for the Persian border, while his four older sons, who had joined his rebellion, covered his retreat. Sokolli and Selim, close on their heels, moved up and sealed the frontier behind them.

Shah Tahmasp was ostentatious in the welcome he gave Bayezid at Tabriz, emptying over his head thirty vases of gold, silver, pearls and jewels, and making him a gift of nine bloodstock horses. But despite this fulsome greeting, Shah Tahmasp intended to sell his unwanted guest for what he would fetch: negotiations began for the extradition of Prince Bayezid.

Prince Selim, on his father's behalf, wrote formally to the Shah, quoting an appropriate line from the Persian poet Sa'adi: 'to do good to the wicked is to do evil to the honest'. Shah Tahmasp riposted neatly enough with a text from the Koran, 'kill idolaters and rebels' – a promising hint. But the Shah went on to demur. Placed as he was, he could hardly betray a guest. Though perhaps Bayezid might be exchanged – for the city of Baghdad? That of course was asking far too much. But the familiar Oriental bargaining had begun; a price would be reached.

At last, on 25 September 1561, the Shah delivered up four of Bayezid's sons and the rebel himself. Prince Bayezid had first been deprived of all dignity – the Shah's men had orders to shave him totally, eyebrows as well as beard, and dress him shabbily, with a rope for a belt. Once in Turkish hands, father and sons were quickly killed off – and to round out his triumph Selim arranged to have the fifth son killed too – a little boy of three who had been left behind at Brusa. As Khurrem's first-born, Soleiman's one surviving ·son and the only living prince of the House of Othman, Selim was undisputed heir.

The men who had first intrigued and then fought for Selim were to be eminent in Ottoman politics all through the years when Turkish rivalry with Spain in the Mediterranean led to outbreaks of war. Selim eventually rewarded the most valuable of his supporters, Mahomet Sokolli, by giving him his sixteen-year-old daughter, Esmakhan, in marriage. (A sultan's daughter was never allowed to bear a son – the unlucky male child would be disposed of at birth by failure to tie up the umbilicus.) Selim's other young daughter, Genher, he married to Piale Pasha, who commanded the navy. Both husbands had in their boyhood been taken up by the *devṣirme*. Sokolli had been the son of the Orthodox parish priest at Sokolic – the Eagle's Nest – in Bosnia. Piale had been exposed as a waif, on a ploughshare outside Belgrade.

Lala Mustafa rose in short order from tutor to the royal children, and the Sultan's spy, to govern provinces and command armies. Mirhmah, the daughter of Soleiman who had married Rustem his Grand Vizier, was now a widow, and for good reasons of her own a fervent advocate of an attack on Malta, the little fortified island which blocked the advance of the Turkish fleet into the Western Mediterranean. Alarmingly strong though the Turks still were by land and sea, courtiers and concubines could dabble from now on in high policy, and this gave the powers threatened in the West a better chance than they had any right to expect.

4

Lions into Hens

Though God be against all persecution to preserve
or increase his faith among the people, yet it is no
reason to look that Christian princes should suffer
the Catholic Christian people to be oppressed by
Turks, or by heretics worse than Turks.
SIR THOMAS MORE: *The Dialogue Concerning Heretics*, 1528

On 15 June 1497, a splendidly dressed corpse was dragged by fishermen out of the Tiber, at the place on the river bank opposite the
ghetto, where garbage was usually tipped. The dead man had been
stabbed. Since he was wearing gold spurs, and had a purse of money in
his pocket, theft was evidently not the motive. He was recognized as
Juan, Duke of Gandía.

The dead Duke's mother had been a tavern wench, called Vanossa
dei Cattanei. His father was Alexander Borgia – Pope Alexander VI – a
man who with his massive, sensual face, huge hooked nose and head
like a soft-boiled egg looks singularly evil, even in a portrait. The
Duke's title derived from an estate at Gandía, near Valencia, on the
Mediterranean coast of Spain, bought for the family with 50,000
ducats of the Pope's money. Probably Juan Duke of Gandía had been
stabbed on the orders of his younger brother, the sinister Cesare
Borgia, whose armed bravos then terrorized the streets and alleys of
Rome on the Pope's behalf.

The Borgias were identified by the Romans with both violence and
vice. They confidently believed that Cesare as well as his father the
Pope had committed incest with Cesare's sister, Lucrezia, angelic-
looking, with butter-coloured hair, blue eyes and a rosebud mouth.
When Alexander VI occupied the throne of St Peter, and used it chiefly
as a means of enriching his illegitimate children, the papacy sank to its
lowest ebb.

Protestant reformers of the early sixteenth century made such rapid
headway because a conspicuous minority of Catholic priests had been

living instances of scandal, if not of quite such extreme wickedness as the Borgia Pope himself. A similar worldly mockery of the priestly function was frequent, even in Spain. The third Duke of Gandía's father-in-law, for instance, was Alfonso, Archbishop of Saragossa. Alfonso, himself an illegitimate son of Ferdinand of Aragon, the 'Catholic King', had by the good offices of his father been installed as Archbishop at the ripe age of nine. The only day in his life on which Alfonso was ever heard to say Mass had been twenty-three years afterwards, when belatedly he had to consent to being ordained priest.

The third Duke of Gandía's wife, Juana de Aragon, was one of Archbishop Alfonso's four illegitimate children by his mistress, Ana de Gurrea. Two of Ana's sons became archbishops of Saragossa in turn. Thus the archbishopric with its revenues and its enormous political influence stayed in the family, and under the direct influence of the crown. This is not to say that the Spanish church of the time was lacking even then in serious-minded men and women, who prayed for better days and tried by their lives to set an example. The widow of the Duke who was done to death in Rome was a woman of exactly this stamp.

She had gone back to Gandía, in the gentle climate of Valencia, and in her widowhood developed the property there until it brought in 30,000 ducats a year, a third of which she dispensed in charity. She built a church at Gandía, and endowed the local convent of Poor Clares. On 28 October 1510, her daughter-in-law, Juana de Aragon, presented her son, the third Duke, a dull and conscientious man, with an heir who was christened Francisco. And which of his forbears would he grow up to resemble?

Young Francisco inherited the prominent Borgia nose. He was a tall and lively boy, equally interested in Latin and hunting, hawking and music. But when he was ten, the calm, orderly and interesting life on the family estates at Gandía was violently broken in upon.

Provoked by the extortions of royal tax collectors, the citizens of nearby Valencia had formed a brotherhood – the *Germanía* – and risen in revolt. Their hope was to break away from the kingdom of Spain, then being rather nonchalantly governed from a long way off by Charles V. The armed citizens were particularly hostile to local land-owners, like Francisco's father, whose over-riding loyalty was to the crown. They wanted to make Valencia a democratic city state.

The cathedral in Valencia – which contains among other relics the Holy Grail, though there is a rival Holy Grail in Genoa – was pillaged by rioters. Having all their lives seen the cathedral administered as a source of patronage for the rich, the men of the *Germanía* made no distinction in their minds between the interests of the church and those of the great landlords. Francisco's father rode out confidently against them at the head of a royal army – only to be defeated by the citizen levies of the *Germanía*. But another army marching up from Andalusia managed to crush the revolutionary brotherhood, and terrorize the *valencianos* back into their old obedience. The Duke and young Francisco went back again to Gandía, where the rebels had turned their palace upside down. Young Francisco had learned a lesson. Everyday life was never quite as safe as they might try to make out.

There was more to come. At twelve, Francisco was sent off to be a page at Tordesillas – where Charles V's crazy mother, Juana la Loca, was kept under restraint. Francisco was intended as company there for mad Juana's fifteen-year-old daughter, Catherine, a future Queen of Portugal, whose young life was being made dismal for her. She could never escape the apparition of a royal mother with wild grey hair, clad in rags, indescribably filthy, and continually shouting out the most heart-stopping blasphemies. Francisco – at twelve a charming, cheerful and self-possessed little boy – was a good friend to Catherine, then and later. But he had perhaps been shown the seamy underside of the dynastic system when a little too young.

Charles V, though ten years older than Francisco, made close friends with him when later on they met. They had much in common. Not only were they cousins, but both were idealistic young men of a religious turn of mind, but with a taste for action. Both were haunted by an unfortunate ancestry – between a Borgia Pope as one's progenitor, and Juana la Loca, there was not much to choose. Each of them tried to avert the consequences by trying to lead a strict and upright life. Francisco was good at dancing and tilting, and was regarded as the best horseman at court, except for the Emperor himself. He put Charles's heir, little Philip, the future King of Spain, astride his first pony – but the young prince was never cut out to be a cavalier.

Francisco as a young man was notorious for one oddity: he never sowed his wild oats. In an imperial court full of beautiful and eager young women, he was never even observed to flirt. His friends were therefore much relieved when he fell passionately in love with and soon married a Portuguese lady-in-waiting, Eleonor de Castro: he was nineteen. At court the pair of them were a great success. During

Charles V's long absences from Spain, Francisco and Eleonor ran his household for him there with efficiency. They were devoted to one another. Eleonor bore Francisco eight children in ten years, and Francisco in the meanwhile became remarkably fat. His valet was overheard to boast that his master's great leather belt could hold three ordinary men. But his contentment was to be undermined by yet more lessons in human transitoriness.

On 1 May 1539, Isabella, the empress whom Charles V loved so deeply, died of fever in childbirth. It was part of Francisco's duty, when her death was reported, to go to Toledo and formally identify her, as his cousin's wife. When the shroud was lifted from Isabella's face, her features were a mass of worms. Under the impact one after another of these sobering occurrences, Francisco's mind became preoccupied with religion. He was nearly thirty.

Charles V appointed him his Viceroy in Catalonia – an exceptionally difficult place to administer. The corpulent young aristocrat would henceforth need to be active. The Catalans live in a principality which straddles the Pyrenees. They have a language and a literature of their own, and are fiercely independent. In those days many of them were going hungry. This was partly the fault of the corsairs, who played merry hell with the coastal trade. The expulsion of the Jews had gravely damaged commerce in the great port of Barcelona. But worst of all, the current of trade was nowadays flowing more vigorously the other way – not across the Mediterranean, but through Seville to America. Thus life in Catalonia was harsh, and the Catalans were in a mood to put the blame on outsiders. Francisco, as Viceroy, had been sent there to diminish this resentment by strictly applying royal justice. But he found the Catalans violently jealous of their local privileges, and their mountainous countryside had become a law unto itself.

Banditry in Catalonia was an organized trade. The roads through the passes of the Pyrenees which linked Spain to France were harassed by *bandoleros*, operating in gangs of up to fifty men, some of them carrying arquebuses – against which armour was no protection. The robbers were often working for the account of provincial nobles, hard to get at because they lived in their own fortified towers up in the mountains. They had highly placed accomplices in Barcelona – even on the city council – glad to sell off the plunder.

Though heavy in the saddle, Francisco began riding out into the mountains, with an escort of thirty soldiers – his entire armed force – systematically hunting down bandits as he might have hunted wild boar. His one short answer to banditry was the hangman's noose. He once brought in so many prisoners that Barcelona ran out of gibbets. He discovered that one of the bandits' accomplices in the city was the bishop – a gambler, and another of those worldly ecclesiastics who had never been heard to say Mass more than once in his life: his cathedral was the *bandoleros'* sanctuary. 'I find in Catalonia,' Francisco reported to Charles V, 'an equal lack of corn and justice.' The Emperor – as usual – was so hard-pressed for ready money that Francisco was financing the administration out of his own pocket.

Outwardly he was nothing more than a busy servant of the crown – reforming, repressing, making sure the people had corn, hanging robbers by the neck. He was casting cannon – on 10 October 1542 he presented Charles V with twelve of them, named after the twelve Apostles. He revived shipbuilding in Barcelona, particularly the construction of galleys – there was even a fanciful project for a seagoing vessel to be worked by steam. But Francisco Borgia was by this time leading a double life. The mortal corruption of the Empress Isabella, the useless death in an attack on a tower at Fréjus of his friend Garcilaso de la Vega, whose splendid poems had exalted military glory – these, added to the unforgotten experiences of his boyhood, were giving his mind a turn which might even be considered morbid. Beneath his rich dress as he rode over the cobbles of Barcelona, or as viceroy took the principal place at banquets, Francisco was wearing a hair shirt. That ever present itch on his bare skin was to remind him – so he wrote in his diary – that he must contend day and night with his Borgia inheritance: 'those two beasts, of hot temper and lust.'

Eleonor and he lived in unbroken amity, and she fervently shared his intensifying religious convictions, but after her last miscarriage he dared not touch her. He slept apart. Taking off his hair shirt at bedtime, the viceroy would lock the door of his room, and privately scourge himself, to break the neck of his carnal desires.

He had also turned author. During this busy time in Barcelona, Francisco wrote and published a little book of devotions, *The Practice of Christian Works*, which was to cause him endless trouble later on. In 1541 he came across a young Savoyard priest called Father Faber, who was travelling through the Pyrenees into Spain. He was one of the half dozen companions who seven years before had stood with Ignatius Loyola on the hill of Montmartre outside Paris, and pledged themselves to form the Company of Jesus. They still hardly numbered more than sixty, all told – but the Jesuit view of how to live in a cruel and corrupt world, as expounded by Peter Faber, struck the young viceroy's imagination.

To enhance the discipline of the soldier and the reforming zeal of the enlightened administrator by a conscious imitation of Christ? To unite the mystically devotional with the intensely practical? This was exactly what Francisco had been looking for. The Jesuits declined all office in the church – no more nine-year-old bishops! They obeyed their General like men-at-arms in battle, and the General put his Society totally at the disposal of reforming popes, in their efforts to put the church to rights. By 1542, Faber was writing to inform Ignatius Loyola that the Viceroy of Catalonia 'is devoted to us, and so is his wife.'

Years before, in 1527, at Alcalá de Henares, Francisco may have caught a glimpse of Ignatius Loyola – slight, shabby, a Basque noble-man limping from an old war wound. Ignatius had come to the university late in life to study – only to be imprisoned twice by the Inquisition, as leader of a small group of students who took their religion too much in earnest for the authorities' liking. The Spanish Inquisition had forbidden Ignatius to meet with others of like mind in public or private for three years. To avoid such interference he completed his studies in Paris – where John Calvin, oddly enough, was his fellow-student, though theologically his diametrical opposite.

Ignatius Loyola had once been a page at court. As a youngster he had fought duels, gambled, had mistresses – but all that was a long way behind him. His mind had a mystical cast – he was not a man abounding in ideas – but he possessed a genius for leadership and organization. The effect upon Ignatius's followers of his *Spiritual Exercises*, involving them in a stringent and prolonged meditation upon the life and death of Jesus, could often change a personality for life. Self-abnegation, deliberate heroism – Francisco, oppressed as he was by the condition of mankind, and tormented by his Borgia blood, could hardly ask for anything better. He determined to quit the service of his cousin, the Emperor, and give up all worldly possessions and authority, so as to serve Christ the King.

But his father died, and Francisco came into the Dukedom. He would first have to go back to Gandía and see to his estates. Loyola in Rome had already been informed of the Duke's willingness to give up all he had and join the Order. His answer was that the Duke of Gandía's first responsibility must be to his family. Let him settle the younger sons in life, and see his girls well married. The Duke might do well to take a doctorate in theology; there was no hurry. Ignatius wanted to avoid scandal. The government in Spain would not be pleased at losing such a useful public servant as the Duke to a new order about which many in high places still had grave doubts. 'The ears of the world,' Ignatius wrote, 'are not strong enough to stand so violent an explosion.' Dukes are used, moreover, to having their own way – a few years of waiting in patience and obedience would test the strength of Francisco's vocation.

The property at Gandía was a world in miniature, and the Duke himself all-powerful there. The estate produced two profitable cash crops – sugar and silk. In the little whitewashed houses across the *huerta*, the womenfolk had been taught how to breed silkworms, and the delicate task of cleaning and winding the sticky thread. From late November to mid-January, 550 men and 200 mules were kept busy at sugar boiling. From four to eight each morning, Francisco prayed and meditated; the rest of the day he administered.

In the stable were forty bloodstock horses; the house gave occupation to 140 gentlemen and pages. Francisco had the town walls repaired, and mounted sixty guns around them as a precaution against the corsairs from Algiers. Their leader Dragut had lately pillaged this coast, carrying off local people as slaves for the galleys or the harem. If they tried it again, they would find themselves up against a local militia numbering 600, stiffened by forty experienced men-at-arms and led by the Duke.

Many of the workers on the estate were Moriscos. They were frugal, skilled, hard-working. The elaborate system of irrigation which made the *huerta* so exceptionally fertile had been the handiwork of the Moors, in the days when they still ruled here. The saying in the province of Valencia was, *que tiene moro tiene oro*: to have Moors working for you was as good as having gold. But their descendants by this time were at the bottom of the social pyramid: of the 150 poorest families in Gandía 120 were Morisco.

These poor, defeated, alienated but necessary people weighed on the Duke's conscience. He spent a great deal of money to buy himself peace of mind. He built a school, and brought in ten Dominican friars to educate the Morisco children and give them a better chance in life:

nothing of the kind was happening elsewhere. He endowed the Hospital of St Mark, which provided ninety-nine beds for the sick poor. In his years of marking time at Gandía, waiting to give it all up, Francisco was estimated to have dispensed 50,000 ducats in charity.

He was also ashamed of being so fat. On the topic of diet, the *Spiritual Exercises* advised the Duke, 'so as the better to overcome every disorderly appetite and temptation of the enemy, if one is tempted to eat more, he should eat less.' As late as 1543, Francisco had been named 'the fattest man in Valencia'. He became a vegetarian, and on this new regimen managed at last to take his great leather belt in by a hand's breadth.

Music and scholarship, architecture and art were to the Jesuits but alternative ways of touching men's souls. Nor were such things neglected at Gandía. For the library of the Jesuit college there, the Duke shipped in an entire ship's cargo of books from France and Flanders. (The college too was open to Moriscos.) Francisco indulged his passion for music, composing liturgical and organ pieces for the collegiate church of which the fragments that survive – eight motets and a mass for four voices – rank him among the masters of Spanish music in his time.

He had built himself an oratory, in the shape of a coffin, to the traditional dimensions of the Holy Sepulchre at Jerusalem. He took to fasting and self-mortification with such single-mindedness that Ignatius had to write from Rome and reprove him: 'it is a higher virtue to be able to enjoy God in different occupations and in all places than only at prayer, in your oratory. As for fasts and abstinences, I wish you to increase not to lessen your strength.' Even after Francisco had been admitted into the Company of Jesus he still went on fasting too rigorously and praying too much. At last Ignatius submitted him to discipline. In all such matters as food, clothing and sleep, Francisco was to obey the orders of a simple but sensible lay brother called Marcos, once a choirboy at Gandía. At night, when Francisco would rather have remained on his knees at prayer, Marcos would put out the light and pack him off to bed.

Eleonor had died on 27 March 1546. In 1548, the rumour got about in Spain that the Duke of Gandía might be appointed Charles V's chief minister. Since this great promotion was the last thing he wanted, Francisco made his profession as a Jesuit, though in secret. Then

Carlos his son and heir married, and Francisco could decently ask Charles V for permission to hand over both title and estate.

He knew that Charles V had no great affection for the Company of Jesus. After his great victory over the Lutheran princes at Mühlberg, the Emperor had hoped that the Council of Trent might reach some kind of working arrangement with the Protestants, by slightly watering down Catholic doctrine. But a Jesuit at the Council called Bobadilla vehemently opposed him, and this left Charles V both baffled and affronted. The German Lutherans were led after all by princes like himself, sensible men who might accept concessions and agree to sink their differences. Charles V had not yet had to cope with the Calvinists – those Bolsheviks of the sixteenth century – with whom no such compromise would ever have been possible.

In the autumn of 1550, on his way to Rome at last, and to every appearance a Duke though secretly a Jesuit, Francisco paid a passing visit to his cousin, Ercole d'Este, Duke of Ferrara – the son of golden-haired Lucrezia Borgia. The Spain Francisco had known all his life, though often violent and carnal, had never been delicately corrupt. But here in Ferrara, served at table by lackeys in the scarlet livery of the Borgias, he caught his first whiff of a decadence which in his own mind must always have been associated with 'rage and lust'.

On the walls were strange astrological frescoes by Dosso Dossi. Women with bare arms and bosoms, frizzled hair, painted faces, sat down to dine with him at a table where the silverware was the handiwork of Benvenuto Cellini. The Duchess Rénée, daughter of King Louis XII of France and a brilliant conversationalist, boasted daringly in Francisco's hearing that she admired Calvin and was going out of her way, here in Italy, to patronize the handful of secret Protestants. Such an admission was no doubt taken at the dinner table for a piece of audacious wit, but such intellectual frivolity in a member of his own class – the ruling class – must have left Francisco horrified. Everyone on either side of the question must by now have been well aware of what the coming decades of religious warfare in France were to prove: a Protestant movement could take hold here in Italy only as the outcome of a destructive civil war. He was forty, a widower, a duke and yet a Jesuit – still moving uneasily in two worlds at once. After Ferrara he turned his back on his old courtly life with revulsion.

Francisco soon discovered that Rome was hardly less vicious than when Cesare Borgia's bravos overran the streets, though perhaps the city was less violent. The current Pope, Julius III, was rather less interested in church reform than in the splendid villa he was having built for himself outside the Porta del Populo, crammed with works of art. Ecclesiastical Rome, however, had taken a distinct turn for the better. Stung by Protestant reproaches, several of the older religious orders had taken a decision to live strictly according to rule. New orders, like the Theatines, were soon to be brought into being by young men eager for saintliness. The Company of Jesus had grown enormously: from only sixty members ten years ago, it numbered 1500 by 1556, most of them highly intelligent volunteers of good family, well educated and blindly courageous.

Francisco met the General himself, Ignatius Loyola – small, lame, soldierly, courteous, and far-sighted or devious depending on whether you approved or disliked what he was doing. From a tumble-down, overcrowded house in the midst of Rome, he conducted an enormous correspondence with his followers all over the world. His secretary was a brilliant and subtle converted Jew, Father Juan de Polanco. Yet another converted Jew, Diego Lainez, who had served as a chaplain in the Tripoli campaign against the corsair chief Dragut and afterwards been papal theologian at Trent, was the order's most incisive intellect. He, like Peter Faber, was one of the seven founding members. When Ignatius died, in 1556, Lainez was to take his place as General.

On his first night under Ignatius Loyola's roof, the former Duke of Gandía doffed his fine clothes, tied an apron around his now diminished waist, and waited on his black-robed brothers at table. He then washed up for them (to his shame he broke a dish). From that time onward, manual labour intrigued Father Francisco, as it did other repentant aristocrats like Tolstoy in time to come. In the small town of Oñate, in the Basque country of northern Spain, where Francisco was sent to make his public profession as a Jesuit priest, 'far from my own company and my friends, having renounced all my possessions', Francisco regularly washed dishes, though he never managed to excel at the no less useful art of cookery. The abbess of the Poor Clares at Gandía, when she heard that the Duke was learning to sweep out a room, sent him a broom as a gift. He shifted dung in a wheelbarrow, but the craft of ploughing was too much for him. He wandered the streets of the little town with a bag over his shoulder, begging alms, and was not even disconcerted at being given a live pig: a peasant joke accepted with good humour.

The local peasants spoke nothing but Basque, and Father Francisco preached his sermons in courtly Castilian, yet a strange duke like this was too good to miss: they crowded his church to the doors. As well as being extremely tall, Father Francisco was by this time quite thin. He had reduced to skin and bone that symbolic mountain of well nourished flesh he had once borne before him. He had assimilated to the poor.

In Gandía, once Francisco's influence was removed, the Borgias had reverted to type. The new Duke, Carlos, contrived to plunge the family into a Valencian blood feud. After a sequence of mortal exchanges, Diego Borgia was obliged to run for cover to the Poor Clares in Madrid. Even Francisco's son Juan, who his father had hoped might make a Jesuit, became a source of embarrassment. After running up 10,000 ducats of debt at the university, he eloped with Ignatius's grandniece, Lorenza de Loyola, an heiress. Recurring temporarily to the Basque nobleman, Ignatius Loyola was furious.

Prince Philip, when about to leave for England and his brief marriage with Mary Tudor, asked Francisco please to go back to Tordesillas, where he had been a page thirty years before, in case something could still be done to ease the distressed mind of his grandmother, Juana la Loca. Madness in those days was taken to be possession by devils. They might baffle a physician, yet a priest might at times grapple with such devils therapeutically. Francisco spent two months of such intercession in Tordesillas, but to his last day there the demented old woman still crouched and gibbered and screamed her blasphemies.

Having served his apprenticeship at Oñate, Father Francisco re-entered the great world. He became spiritual adviser to the Regent Juana, who always went veiled and was waiting only to be relieved of her political charge so as to enter a convent. Francisco even when a young courtier had never been thought of as a ladies' man, and physically he was by this time a walking skeleton. But there was no stopping spiteful tongues. Sensitive even to a glancing threat to his authority, Prince Philip heard the evil gossip from afar, and took note. A duke become a priest, worse still, a Jesuit, who had the ear and confidence of the Regent, would be an uncomfortable anomaly in the rationally organized and centralized government he had in mind to impose on Spain.

In Lent of 1555, when Juana la Loca lay dying, Father Francisco was sent once again to Tordesillas. This time the concentrated attention of the priest she had known as a boy had its effect. Juana's lifelong derangement became at least intermitted. When asked if she died in the Catholic faith and wished to receive the sacrament, Juana la Loca was distinctly heard to say 'Yes.' Father Francisco was able to console Charles V with the news that after decades of loud blasphemy his mother's last words had been, 'Crucified Jesus, be with me!' The change Father Francisco's presence had worked in the unhappy woman was regarded all over Spain as a miracle: a man who gains this kind of reputation when others have failed inevitably makes enemies.

In 1556, Charles V got his own way at last, and retired to the monastery at Yuste. His Hieronymite confessor there, Fray Juan de Regla, once a peasant, had a rough side to his tongue. He scented a rival in Father Francisco. He did his best to convince the Emperor that these new people, the Jesuits, if not outright agents of Satan, were at the very least spies of the Grand Turk. The fact that some of the most eminent Jesuits were converted Jews served to verify Juan de Regla's suspicions.

Melchior Cano, the Dominican who was to preach at such length during the auto-da-fé at Valladolid, began surreptitiously furnishing the Hieronymite monks at Yuste with arguments to discredit Father Francisco. The Jesuits, Cano wrote, hoping his words would be repeated in the ear of Charles V, 'change the gentlemen who fall into their hands from lions into hens, soldiers into women, gentlemen into merchants'. When the old friends met again, Charles V confided to Luis Quixada that he found 'Father Francisco very different'. The two men still had this much in common, that to gain peace of mind, one had renounced a dukedom, the other a worldwide empire.

On 28 December 1556, Charles and Francisco had a serious conversation lasting three hours, during which Francisco tried to clear up all misunderstandings. 'I told him all about the Company,' he informed his superiors in Rome, 'of which he did not have a good opinion, owing to unfavourable information. I won, thanks to the great strength which God grants to simple straightforwardness and truth.'

'I must believe you,' had been Charles V's reply to his cousin, 'as I have always found you truthful.' Francisco had tried to impress on him that 'the Company combined the active and contemplative lives, Mary and Martha, so that it was the best imitation of Christ.' To rub it in that Jesuits were not hens, Francisco introduced his companion, Father Bartolomé Bustamente, whom Charles V had last met twenty-one years before, on active service, at the time he captured

Tunis. After this shrewd and courtierlike counter-stroke, Charles V began to feel that the Jesuits might be men after his own heart, and told Luis Quixada to make them a donation in his name of 200 ducats. Nothing splendid – but then, as ever, Charles V was short of ready cash. In September 1558, when Charles V died, it was discovered that so as to make sure his exact wishes would be carried out, he had made Father Francisco his executor.

When Father Francisco arrived in Valladolid to preach the dead Emperor's funeral sermon, he found the atmosphere changed for the worse. Melchior Cano, as the theologian who supported the King against the Pope, occupied a high place in the reorganized Inquisition. He was giving currency to an argument often used against the Jesuits – that the money they collected for their cause and sent to Rome was so much gold lost to the kingdom. But this was an argument for simpletons.

King Philip's real if silent objection to the Jesuits, as indeed to the Knights of Malta, or for that matter to converted Jews, whom he also mistrusted, was that they were cosmopolitan. They would never be completely under his thumb. Philip proposed to hand down a unified kingdom and empire intact to his successors. God's regent in Spain's enormous empire was to be Philip himself, in his cell at the Escorial, at a wooden table covered with piles of paper, having the last word in every secular decision over half the known world.

But the Jesuits, too, saw themselves as serving God. Since King Philip – apart from certain lapses – acted in the light of conscience, as a just prince should, they were obliged in secular matters to do him willing service. But their primary obedience here on earth was to the Pope, as spokesman for all Christendom. This primary loyalty of theirs was what galled Philip. The nation-state was then a novelty, and its chief instrument in Spain was the Inquisition, which relied ultimately on torture. The moral obligation which consequently might at times be placed upon others to stand up to Leviathan was a stumbling block in King Philip's path, and he knew it.

In 1558, in the fearful calm before that spectacular auto-da-fé at Valladolid to which Magdalena de Ulloa was to bring young Gerónimo, Father Francisco sent this warning to another Jesuit called Ribadeniera: 'Lutherans have been unmasked here, and plenty of people are saying in court and in Castile that we are the cause of these errors, that I have been arrested or we are about to be burned. Such is the common talk.' The Inquisitor-General stopped Father Francisco from leaving Valladolid. He was ordered instead to go to the prison where the Inquisitors were holding the sister of his son-in-law, Doña María Henriques. He was to tell her what her punishment would be. 'I had to comfort and strengthen her,' Francisco wrote to Father Lainez in Rome, 'to help her to submit bravely.' Melchior Cano, with a star preacher's gift for a barbed phrase, had already publicly described the Jesuits as 'predecessors of anti-Christ'. The Inquisitors were ready to deliver their meticulously prepared blow at Father Francisco himself.

The little doctrinal book, *The Practice of Christian Works* – written when Francisco was still viceroy in Barcelona, and long before he was granted his doctorate in theology – had lately been printed again, obscurely, in the provincial town of Medina del Campo, in a pirated edition. Into the text some unknown hand had slipped passages of a Lutheran tendency, not to be found in the first edition.

When *The Practice of Christian Works* was condemned as heretical, Francisco's many friends were obliged in the atmosphere of terror then prevailing to hold their tongues. Meanwhile scandalmongers in a cleverly orchestrated outburst were doing all they could to demolish Father Francisco's character, with their tall tales of his friendship with the Regent Juana, his pernicious influence over the dead Emperor, the rumour that with Juana la Loca he had worked a miracle. For King Philip, such causes of complaint against Father Francisco could at the most have been irritating pinpricks. But they were being cleverly transformed into pretexts upon which the Inquisition could fasten, to use against him.

Despite his shabby robe and gaunt, saintly face, Francisco still had the preternaturally alert social instincts of an old courtier. He moved without warning away from the danger – not in the direction expected of him by the familiars of the Inquisition, to Rome, but sideways and backwards to Portugal, where Catherine, his boyhood friend, was now Queen. As soon as Father Lainez got to hear, he ordered Father Francisco somehow to make his way to Rome: he was a man under obedience. But the political use now being made of the Spanish Inquisition had shaken Francisco profoundly. His health broke under the strain. Being compelled to act disobediently after having accepted Jesuit discipline was psychologically perhaps the last straw.

While he was convalescent in Portugal from fever, gout, bladder trouble and nervous paralysis, word came to him that King Philip was striking out at the errant members of the Borgia family: no one, whatever his wealth, rank or past services, must elude royal justice. Diego Borgia was plucked from his sanctuary with the Poor Clares in Madrid, and his head was hacked off. Felipe Borgia, who had also killed in the blood feud, skipped overseas to Africa in the nick of time. Then Father Francisco, having regained a measure of health in peaceful Portugal, contrived to make his way back to Rome – where an even greater part in the crisis of his times awaited him.

5
The Kingdom in a Noose

The world is not evenly divided. Of its three parts, our enemies
hold Asia as their hereditary home. Yet here, formerly, our Faith
put out its branches; here all the Apostles save two met their
deaths. But now the Christians of those parts, if there are any left,
squeeze a bare subsistence from the soil, and pay tribute to their
enemies, looking to us with silent longing for the liberty they have
lost. Africa too, the second part of the world, has been held by our
enemies by force of arms for two hundred years or more, a danger
to Christendom all the greater because it formerly sustained men
whose works will keep the rust of age from Holy Writ as long as
the Latin tongue survives. Thirdly, there is Europe. This little
portion of the world which is ours is pressed upon by warlike
Turks and Saracens: for three hundred years they have held Spain
and the Balearic Islands, and they live in hope of
devouring the rest.

WILLIAM OF MALMESBURY: *Gesta Regum*, 1125 (quoting the
speech of Pope Urban II to the Council of Clermont, 1095)

For Italian merchants trading in the eleventh century from Amalfi to
the Holy Land, a load of Christian pilgrims was a profitable cargo. In
Jerusalem, as an act of charity, they set up a hospital for sick pilgrims
near the church of St John the Baptist. In course of time, other such
hospitals were endowed along the pilgrim road which crossed
Provence and went the length of Italy – and on 15 February 1113, Pope
Paschal took the Noble Order of the Knights of St John of Jerusalem
under his protection, charging them to care for pilgrims who fell sick
on their journey, and give them armed protection as they travelled.
For their badge, the Knights wore the distinctive eight-pointed cross,
rich with pious symbolism, which had been inscribed on the banner of
Amalfi – the present-day Maltese Cross.

In 1099, crusading knights from Western Europe managed to recapture Jerusalem from the Moslems who had gained possession of the
Holy City over four centuries before, when the followers of Mahomet
exploded out of Arabia. They set up little Latin kingdoms along the
eastern shore of the Mediterranean, so that the inland sea became what
it had been once before, briefly, in antiquity, and was to be again in the

first part of our own century: a Christian preserve. The Knights of St John, together with their rivals, the Knights Templar, were the shock troops of the Latin kingdoms in the Levant – the military corps d'élite. But even before the Ottoman Turks burst out of their little principality in northern Anatolia and began once again spreading Islam by the sword, the Arabs under Saladin were pushing the Crusaders out.

Their little kingdoms along the mainland collapsed, the Holy Land fell once again under Moslem rule, and the Knights of St John retreated to nearby islands – first to Cyprus, then to Rhodes, which was their base from 1309 to 1523. In gratitude for their services, pious crusaders and returning pilgrims had by this time endowed them with estates scattered all across Europe, from which they drew rents – by tradition spending a third of this income on arms, and on the upkeep of hospital and headquarters. Their rivals the Templars went in for international banking, made too many enemies, and failed to survive. But the Knights of St John as well as being combative and acquisitive were compassionate. On Rhodes, as they waited patiently for a second chance to liberate Jerusalem, they went on treating all the sick who arrived at the doors of their hospital, Christian, Jew and Moslem alike, on terms of equality – they would even nurse their wounded enemies back to health and strength.

The Knights took to seafaring. From the harbours of Rhodes and Halicarnassos they preyed on Moslem shipping. The Ottoman Turks, who had taken Constantinople and were to extend their empire all along the coast from Greece to Egypt and beyond, were their chief prey, and in the end the Knights' piracies made Rhodes too hot to hold them. In 1480 a Turkish expeditionary force landed on Rhodes from 140 ships but after a fight lasting ten weeks they were driven out. The Knights, under Pierre d'Aubusson – 'Ye have swords, messires, use them!' was his famous exclamation – had killed 6000 janissaries. Sultan Mahomet II, conqueror of Constantinople, swore revenge, but as well as swordsmen the Knights were masters of firearms and fortification – a Turkish onslaught in 1485 was again defeated.

But in 1522 Soleiman the Magnificent landed 200,000 men on Rhodes – an army outnumbering the Knights and their followers by a factor of twenty to one. The siege of Rhodes, even so, went on for six months, and cost Soleiman 90,000 men – nearly half his army. When the Knights finally gave in, Soleiman showed no resentment, but magnanimously allowed them to leave Rhodes with all the honours of war. 'It weighs on me somewhat,' said the twenty-eight-year-old

Soleiman, on 1 January 1523, as he watched the white-headed Grand
Master, Philip Villiers de l'Isle Adam, lead his men down to the ships,
'that I should be coming thither to chase this ancient Christian warrior
from his home.'

Military Knights entering the Order of St John were usually the
younger sons of great families; they were expected to prove an impec-
cably aristocratic descent. Conventual Chaplains did not bear arms.
The family origin of Lay Brothers need only be 'respectable', and their
sole concern was fighting. According to whether he came from
France, Provence or Auvergne, Italy, Aragon or Castile, Germany or
England, each Knight was allotted to his *Langue*. Those who spoke the
same language and messed together in the celibate brotherhood of the
same Auberge also shared duty on one particular stretch of the castle
wall. They were all ruled over by a Grand Master, who was voted into
office by the Knights themselves, and then confirmed by the Pope. In
all other respects the Order was sovereign, and on Rhodes had even
coined its own money.

Over the centuries, the Knights of St John had had their ups and
downs. Material prosperity might continue to sap their will, until
eventually an outstanding Grand Master applied the rule firmly and
revived their crusading spirit. The religious obligation laid upon the
Knights of nursing the sick had in the long run a tonic effect upon
them. From classical Greek medicine as interpreted by the Arabs they
had learned much. But the Knights had also made valuable discoveries
of their own. The cutting up of dead bodies was frowned upon at the
time by both Moslems and Christians. But the Knights went on
observing a custom invaluable to science, of allowing a Knight on his
deathbed to do medicine one last service by willing his body to his
comrades for dissection.

After the Knights of St John had been driven out of Rhodes, their
aged Grand Master, de l'Isle Adam, wandered for seven years around
the courts of Europe offering their services. But as a volunteer fighting
force in a time of intensifying nationalism, the Knights had two grave
drawbacks. They owed fealty not to the monarch who might consent
to employ them, but only to the Pope. And they were forbidden by
their oath to wage war on other Christians: they were available to fight
only the enemies of all Christendom.

Their Grand Master at last found a kindred spirit in the Emperor

Charles V. If Sultan Soleiman could make use of the corsairs of North
Africa as his naval irregulars, why not employ the Knights against
him in a similar way? In 1530 they were allowed to settle in the bare
and windswept archipelago of Malta 'in order that they may perform
in peace the duties of their Religion,' wrote Charles V, 'and employ
their forces and arms against the perfidious enemies of the Holy Faith.'
His viceroy on Sicily was to charge them only a nominal yearly rent – a
falcon. They changed their name to the Sovereign and Military Order
of the Knights of Malta.

Two stony and windswept islands, Malta and Gozo, stand plump in
the straits between Europe and Africa, sixty miles from Sicily and 180
from Tunisia. Except for a few springs, the islands depend for their
water on rain caught in cisterns – and there was in those days so little
vegetation that thistles and dried dung were commonly used as fuel.
But Malta though agriculturally poor had a splendid harbour. With
the Knights established on Malta, no Turkish fleet could enter the
Western Mediterranean without exposing its lines of communication
to the enterprising harassment of the Knights' war galleys.

The Maltese were fervently Catholic and fiercely independent.
They had suffered endlessly from corsair raids. At Mdina, the ancient
capital, the Grand Master pledged his word to maintain Malta's
ancient rights and liberties – and though the Maltese aristocracy may
have resented the presence of the Knights, the common people were
not sorry for their protection.

In a world where gunpowder and the printing press were becoming
implements of dominion – where nation-states had begun to flourish,
and explorers were mapping America – the Knights of Malta had an
archaic air. They still fought in armour – and only against Moslems.
They were a relic of the Crusades. In 1540 the English King, Henry
VIII, had ordered that all those English Knights who refused to deny
their fealty to the Pope should have their heads cut off – forcing such
an oath upon them made it easy for him to grab the land held in trust
for the Order by the English Grand Priory. The *Johanniterorden* – the
German branch of the Order – survived Luther's Reformation only by
becoming Protestant. The Knights were an anachronism, an aristocratic survival. Driven out of Rhodes by Sultan Soleiman, chivvied
eventually from their other refuge in Tripoli, harried by German
Lutherans and by an English king who had the impudence to call
himself Defender of the Faith, it might well seem that their day was
done. What could a few hundred men in armour do, against the

massive seaborne attack likely to be launched upon them one day soon by the invincible Turk?

From Tripoli to the borders of Morocco, the North African corsairs looked upon Soleiman the Magnificent as their overlord. He had garrisoned Algiers, their most important base, with 2000 of his janissaries. The corsairs were his eyes and ears, the probing point of his sword. At the end of the Mediterranean furthest from Constantinople they gave him a naval presence which he could repudiate whenever it suited his diplomacy. And they cost him nothing: indeed, since the Sultan was their suzerain the corsairs let him have 20 per cent of all their plunder.

In summertime, when they went out cruising on the account, what the corsairs wanted most were captives. Ransoms could be negotiated for the richer ones, and if the poorer men taken captive refused to give up their Christianity they could be set to work as slaves – for most of the year as building labourers and market gardeners, but for three or four months in summer, as galley slaves. In Algiers these foreign slaves were housed ashore, not too uncomfortably, in slave barracks called bagnios. A priest who had been taken prisoner was allowed to say a daily Mass for them, since the observant corsairs had noticed how much more willingly a prisoner who was devout did his work. In the slave market of Algiers, a pig-headed and possibly heretic Englishman fetched a third the price of a Catholic Spaniard.

Algiers only fifty years earlier had been a small and exposed anchorage. The change came when refugees began arriving across the straits of Gibraltar – Moors expelled from Granada, Jews, mainly from Aragon, who would neither give up nor dissimulate their religion. Some of the Moors who had once lived in Spain took to the sea, and got their own back as pirates. Jews now settled in Algiers made use of their international connections to arrange ransoms, market plunder and smuggle in war supplies, particularly from Marseilles. Enriched beyond measure by this endless flow of stolen goods, ransoms paid in cash and abundant cheap labour, Algiers prospered, soon becoming a handsome walled city of villas set in gardens. A horde of Christian slaves was set to work on the building of a mole out to an offshore islet – by 1560, this artificial harbour was big enough to shelter a fleet.

The corsairs had gone cruising at first in galliots – lateen-rigged open boats, rowed by a dozen oarsmen and sometimes mounting a brass bow chaser. Except for its lateen sail, a galliot was not unlike the oared ship in which Odysseus and his comrades had voyaged, in Homeric times. But as Algiers and other corsair cities along the coast prospered, they began to launch war galleys, each rowed by up to a hundred slaves – less robust than a Spanish war galley, and less heavily gunned, but handier. A couple of such war galleys, crammed with armed men, would lead out a flotilla of nimble and vindictive little galliots. And such a raiding force had nothing to fear from anything but the kind of large cruising naval squadron that Don John of Austria was sent to command, on his first active service.

Whether launched from a slipway in Barcelona or in Algiers, no new galley could move out to sea until a full complement of rowers had been found for it – just as a modern ship of war is useless until equipped with an engine. With galley fleets on both sides growing larger, a sinister hunt began around the Western Mediterranean for human motive power. In 1555 Sultan Soleiman sent the corsair leader, Dragut, in consort with his own admiral, Piale Pasha, to bring back slaves from southern Italy. They took and enslaved every living soul in the city of Reggio, across the strait from Messina. In a similar raid on Corsica, Dragut made slaves of 6000 citizens of Bastia. No one at sea or on shore was safe.

Even famous captains ran the risk of finding themselves chained to an oar. Jean Parisot de la Valette – elected Grand Master of the Knights of Malta in 1557 – had been caught sixteen years earlier by a corsair called Kust-Ali. La Valette spent twelve months tugging a Turkish oar to the flick of a whip before he could be exchanged. And the corsairs' greatest leader, Dragut, had also done time, at the oar of a Genoese galley.

Dragut was born of Greek parents, Orthodox Christians, at Charabulac on the coast of Asia Minor, but a Turkish governor took a fancy to the boy and carried him off to Egypt. After learning the trade of gunner and serving the Mamelukes (who earlier had disdained artillery as a 'dishonourable weapon', only to be defeated by the Turks in consequence) Dragut went to sea with the Sultan's famous admiral, Barbarossa. The men under his command were said to 'fear Dragut more than they feared death itself' and his exploits against the Christians earned him the complimentary title of 'The Drawn Sword of Islam'. Yet in 1549, the famous Dragut, too, had been laid by the heels, when the thirteen ships he commanded were neatly trapped under the guns of a Corsican fortress by one of Andrea Doria's more disreputable kinsmen, Giannatino. ('What! Am I slave to that effeminate catamite?' stormed Dragut, when he saw there was no way out.) Dragut served four years before Barbarossa handed over the very large ransom – of 3000 ducats – which the Genoese had decided to ask for him.

In 1559, several of the Christian states who suffered from this annual corsair slave raiding had managed to patch up their differences. Warships from Spain, Florence, Genoa, Sicily, Naples and Monaco, together with a squadron from the Papal States, joined forces with the galleys of the Knights inside Malta Grand Harbour. To the number of 200 sail they proceeded south past Tunis until they came near an important corsair base called Djerba – in antiquity, the Isle of the Lotus-Eaters.

Overwhelmed by their sudden arrival and massive presence the corsairs on Djerba gave in quickly – and the victors imposed on the island an annual tribute of 6000 ducats, four ostriches, four gazelles, four stallions and a camel (since some of the allied monarchs had private zoos). But the following spring Piale Pasha and Dragut arrived off Djerba with a Turkish fleet, and on 14 May 1560 took the allies by surprise, trapping their ships on a lee shore. The Turks sank or burned twenty Christian galleys and twenty-seven store ships, wiping out the entire papal squadron. They put 14,000 troops ashore, and the fight for the island lasted eighty days, Don Alvaro de Sande and his men yielding only when Djerba's brackish water supply had given out. Djerba was lost, and the allied fleets had for the time being been reduced to impotence.

Stripped of mast and rudder, the Christian galleys made prize at Djerba were towed in triumph up the Bosphorus to Constantinople, the leading vessel, as a mark of humiliation, dragging in the water a banner, captured from the Spanish army, depicting Christ on the cross. Don Alvaro de Sande and his men were paraded, three by three, in chains, through the city streets. But Don Alvaro himself had put up such a good fight on Djerba that the Turks offered him command of one of their armies fighting against Persia. Of course he must first abjure his fealty to King Philip and the Faith. Don Alvaro told them that he would rather go on living in chains.

At the final Council of Trent the idea had again been mooted of a unified Christian resistance to the Turks. This idea had been around for a long time, and when tried out had led nowhere. The days of the Crusades were long over, and the abject defeat on Djerba was no encouragement to forming larger alliances. Hard-headed men were pointing out, now as before, that it was simply a matter of political arithmetic. Spain, though the most powerful Christian state in the Mediterranean, could simply not built enough galleys, on her own, to challenge the Turks, even if King Philip had the will and the money to embark on such an arms race – and he had neither. Catholic France, always envious of Spain, was a tacit ally of the Grand Turk's, and in the past had even let the Turkish fleet make use of the French naval base at Toulon. Catholic Venice had a very large fleet indeed. But most of her war galleys were laid up, while Turks and Venetians – to whom the Sultan had granted valuable commercial privileges – did a thriving business together. The proposal made by a handful of visionary priests for a Holy League against Turkish aggression was thus shown to be hopelessly impractical.

King Philip was having bad luck with his warships. In 1562 he lost twenty-three of his galleys, wrecked in a gale on a rocky shore at Herradura. Next year the corsairs captured seven more of his galleys in an ambush off the Lipari islands. Thus, for the time being, Spain's entire naval strength in the Mediterranean was weaker than the single corsair force under Dragut operating just then off southern Italy, of which the viceroy reported from Naples that 'Dragut with 35 vessels hath held the kingdom in a noose'. Until his lost galleys could be replaced, King Philip had to step with care. On a visit to Valencia in 1563, he had been obliged to look on while a corsair galliot three miles offshore boarded and made prize of a Spanish coaster. Word came to him that corsairs had landed on the coast near Granada and taken 4000 prisoners; they raided Malaga in broad daylight. Intelligence reports were also beginning to reach Madrid that the Moriscos of Granada, who had lived fairly peaceably for the past thirty years, were taking these corsair raids as an assurance that if only they asserted themselves, the Turks were sure to come to their aid.

The Knights of Malta, numbering only a few hundred men and possessing less than a dozen galleys, were all this time, however, taking the war to the enemy. The Chevalier Mathurin Romegas, a masterly seaman, led them out on piratical raids so audacious that he provoked the Turks to anger. In 1561 he took several valuable cargoes in the delta of the Nile itself. In 1563 he captured eight more of the Sultan's merchant ships there, bringing back with him to Malta 500 slaves, white and black, to row the Knights' galleys and work with pick and shovel on the harbour fortifications.

Chevalier Romegas's next exploit earned him the bitter enmity of those mistresses of intrigue, the matrons of the Sultan's harem. As his squadron of seven galleys was cruising between Zante and Cephallonia, he came up with a very large Turkish merchantman, carrying a freight worth 80,000 ducats – a cargo of Venetian luxuries on their way to Constantinople. The fight was sharp and costly, since 200 janissaries had been placed on board to give the ship special protection. After the Turkish merchantman was taken, Romegas found several notabilities on board, for whom the Turks might pay a high ransom, including the nurse of the Sultan's favourite daughter Mihrmah. The costly cargo had been a speculation, financed by Kustir Aga, chief eunuch of the seraglio, and both Mihrmah and other harem matrons had taken shares in it, in the confident expectation of a large profit.

The furious old ladies at once went to work on Sultan Soleiman's more vulnerable side – his piety. He could hardly enter his own harem without being tartly reminded that the slaves now rowing the Knights' galleys for them were Turkish prisoners. When he went down from Seraglio Point to Friday prayers in the great mosque built in his name between the Bosphorus and the Golden Horn, the sermon after prayers echoed the same theme. 'Only thy invincible sword,' proclaimed the Imam, 'can shatter the chains of these unfortunate people, whose cries are ascending to heaven, and afflicting the ears of the Prophet of Allah.'

The Turkish cabinet – the divan – sat four times a week to discuss the business of the Empire, and very often, so far as appearances went, in the absence of the Sultan. But the viziers were all well aware that Soleiman might be hidden behind a wooden grille let in the wall, and listening to what they had to say. So they voiced their opinions with care, taking into account all the pressures that the Sultan himself might be under: a bad guess could cost a man his head. Well aware of the agitation in the harem, the viziers tended therefore to emphasize the advantages of an attack on Malta, and play down the difficulties. There were other options, and if Soleiman had been left in peace to make up his own mind, some of the viziers – Sokolli was one –

thought he might have preferred an offensive in Hungary. The Emperor, having sought a peace with Soleiman the Magnificent in 1562, was buying him off with presents. But the Turks had a poor opinion of the soldiers who just now stood between themselves and Vienna. ('So many women, and we have beaten them as many times as we have come to blows.') Along the wild Hungarian borderland there was always enough trouble for some incident somewhere to furnish a pretext for war. But as the argument proceeded, in and out of the divan, it became clear that the harem was winning: the next target would be Malta.

Old Dragut's opinion had already been sought. His blunt advice on Malta was, 'Unless you have smoked out this nest of vipers you can do no good anywhere.' Another of Soleiman's sea captains had warned the Sultan not to underestimate the Knights. Their galleys, he said, 'were not like others. They have aboard a great number of arquebusiers, and of Knights who are dedicated to fight to the death'. Another adviser, describing Malta as 'this cursed rock', had told the Sultan, 'if you do not decide to take it quickly, it will in a short time interrupt all communications between Africa and Asia and the islands of the Archipelago.'

To Soleiman himself, the Western Mediterranean represented both a mass of tempting plunder and a religious duty. At one time the larger islands there, Sicily, Sardinia, Majorca, had all been under the sway of Islam, as indeed had Spain itself. In October 1564, the divan met to take its formal decision, in the light of the evidence, as to where next the Ottoman Turks, a people organized for war, should take the offensive. The rocky little island might be barren of crops and short of water. But if only the Turks could take Malta quickly, its great harbour would serve as the base for yet another leap forward – a landing, for instance, on the wheat-growing island of Sicily, only sixty miles to the north. The corsair chiefs knew the Sicilian coast like the back of their hand; the Sicilians were known to resent Spanish overlordship. There would be nothing between Malta and Sicily to oppose the Turkish fleet but a squadron of thirty galleys under the Spanish viceroy – an old and hesitant veteran called Don García de Toledo. From Malta it would be feasible to land directly on the southern shores of Italy, or even to cross over to Spain, where the Moriscos were waiting. With Malta taken, the Turks next year could keep the whole Western Mediterranean on the jump.

The Turkish High Command had by this time precise and recent information about the state of Malta's Grand Harbour, which La Valette and his men were still working against time to fortify. Two of the Sultan's military engineers, a Slav and a Greek, both renegades, had landed on Malta not long since, dressed as fishermen, and had 'noted every gun and measured every battery'. The building work there, so they reported, was a long way from finished. In their professional opinion, 'Malta could be taken in a few days'.

Soleiman the Magnificent was seventy, and despite his abstemiousness he too was beginning to suffer from gout. Since the capture of Malta itself was to be no more than a rapid preliminary to some more important landing further on, no one was surprised when the old Sultan decided for once not to lead his men in person. The fleet was entrusted to Piale Pasha – a decision which pleased both the harem and the men grouped around Prince Selim, the heir apparent. Piale Pasha had the support of the harem because he was married to Selim's daughter, Genhir. He had been given the credit when he was thirty-five for driving the Knights out of their forward base at Tripoli – though without the help of old Dragut on that occasion, he might not have been so lucky. His slave raids though profitable had been a walkover. He was an admiral who so far had never been tested against severe opposition.

Dragut at nearly eighty was judged to be too old and perhaps too opinionated for the supreme command against Malta, but he would turn up there with his men, in time to help. The old corsair passed on two pieces of good advice: start early, and detach fifty galleys to threaten Spain itself, thus making it more difficult for the Spaniards to assemble a larger fleet against you.

On 29 March 1565, Soleiman the Magnificent went down in procession to the Golden Horn, where the Malta fleet had been drawn up for his inspection. Of the 180 ships in the famous horn-shaped bay, 130 were war galleys. Several of the supply ships in the tail of the fleet had been provided for the Sultan's service by the Jews of Constantinople. They too were enraged with the Knights – 'those most evil monks of Malta' – for their recent practice of rummaging Christian merchantmen, which previously they had let alone, so as to take out, in their jocose phrase, *ropa de judios*, that is to say, any merchandise consigned to Jews trading under the Sultan's protection, but sent for safety in the hold of a Christian ship.

Jovial and cunning Ali, the Grand Vizier, came down to bid the two leaders goodbye – Piale, about whose capacity as admiral he had his private doubts, and the sixty-five-year-old army commander, Mustafa, brave but obtuse, a lineal descendant of the Prophet's standard-bearer, and therefore a lucky personage. In 1522, as a young man, Mustafa had fought against the Knights on Rhodes. As the two leaders went aboard the flagship, Ali was heard to remark ironically, 'There go two cheerful fellows, always glad to partake of their coffee and opium, off on a pleasure cruise among the islands.'

Soleiman's fleet for Malta was carrying 40,000 fighting men, including 6500 janissaries armed with long-barrelled German arquebuses, the best procurable. One ship carried a siege train; another was freighted with 6000 barrels of gunpowder. In obedience to tradition, the Sultan himself fell in with the janissaries, just like any other private soldier, and lined up with them to draw his pay. Then Soleiman toasted his comrades in sherbet from a great beaker – to be given back afterwards to the janissaries filled with gold pieces. 'We shall see each other again,' he told them, repeating the familiar toast, 'at the Red Apple.'

Ripe, bright, and full of juicy plunder, the Red Apple was Rome.

News that a large Turkish war fleet was being got ready for sea had filtered through to Vienna by the last days of 1564. Don García de Toledo, in Sicily, heard the news from his own spies, independently, and wrote warning King Philip to be free of other Mediterranean entanglements by April of 1565 – trouble was on its way. By January 1565 Spanish intelligence knew for sure that the objective was Malta. Merchants from neutral Ragusa reported the first twenty Turkish galleys through the wind-tossed Dardanelles before the end of March – the Turks had evidently taken Dragut's advice about making an early start. Then, from a merchant in Constantinople well disposed towards the Knights, La Valette their Grand Master procured a secret copy of the Turkish war plan, written in lemon juice between the lines of a bill of lading.

6
Malta Besieged

Many more difficult victories have fallen to your
scimitar than the capture of a handful of men in a
tiny little island that is not well fortified.
VIZIERS OF THE DIVAN to Soleiman
the Magnificent, October 1564

Jean Parisot de la Valette, the Grand Master of the Knights of Malta, was described by the French writer Brantôme, who knew him when he served there, as 'tall, calm, unemotional, handsome.' He was related to the Counts of Toulouse, whose forbears had served on Crusade under St Louis. La Valette had left his home in Gascony to join the Order when he was twenty – he was now seventy-one.

The brethren had been well aware that in choosing La Valette they were electing a Grand Master who would be an enlightened disciplinarian – a man, in their own words, 'capable of converting a Protestant or governing a kingdom'. La Valette obliged his Knights to keep strictly to their vows. He put down duels, drinking and dicing, and maintained a regular observance in religion. The severe and fervent mood encouraged elsewhere in the Roman Catholic church by the Counter-Reformation was already apparent in Malta in 1565, the year the island was placed in such jeopardy.

The Turkish war plan, sent secretly from Constantinople, was decoded and translated for La Valette by his Latin Secretary, an elderly Knight of the English *Langue* called Sir Oliver Starkey, who had managed to elude the axe of Henry VIII's headsman. As a confidential warning, copies of the plan were sent to all the crowned heads of Europe. La Valette then had Sir Oliver send out a General Citation – ordering any Knight who might find himself at a royal court, or busy with one of the Order's estates elsewhere, to come in at once to headquarters and do duty. From all over Europe, members of the Order took horse and ship for Malta.

The Spanish King's viceroy in Sicily, Don García de Toledo, sailed across to Malta for consultations, bringing with him his younger son, Federico. The boy – 'a promising youth, who took the habit' – had told Don García of his wish to join the Order. Federico stayed on in Malta for the siege. Don García agreed with La Valette on the need to ship out useless mouths and to fetch in wheat, which the Knights stored in the underground galleries they had prepared cut from the solid rock and sealed with a sandstone plug. Water on this dry island was also an important munition of war. Inside the unfinished fortifications on both sides of Grand Harbour, clay jars filled with drinking water had been sealed and stowed under cover. From their influential friends abroad, the Knights begged munitions and supplies. The Duke of Tuscany sent them 200 barrels of excellent gunpowder – a trifle, compared with the shipload the Turks were bringing with them, but in the event, those barrels were to make all the difference.

At the first head count that spring there were 541 Knights on Malta. Between three and four thousand Maltese were also eager to serve against the Turk. Powder was so short that men volunteering could be allowed only five practice shots with an arquebus at a mark before they were sent into action. By 18 May – the day the enormous Turkish fleet was sighted offshore, sailing in three divisions – 700 Knights had returned to their place of duty on Malta.

The Turkish galleys were first seen at dawn, fifteen miles offshore, by a sentry placed high up on the walls of St Elmo – a fortification in the shape of a four-pointed star, up on Mount Sciberass, northward across Grand Harbour from La Valette's headquarters in Castle St Angelo. The Turks came slowly closer, in a crescent formation which spanned the horizon. They anchored in a bay to the south of Grand Harbour, a malarial place called Marsasirocco, and began to land. By 20 May they had put 23,000 troops ashore. After dark an Italian Knight called Giovanni Castrucco ran Piale Pasha's inefficient blockade of the island in a small fishing boat, and headed for Sicily. He bore to Don García a personal message from La Valette: 'the siege has begun. The Turkish fleet is close on 200 ships. We await your help.' Piale Pasha and his fleet had made an unexpectedly swift passage from the Levant – Genoese merchants only two weeks before had reported him as loading biscuit and troops on Chios. He had taken the Knights by surprise.

While the Turkish fleet was still offshore and slowly approaching, La Valette had led his 700 Knights into chapel, to confession and then to Mass. he spoke to them frankly and yet encouragingly of what they would have to face. 'A formidable army composed of audacious barbarians,' he is reported to have said, 'is descending on this island. These persons, my brothers, are the enemies of Jesus Christ. Today it is a question of the defence of our faith – as to whether the Gospels are to be superseded by the Koran. God on this occasion demands of us our lives, already vowed to His service. Happy will be those who first consummate this sacrifice.' When chapel was over, said an eyewitness, the Knights 'went out from thence as men who had received a new birth.'

Castle St Angelo on the southern shore of Grand Harbour – La Valette's headquarters – was protected on its landward side by a long curtain wall, and the defence of this wall was the duty of the *Langue* of Castile. Over on the harbour's northern shore ran Mount Sciberass, a high and narrow spit of rock, and near its headland the star-shaped Castle of St Elmo, as yet unfinished, served as a defensive outwork to Grand Harbour. On the far side of Mount Sciberass, and out of sight from Grand Harbour, ran another long inlet called Marsa Muscetta. Malta is windswept, and Piale Pasha the Turkish admiral, fearing for his ships, thought Marsa Muscetta would make a safer anchorage than the bay where the soldiers were being put ashore. But the anchorage at Marsa Muscetta would be dominated by the guns of St Elmo. Piale therefore proposed to the soldiers that they begin by taking the inconvenient outwork for him – a matter, said the Turkish Chief Military Engineer, of four or five days.

Meanwhile Mustafa, commanding the army, made his first tentative and inconclusive attack on Castle St Angelo itself head-on, against the curtain wall held by the *Langue* of Castile.

They had been deliberately misled into making this wrong choice by a Knight called Adrien de la Rivière, who at the head of some Maltese irregulars had kept the Turks under observation as they landed. La Rivière had been wounded and taken prisoner, and Mustafa, the Turkish army commander, handed him over to the torturers, with orders that they were to make him tell which was the weaker side of Castle St Angelo. The captured Knight was put to the bastinado – slow and repeated blows by a rod on the belly and the soles of the feet, which lead eventually to an agonizingly painful death by internal haemorrhage. La Rivière before he died of this treatment managed to make his Turkish interrogator accept as the truth what were two heroic lies – that the castle's weak place was the curtain wall and that

Don García on Sicily planned to use his galleys aggressively, and would soon be landing a relief force: precisely the news the Turkish leaders least wanted to hear.

At the curtain wall, the Turks ran into trouble. They had been sent into attack under the unexpected fire of La Valette's two new batteries, mounted on the castle roof to dominate all the approaches from landward. Then from the sally port in the curtain wall itself, which they supposed to be weakly held, out poured the Spanish Knights in such force that this first attack was humiliatingly driven off.

The Sultan's commanders were by this time in two minds. Mustafa thought that St Elmo might be safely ignored. He would rather concentrate his force on taking Castle St Angelo and thus capturing Grand Harbour. Piale Pasha – who owed much of his promotion to harem intrigue – wanted no wrecked galleys to be scored against him. If his ships were at risk, so was the army and the whole enterprise. He insisted on being provided with a better anchorage at once. Ships, he pointed out, were costly. Men were not.

After their rebuff at the curtain wall of Castle St Angelo, the Turkish army leaders felt bound to defer to Piale, so they consented to take St Elmo for him. This was a blunder. Successfully reading their minds, La Valette sent sixty-five Knights and 200 soldiers across Grand Harbour in boats, after dark, and up the steep incline of Mount Sciberass, to reinforce St Elmo's garrison. So long as the Turks could not stop him doing this, St Elmo would go on being a thorn in their side. In the meantime a mass of turbanned soldiers had occupied the heights of Mount Sciberass. As they hacked emplacements for siege guns out of the bare rock, they were looking downhill on St Elmo.

At the best of times Malta could hardly feed itself – much less an invading army five or six times larger than the entire population. To feed their 40,000 men the Turks needed to ship in vast quantities of rice and beans, and if they were held up on Malta for much longer than their commissariat had planned, their soldiers would go hungry. But as teams of oxen and long lines of harnessed galley slaves began to haul their siege guns the four and a half miles from their original landing place at Marsasirocco to the new gun emplacements on top of Mount Sciberass, it was still the month of May. Grass as yet unwithered grew brightly green in the cracks between the rocks, and the appalling heat of summer still lay ahead. The Turkish leaders had an entire campaigning season ahead of them. There was no possibility of mining through the solid rock under St Elmo so as to blow its walls skyhigh.

They must be breached by unremitting gunfire. Up to the crest of Sciberass had been manhandled two culverins, throwing a 60-pound ball, ten 80-pounders, and a huge and famous basilisk which threw balls of iron, stone or marble weighing 180 pounds. Earth to protect the gun emplacements was being carried up the hillside on men's shoulders in thousands of sacks, under fire from the snipers along St Elmo's ramparts.

The first Turkish cannonballs had already begun methodically to pulverize the sandstone and limestone walls of the little fort when old Dragut with 1500 of his corsairs arrived off Grand Harbour. He had expected that by this time the capture of Malta would be well in hand. When he saw how Mustafa and Piale had been led astray by a sideshow like St Elmo he was full of contempt. They would have done better, he told them, to occupy the whole island and make their blockade complete, so as to cut off all communication with Sicily and prevent outside help arriving. Then St Elmo must have fallen eventually, of its own accord. Dragut already knew from his spies in Sicily that Adrien de la Rivière's 'relief force' – the threat which had made Mustafa and Piale hesitate – could not possibly be ready for at least two months. The King of Spain showed no serious intention as yet of risking his galleys. 'It is a thousand pities,' Dragut declared, 'that the attack on St Elmo was ever begun. But now that it has,' he conceded, 'it would be shameful to give it up.' To Malta the Turks had, as usual, brought an overwhelming surplus of men. What they lacked was time.

Dragut landed heavy culverins from his galleys, and had his corsair gunners bombarding St Elmo from a battery on the seaward side too; he increased the Mount Sciberass battery to sixty guns. As army commander, Mustafa had his quarters in a silk-lined tent. Old Dragut, at eighty, went to live in the forward trenches, with the artillerymen. Under their coordinated and remorseless bombardment, St Elmo became 'like a volcano, spouting fire and smoke'. According to a careful account kept by one of the Knights, during an average day and night over 6000 cannonballs smashed into the little fortification. Soon there would be not much more than a star-shaped mass of rubble to defend.

In combat a Knight wore a suit of armour which weighed about 150 pounds. Under his metal outer shell was a leather or quilted jerkin to reduce bruising. This suit of armour was made for each Knight individually, like bespoke clothing, and fitted him well, with joints that bent readily at ankle, knee, wrist and elbow. Though covered with steel plates from head to foot, and moving therefore with massive deliberation, a Knight in his armour could dominate the cut and thrust in hand–to–hand fighting, since the great weight of metal was borne evenly over the total surface of his body. Thrusts from others made little impression on him, and his own blows were all the weightier. Only an arquebus shot fired at short range was at all likely to kill him.

Each Knight as he plunged into a mêlée, wielding his great two–handed sword, would be backed up by his own group of men–at–arms, less well protected but more nimble, who wore pot-shaped helmets and a leather jerkin or a coat of mail to protect the body. They were like infantry in a modern offensive, backing up tanks, but since they were more vulnerable than the slower moving man in armour who led them, casualties among men-at-arms were proportionately higher.

Among the Knights there was a difference of opinion about which helmet to wear. Some argued for a close–helm, with a movable visor which could be locked down, so that the entire face was hidden. Others preferred a Venetian salade – with its long nosepiece, like a classical Greek helmet – which though guarding only part of the face gave a better all–round vision. The drawback was that a chance blow at a certain angle could knock the salade off a man's head and send it spinning.

Inside St Elmo, a hand–picked force of Knights in full armour, each backed by his group of men–at–arms in buff or mail, kept their heads down under the monotonous and endless bombardment of the Turks' big guns. When the enemy did decide to attack, they all knew what to expect. Breaking from the cover of the artificial earthworks around their gun emplacements, a vast mass of Turkish soldiers would pour downhill, firing arrows from their short bows with astounding rapidity, wielding scimitars, a few in breastplates, many with round shields, but with many more turbans among them than helmets. If the janissaries should be sent into this particular attack, the bravest among them would be suicidally conspicuous, on account of the ostrich or egret feathers they continued to wear as badges of honour, even on the battlefield.

Early in the morning of 3 June 1565, the guns went silent. Down the rocky slope of Mount Sciberass towards the partially crumpled walls of St Elmo came the tide of robes, breastplates, tall feathers, white turbans, which everyone had been waiting for. The Turks in this first attack were going headlong for the ravelin – an unfinished protective earthwork to the northward, beyond the perimeter of St Elmo's walls. If they captured the ravelin they could mount guns there, and bombard the northern face of the ramparts point-blank.

Emerging through a hail of fire, the janissaries reached the very walls of St Elmo. Some knelt to fire their arquebuses through the grid of the portcullis, others shouted for scaling ladders to get them over the top. A mass of janissaries were climbing upwards when wildfire came down on their heads. Fighting men transformed into living torches turned and broke from the Turkish ranks, to run uphill again, screaming. Those few janissaries who did crest the battlements clashed with men clad in an armour which blunted the edge of cold steel. At noon, when the fighting ended, the Turks had taken the ravelin, they could move some of their guns up much closer, but none that day got inside the walls. For this small advantage they had lost 2000 men – most of them crack troops. In meeting their attack, seventy men-at-arms and ten Knights had been killed.

After dark, La Valette ferried 200 fresh men the half mile across the harbour, and thence up the steep track to St Elmo. Next day at dawn it was for the Turks as if the garrison they fought so hard the day before had been miraculously renewed.

Wildfire was a weapon devised long ago in Byzantium, and useful particularly against an enemy who fought in flowing robes. The Knights with their scientific cast of mind had been working to improve it ever since the Crusades. To the oncoming Turks in their attack the day before on the ravelin, wildfire had been served out in three forms. Into a clay pot with a narrow mouth 'of a size that could be thrown twenty to thirty yards' had been crammed a clever mixture of combustibles, some of them sticky – saltpetre, powdered sulphur, pitch, resin, turpentine. The pot was lashed up with a cord of slow match, and fire applied to the loose shank. When the pot hit its human target and smashed, the glowing cord set fire to what was inside.

When hard pressed along the walls of St Elmo, the Knights had also used the trump – a long metal tube serving as a flame-thrower. 'It continues for a long time,' ran the description, 'belching vivid furious flames and large, several yards long.' But the newest form of wildfire –

which to Turks climbing up the battered walls of St Elmo had proved
the most disheartening – was the recently perfected hoop, 'of lightest
wood, first dipped in brandy, then covered with wool and cotton,
soaked in combustible liquors and mixed gunpowder and saltpetre.'
The hoop having been set furiously alight could be picked up with
tongs and dropped neatly over the heads of a group of men climbing
upwards, trapping them together inside a deadly ring of fire.

To the Turks, these celibate pirates who carried an inexplicable
Maltese Cross on the mainsail, wore armour, wielded huge swords,
and prayed before battle had always been hatefully unnerving. Word
began to go about in Mustafa's army that La Valette must be in league
with Shaitan: 'how else could infidels like these make headway against
the Chosen of the Prophet?' Islam's less rational aspects were also
given expression by the Dervishes – wandering prophets, who voiced
impulses of fanatical revivalism and popular discontent, and were
listened to chiefly by the poor. Dervishes followed the camp, and had
an acknowledged usefulness as religious agitators. When, in their
second assault, on 7 June, the Sultan's crack troops leading the masses
of the Turkish feudal levy went hell for leather yet once more against
the walls of St Elmo, they were encouraged by loud, screaming cries
from the Dervishes, who had worked themselves up into a frenzy.
'Lions of Islam! Now let the Sword of the Lord liberate their souls
from their bodies! Their trunks from their heads! Liberate spirit from
matter!' The Sultan's war against the Knights of Malta had already
been proclaimed holy – a jihad – so that any Moslem who fell fighting
had an assurance of going straight to paradise, there to sense an endless
spasm of joy in the arms of a houri. The janissaries were again hurled
back. Three days later, on 10 June, the Turks tried an attack after dark:
inside St Elmo sixty met their death that night, but of the Sultan's
men, 1500 attained the paradise their Dervishes had promised them.

The Catholic soldiers too had been provided with an incentive to
courage: a Bull of Pope Paul IV's had recently granted plenary
indulgence to all who met death in the fight against the Moslem
invader. Thus the Maltese volunteers, deeply pious Catholics then as
now, were confident that they would die with their sins wiped clean.
Their heaven, though less sensually gratifying than their enemies',
had been secured to them as well.

To La Valette, the ongoing defence of St Elmo posed a perilous
equation. His brethren to a man were willing to go across the water
after dark, and up Mount Sciberass, there to confront an inevitable

doom. By dealing out their lives, one by one, like counters in a game of death, he was buying time for Europe. Word of this extraordinary resistance inside St Elmo had already reached the mainland, and was arousing breathless admiration. But the Knights were a handful, and at this rate they would all be spent – all be gambled away – before help came from Sicily. Where was the relief force?

After the attack of 7 June, the Council of the Order had met in Castle St Angelo, to discuss whether or not to evacuate St Elmo. After opinions had been exchanged, La Valette read them all a letter from Sicily, just arrived through the blockade. Dragut's secret information had indeed been correct. According to Don García de Toledo, the earliest date on which help could possibly be hoped for was 22 June.

In the letter was one ominously significant request. Don García asked the Knights to send over to him their five remaining galleys, though, as well he knew, manning and equipping them to run the Turkish blockade would cost the defence of Malta about a thousand men. La Valette understood what this meant. Don García must simply be reiterating his orders from Madrid. King Philip had evidently written off Malta – he expected the Knights' defence to fail. The Spaniards were raising 10,000 troops in Naples – but to defend that kingdom if the Turks should get that far. Very well, said La Valette – and the Knights understood what he meant, and why. Every defensible position on Malta must be held to the last man. The alternative was letting the Turks pour into the Western Mediterranean. By now, as well as being a stumbling block to the Turks, the Knights' tenacious defence of St Elmo had become to their friends on the mainland a great symbol.

For Don García, doing the duty laid down for him as Viceroy of Sicily, galleys that summer had very nearly the significance of fighter aircraft in the Battle of Britain. If the Turks tried, later, to land on Sicily or the Italian mainland, only galleys could hold them up – therefore every single one was precious. To King Philip in his bare cell in the Escorial, meditating the danger in all its aspects, and with more information in front of him than anyone else, what really mattered were not the brave impulses of romantic young hotheads like his half-brother, Don John, but the paramount need to keep the strongest possible Spanish galley squadron intact until the final moment. Piale Pasha was now screening Malta from Sicily with 100 Turkish galleys – so that putting a relief force of any useful size on Malta might mean a costly sea battle. If a large number of galleys were lost in that battle, the coast of Italy and the islands would be left wide open. And when had the Turks last been defeated at sea – or for that matter, on land either?

Don García sedulously obeyed the orders sent him by the Prudent King – including the insufferable one, asking the Knights to send in their five galleys – but he had been a brave man in his day, and had more confidence, personally, in the Knights than King Philip was showing; moreover, his young son, Federico, was on Malta. So whenever he could, Don García exceeded his orders. Two of the galleys belonging to the Knights themselves – and therefore, not strictly speaking under King Philip's direct control – in company with two of Don García's own, managed to slip through Piale's blockade in June, and carry across the men come from all over Europe to die with La Valette. Forty-two were Knights – latecomers, many from Germany, who had been obliged to cross the Alps. Of the twenty-five gentlemen-volunteers, at least two, listed as Juan Smilt and Eduardo Stanle (John Smith and Edward Stanley?), were almost certainly English. The new arrivals made their way successfully through the Turkish lines, and came as a welcome reinforcement into Castle St Angelo.

By now, nearly all the men keeping the line within the ruined 800-metre perimeter of St Elmo had minor wounds – and powder was running short. In their night attack on 10 June the Turks had used *sachetti* – sticky little fire grenades, which clung to armour, and burst into flames on impact. A Knight hit by a *sachetto* had to clamber at once into a nearby water barrel, to avoid being roasted alive inside his armour.

On 14 June, the Turkish command sent out a trumpet under a flag of truce to the pile of rubble which once had been a fort, offering the Knights a safe-conduct out of St Elmo if they would yield up the place. Rumours were reaching the Turks of the defenders by now being at odds with one another, and this disagreement they were hoping to exploit. In fact the younger and more impatient Knights had begun to doubt if St Elmo could hold out any longer. They now wanted to sally forth from the ruins, all together, sword in hand, to fight in a mêlée with the Turks until they had been killed to the last man. Knights of longer experience were inclined to think that St Elmo could hold out a little longer, and their arguments convinced La Valette. 'The laws of honour cannot necessarily be satisfied,' he told

Chevalier Vitellino Vitelleschi, spokesman for the younger and more hot-blooded Knights, 'by throwing away one's life when it seems convenient. A soldier's duty is to obey. You will tell your comrades that they are to stay at their posts.'

The human cost of continuing to hold St Elmo might be high, and the chances of seeing a relief force arrive remote, but the Turks, too, were wearing away up there on Mount Sciberass. The Knights could see enemy dead heaped in piles around the ramparts. Up and down that unhealthy landing place at Marsasirocco, ever longer lines of tents were being pitched to hold the Turkish sick and wounded. There was an outside chance that, despite the huge army the Turks had landed, the life-and-death equation on Malta might ultimately be resolved in La Valette's favour.

At dawn on Saturday 16 June came what the Turks meant to be their final and overwhelming assault. They began by posting 4000 snipers with arquebuses around the walls, to pick off any defender who showed himself above the line of rubble. So many janissaries – the backbone of the Turkish army – had already been lost on Mount Sciberass that the place of honour in the first attack was this time given to the Iayalars – a corps less well trained than the janissaries, but famous for their reckless courage.

Downhill towards what was left of Fort St Elmo came the Iayalars, 'clothed with skins of wild beasts,' armed with 'gilded steel helmets, round shield and scimitar'. As they raised their bloodcurdling yells, tambours, trumpets and the ululations of the mullahs added to the din. The Iayalars, all high on hashish, were utterly reckless: at an enormous loss their attack was beaten back. Mustafa then threw in his janissaries: they too were held. The Knights in this affray lost 150 men, the Turks 1000.

To reinforce St Elmo that night, La Valette called generally for volunteers, since all who crossed the harbour would be going to certain death. Thirty Knights came forward and 300 soldiers, many of them Maltese, together with two young Jews, civilian volunteers, who though not sharing the religion of the Knights – indeed, abhorring it – had been so inspired by Malta's resistance that they were willing to die in good company.

On 18 June, a cannonball fired from St Elmo at a group of high-ranking Turkish officers hit a dry-stone wall nearby. One of the Turks standing there was Dragut – a splinter of rock hit the side of his head, and blood poured from ears and mouth. He was carried to a nearby tent, mortally wounded. The old man whose prestige and experience had managed to unify the Turkish command on Malta was thus removed from the scene – though the tough old corsair lingered on the verge of consciousness for long enough to hear that in a last attack on 23 June, the ruined shell of St Elmo had fallen. Dragut's body was taken across to Tripoli for burial by the man who was to succeed him as leader of the corsairs, an Italian renegade, clever, cruel and scabby-headed, known to his enemies as Ochiali.

In a siege of thirty-one days the Turks had lost more than 8000 men around the walls of the outwork – nearly a quarter of the fighting force they had embarked under the Sultan's eyes at Constantinople. 'If so small a son has cost us so dear,' Mustafa bewailed, 'what shall we pay for the father?'

That night the exasperated Turks took a bloody revenge. From the ruins of St Elmo they could now look across the night water to the glitter of lights in La Valette's headquarters and the Maltese suburb nearby. Knights wounded and dead littered the rubble of the fortifications after the Turks' last assault. Each was stripped of his armour. Hearts were ripped out, heads chopped off, and into the naked breast of each man a cross was cut. Each dead Knight was spreadeagled and nailed down by his hands and feet to a crucifix made of planks, then floated out, so that the night breeze carried the grim little flotilla across the half mile of harbour water. By daylight, four floating crucifixes with their decapitated burdens had been washed up by Castle St Angelo.

For the Ottoman Turks, astounding cruelty here as elsewhere was state policy. The leaders knew precisely what they were doing. The theatrically sadistic gesture was a sop to their own men – a gratification of sorts for having fought so hard and lost so much to capture a place which in the end was virtually useless. Such a gesture was hardly likely to shake the nerves of the Knights over there in Castle St Angelo – pious, arrogant, contemptuous, and perfectly convinced that the soul survives the body – though it would anger them. The Turks were aiming to crack the morale of the Maltese. Had not those defiant Catholic peasants and fishermen, time and again during the past twenty-five years, seen their womenfolk raped and their own children and neighbours carried off into slavery? Had they not thus been impressed from earliest childhood with an instinctive fear of the banner which today floated over St Elmo – a star and a crescent moon, reflected in a river of blood? If only the nerves of their Maltese comrades in arms could be shaken, the handful of Knights would have to bear the brunt.

Nothing else that we know about La Valette allows us to suppose that he enjoyed personally the reprisal which in his judgement had now been forced upon him – and though it rallied the Maltese it stained his reputation. He ordered all the Turks so far taken prisoner to be led out and have their heads cut off. Then from the battery on the roof of St Angelo he shot them across the harbour towards the enemy in St Elmo, as grisly cannonballs.

Malta was by this time in the grip of summer heat. The environs both of Mount Sciberass and of the Turkish camp stank of putrefaction, because the soil on Malta was too thin to bury in mass graves the thousands who had already been killed. The Turks were known to be suffering from dysentery, enteric fever, malaria. The Knights of Malta, with their knowledge of hygiene, had always regarded Constantinople as a great plague spot – the focus of all the epidemic diseases which might come out of Asia. La Valette began to fear an outbreak of plague.

The fleet of Turkish war galleys which Piale Pasha had brought to Malta was in itself about half as large again as any fleet King Philip could reasonably hope to combine against him. His decision to let the Knights take the brunt rather than risk his own galleys displayed Philip's usual prudence. But his choice had made clear to the rest of Europe precisely what were the limits of the King of Spain's vaunted readiness to fight for the Faith. He would defend the needs of Christendom only when they coincided with the vital interests of the Spanish Empire. On 3 September 1565, the English diplomatic agent in Madrid was to report home to the government of Queen Elizabeth that 'the King has lost a great deal of reputation by not succouring Malta.' At the height of the siege, and sensitive as ever to the realities of European politics, Elizabeth herself had warned that 'if the Turks should prevail against the Isle of Malta, it is uncertain what peril might follow to the rest of Christendom'. Elizabeth, the daughter of the schismatic Henry VIII, was kept on her throne with the help of extreme Protestants – followers of John Calvin. But in her private opinions she herself kept her distance from them. Elizabeth had deeper discernment, and was aware that if the Turks came in victorious, so that the Crescent prevailed against the Cross, then Europe as a recognizable society with its inherited moral values must change for the worse; the world Englishmen had always known would disappear.

On Malta the Turks were running short of food and dropping in their tracks from fever, but they could still put 15,000 men into the field. In the fighting so far, La Valette had lost a third of his entire infantry force. Of his 700 Knights – and some in that total were of course old men or invalids – 120 were gone. They still held Castle St Angelo and the suburbs nearby. But if St Angelo went, so did Malta. And where was the promised relief force?

By a bitter coincidence, on the very day that the Turks made their decisive assault upon Castle St Angelo itself, a council of war was convened by Don García de Toledo at Messina in Italy, to reach a decision as to the relief of Malta. The Spaniards had been scraping up galleys wherever they could – by the time Gianandrea Doria arrived in Messina with his Genoese contingent, Don García should have at his command a fleet of over ninety warships: ample to run the blockade and land an expeditionary force on Malta, if he dare take the risk. Don García had commanded his first galley at the age of nineteen – he was now old and crippled with rheumatism. In his long career, when Christian galleys confronted the Turks he had seen them nearly always put to flight. Philip had chosen Don García as his viceroy in Sicily because he was cautious. However much impulse might tug him, he would never do anything rash.

The council at Messina that day was split between the 'bold', who wanted to send off sixty galleys at once, crammed to the gunwales with armed men, and the 'practical sailors' as they called themselves – the pessimists – who by this time had managed to convince themselves that over on Malta the Knights must surely be at their last gasp. Some went so far as to suggest that the Knights should be told to yield to the Turks on terms – as they had done many years since on Rhodes, when Sultan Soleiman let them all leave with the honours of war. But the days when such chivalrous magnanimity could be expected from the Turks were over. And Malta was more important than Rhodes. Malta was the key to the Western Mediterranean.

The council proved to be evenly split, so a supine decision was taken – to do nothing until Gianandrea Doria arrived. Such was Doria's repute as a man who kept an eye on his own commercial interests and never took long odds that the 'practical sailors' were quite sure he would cast his vote their way.

Gianandrea's uncle, the great Prince Andrea, had lingered on to the age of ninety-three, his death being hastened, so it was said, by the shock of hearing, in 1559, that the Christian expedition to Tripoli had been defeated. Four thousand Spanish prisoners were shipped back as slaves to Constantinople after this disastrous encounter. Gianandrea Doria, then only twenty-one, had been entrusted by his famous uncle with the command of fifty-four valuable war galleys. In the débâcle, Gianandrea Doria had done everything he could – to the point of appearing cowardly – so as to get the Genoese galleys away intact. Yet this disreputable conduct on the part of Gianandrea Doria – ugly, proud, subtle, with dark sunken eyes – had not lost him the confidence of his no less prudent paymaster, King Philip of Spain.

The council at Messina had to wait another ten days for Gianandrea Doria to arrive – while on Malta the fighting reached its crisis. Yet when the young Genoese admiral came into the council chamber, to everyone's surprise he was emphatic for action. The Genoese were bankers; they took no great risks, but they saw things clear and cold. The Knights' astonishing resistance had apparently convinced them that the tide of Turkish aggression into the Western Mediterranean might be on the turn – that Malta was too valuable to lose. Don García – whose young son Federico had been killed in July in the defence of Castle St Angelo – abruptly took sides with Gianandrea Doria. The 'practical sailors', wondering, as the vote went against them, whether perhaps King Philip had changed his mind and his secret instructions, were overruled. The council now agreed that 8000 men must be sent to the relief of Malta before the month was out.

If such help were ever to arrive, La Valette needed it sooner. Yet he found an ingenious way to turn even this half-hearted and belated decision to his advantage. Into the Turkish camp La Valette introduced false evidence so cleverly convincing that the Sultan's generals all acted on the assumption that any day now Don García would land 16,000 fresh troops on Malta – or more than in their present condition the Turks could hope to withstand.

To reach the walls of Castle St Angelo, the Turks had had to fight every inch of the way – through the Maltese suburbs from one direction, and down the length of Grand Harbour from the other. On the day when they assaulted the castle itself – 7 August 1565 – and the trumpet inside St Angelo sounded for the counter-attack, La Valette at the age of seventy-one was found to have donned his armour like the others, ready to sally forth at the head of his men-at-arms. Before the bloody scrimmage began, the Knights standing near him protested that as their Grand Master his life was too valuable to risk. La Valette is said by the chronicler to have answered, 'I feel assured that if I and those in command fall, you will fight on, for the honour of the Order and the love of our Holy Church.' In these words, whether uttered or not (and perhaps they sound a little too consciously noble to be verbatim), La Valette put his finger on one good reason for the Knights' military effectiveness. His own leadership counted for much, but he led a military élite, in which every member was not only prepared to die without hesitation for the religious doctrines he had been bred up to defend, but in any crisis was ready to act – to give a lead to those nearby. Therefore so long as one single Knight remained alive on the island and in arms, Malta was not yet lost.

As old La Valette grasping his two-handed sword went out on 7 August to play what part he could in the mass sally from St Angelo, word came to the Turks as they fought in the deadly mêlée under the castle walls that Maltese irregular cavalry dashing out from Mdina had made a destructive raid on the Turkish camp. This discouraged them. The Turks had from the very first shown dread of being cut off from home by losing their ships. Now their shore base was not safe, either. Too much time had slipped by – in the mishandled siege of Malta, all momentum had been lost. Unless Grand Harbour could be won and used – and the Knights had not yet been driven from Castle St Angelo, which dominated the anchorage there – the Turkish fleet dare not winter off Malta's wind-smitten shore. If the army lingered into autumn on the island it would go hungry; with no ships to bring in rice and beans it would very soon starve. Already the Turks were falling sick. They were short of everything they needed. They were nearly a thousand miles from home.

Don García accepted the plan that his sixty best galleys should make a rapid passage to Malta, each carrying 150 armed men – but let them be put ashore quickly, with no one hanging about to see what would happen next. The remaining thirty or so galleys were meanwhile to screen the King of Spain's possessions in Italy from any unexpected move by the Turkish fleet. But the work of getting ready this relief flotilla was allowed to drag on, so that the sixty galleys for Malta, with their expeditionary force on board, did not in fact quit Sicily until 26 August 1565.

The wind in the strait between Sicily and Malta is violently unpredictable – on Malta itself, only one day in ten is calm. Tugging their way south, the sixty galleys ran into 'a tempest the like of which few sailors had seen before.' This foul weather went on without a break for two weeks. Luckily the storm was also playing havoc with the Turkish fleet off Malta, thus doing its bit to demoralize the Turkish soldiers ashore, who were beginning to wonder if they would ever get home. Back limped Don García's sixty galleys, baffled, to a landfall at Trapani on the extreme western tip of Sicily – where 1000 soldiers who had had enough of being seasick promptly deserted.

Gianandrea Doria, however, having made up his mind that Malta must be relieved, began exerting all his powers as an organizer and by 5 September he had the sixty galleys heading south again. A couple of days later – after one or two of the blunders which occur as it were spontaneously when leaders are not all of the same mind – they fetched up at their rendezvous in the strait between Malta and Gozo. Don García managed to land his troops in Melliena Bay in only ninety minutes. Knowing that King Philip would still be morbidly preoccupied about the safety of his galleys, the stiff-jointed old admiral wrote a despatch reporting proudly that he had set 9600 men ashore 'without the loss of a single oar'.

Leaving the bewildered troops on the beach, the galleys turned their iron beaks to seaward, and went away from danger as fast as they could, their banks of oars rising and falling in precise cadence like huge wooden water beetles. The men left on shore had no pack animals, and no very clear idea where they were. But they managed to scramble across to Mdina, Malta's inland capital – only to discover that the siege was virtually over.

The Turks still outnumbered the force Don García had put ashore, but they had had enough. They were striking camp and taking to their ships. The Sicilian and Neapolitan infantry, just arrived on the scene and full of fight, wanted at least to exchange a few heroic blows with the hurriedly retreating Turks, but La Valette held them back. Let the enemy soldiers go away freely, was his advice. Don't lay a finger on them. Let them take their pestilence with them. By 12 September, the last Turkish lateen sail had disappeared over the eastern horizon.

At this time of year in Constantinople – the end of the summer campaigning season – the mob had for many years past grown accustomed to the glad news of a victory – often indeed to a spectacular procession through the streets of slaves and plunder. The disaster on Malta could not be hidden from sight. The Turks had lost 31,000 men there, or three quarters of their force – and all the survivors had to show for it were epidemic sickness and wounds. This absolute and unprecedented defeat was confirmed in the Golden Horn by 6 October. From that day onward, 'Christians could not walk in the streets of the city for fear of the stones that were hurled at them by the Turks, who were universally in mourning one for a brother, another for a son, husband or friend.' Soleiman the Magnificent had made it his rule to listen impassively to all the news that came to him, good or bad. But this time he was stung to an exclamation: 'I see that it is only in my own hand that my sword is invincible!' He at once began planning to redeem this humiliation by a future victory.

On 12 December a diplomatic report sent from Constantinople spoke of an army of 200,000 men being got ready for next spring, for the Sultan himself to lead into Hungary. Soleiman had at the same time set on foot an ominously large programme of galley building, as if to give open warning to the countries around the Western Mediterranean that he would be back.

Of the Knights who defended Malta, 250 were dead by the end of the siege, and nearly all the living were crippled with wounds. The men on Malta capable of bearing arms, including La Valette's Maltese volunteers, had perhaps numbered as many as 9000 on the day the Turks landed. Only 600 were left fit for service. All over Europe, these men were the heroes of the hour. When the news reached London that Malta was safe, church bells rang for joy, and at Queen Elizabeth's bidding the Archbishop of Canterbury ordered a Form of Thanksgiving to be used in English churches 'thrice weekly for six weeks'. Philip of Spain tried to make his amends by sending the Grand Master a sword of honour, filched later by Napoleon when he plundered Malta, and now on display in the Bibliothèque Nationale, engraved with the punning compliment, *Plus quam valor valet Valette.*

King Philip sacked Don García de Toledo from his job as viceroy in Sicily. The King's elderly and loyal scapegoat went off to soak his rheumatism in the hot baths of Naples, the last service he could do his

King being to take the blame in silence. His post as General of the Sea was given to young Don John.

Help in reconstructing Malta as a fortress island poured in, donations to rebuild the shattered walls coming from all over Europe. King Philip himself – who cannot have felt happy about the way he had misjudged the Knights – sent them 30,000 ducats in cash, the value of 20,000 ducats in supplies and lent them 6000 of his own infantry-men to stiffen the garrison. He himself started building new galleys in earnest – forty in Barcelona, twenty in Naples, twelve in Sicily. The Pope offered La Valette a cardinal's hat, but he declined the honour, preferring to spend the rest of his life building an impregnable strong-hold to the north of Grand Harbour, now named in his honour Valetta. The old hero died on 21 August 1568, after a stroke brought on by hawking all day in the hot sun. He lies buried in the crypt of St John's Cathedral, next to his close friend and Latin Secretary, the English Knight Sir Oliver Starkey.

His plans for Valetta included a great hospital, with a ward 502 feet long, where the sick and wounded of every religion and condition, Catholic, Protestant, Orthodox, Moslem or Jew, slave or free, might be nursed back to health on terms of equality. This time, however, Catholics were to be bedded down separately from schismatics, heretics and paynim, as if in such times as these religious controversy might be yet one more infection to avoid. The Knights – military aristocrats discharging their religious duty as male nurses – were remarkable innovators in their treatment of illness. They specialized in diseases of the eye. They were among the first to discern the value of quarantine, in fighting plague. The mentally afflicted, handled with brutality elsewhere, were regarded on Malta, and almost nowhere else, as suffering from a sickness of the mind. Each patient had his own bed – very uncommon at the time – and the Knights fed them all off silver plate 'for the decorum of the Hospital and the cleanliness of the sick.'

In 1566, the year after the Turks were beaten on Malta, the only mint in the Ottoman Empire which issued gold coins – at Cairo – devalued them by 30 per cent. Not only had the Turks failed for once to make war pay, here was a clear sign that their currency was being touched by the malaise of inflation. From then on, for trading countries to ship bullion to the Levant became astonishingly profitable. Piracy from convenient bases on the Atlantic seaboard – in France, England, Holland, Ireland – against Spanish treasure ships returning from America, or proceeding up–Channel, was a game that paid hand over fist. Thus the Turkish defeat on Malta had a distant outcome in gunfire on the Spanish Main.

After the Knights of Malta had proved that the Turks were not invincible, a sense of confidence began to grow, particularly among the young – and in men's minds was soon associated with the enormous effort towards inner renewal being made by the Roman Catholic church. The new mood was exuberant – of gaiety in the presence of danger – and there were signs of it, everywhere, in the emerging art of the baroque. This distinctive tone of voice still resounds in Othello's courtship of Desdemona, and echoes of it can be caught, distantly perhaps, and with a nostalgic dying fall, in the lyric verse of the English cavaliers.

7
The Morisco Revolt

Rather than suffer the slightest thing to prejudice the true religion
and service of God I would lose all my States, I would lose my life a
hundred times over if I could, for I am not and will not be a ruler
of heretics.

KING PHILIP II to Pope Pius IV, 1564

When the Moorish kings of Granada succumbed in 1492 to the
newfangled siege artillery brought against them by Ferdinand and
Isabella, over 700 years of Moslem rule in Spain came to an end. The
defeated Moors around Granada were allowed by treaty to keep their
property. They could live under their own laws and customs, wear
Arab costume and practise their religion.

Moriscos elsewhere in Spain, particularly in Murcia and Valencia,
had been forcibly 'converted' many years before. They probably
numbered 100,000, and most of them were agricultural labourers or
small dealers – men who having lost one faith without gaining another
had become disheartened. In Granada, however, even though their
kings had been defeated, rich Moors went to the mosque clad in silk.
Though the Inquisition lost no time in making an auto-da-fé of Arabic
manuscripts, the Moors of Granada were deeply imbued with Islamic
culture and well aware of their own history. A people with their own
literature, religion and history have a strong sense of identity and a
good chance of survival. In a time of trouble they are likely to throw
up their own natural leaders.

In the years following the *reconquista*, several minor revolts at
Granada gave the Spanish authorities the pretext they needed for
altering the easy-going terms of their treaty. The Moors there were
given their historically fatal choice: baptism or emigration. Since the
Moors in Granada were materially well off, most of them, rather than
leave what they possessed, went through a pretence of changing their
religion. Some were herded into cattle pens, where they had stoupfuls

of holy water flung at their heads, in lieu of baptism. There were 40,000 of these Moriscos in and near the city, outnumbering the Old Christians of Granada by a factor perhaps as large as ten to one. When a Turkish fleet sailed westward, a special watch was kept on them. Everyone knew their conversion was only skin-deep.

A child born to a Morisco family had by law to be taken to the church of the parish for baptism, but the family would troop back home afterwards, lock themselves in, and give the child what henceforth would be its real if secret name – a Moslem name. Boys when they reached puberty were circumcised behind closed doors. After their compulsory marriage service before a Catholic priest, a Morisco couple would hold a secret Islamic ceremony at home. In 1526, with the corsairs beginning to establish themselves threateningly in Algiers and elsewhere along the coast, the Emperor Charles V was persuaded to issue a decree called the Pragmatic, meant to limit the danger of this internal enemy. Moorish dress and Moslem names were to be banned, traditional songs and dances prohibited. The Pragmatic even abolished the *hammam*, the public hot baths, customary in Moslem cities, where neighbours foregather once a week to soak and shampoo and gossip – perhaps to plot.

The Pragmatic was never enforced, though it remained a threat hanging over the Moriscos' heads. Rumour had it that the Emperor – short of ready cash as usual – had been sweetened by a large bribe held out to him by the wealthy Morisco businessmen of Granada. Whether or not he took their money – and he may not have done – Charles V never subscribed so readily to abstract principles as did his son Philip.

After 1526 the Moriscos were reasonably quiet and uncommonly prosperous. Then came the Turkish attack on Malta when royal galleys of the coastal patrol were sent off to Sicily, leaving southern Spain almost defenceless. The corsairs from Tetuan landed that summer at Motril, and lorded it demonstratively for a while within easy striking distance of Granada. Royal spies discovered not long after that some of the more high-spirited Moriscos had made plans, if Malta fell to the Turks, for seizing power in Granada.

Though in a minority, the Old Christians of Granada looked down on the Moriscos as a people their forbears had defeated – a flock to be fleeced. Morisco women in particular were fair game, and since by custom they were veiled in the street or locked up at home, Moriscos found the insult hard to swallow. 'The Old Christians have driven them to desperation by their arrogance, their thefts, and the insolence with which they take Moslem women,' King Philip's secretary was confidentially informed in 1569 by Francisco de Alava, later ambassador to France – a local man who knew Granada well. 'Even priests,' his report went on, 'are not exempt: an entire Morisco village begged the archbishop to "remove the priest or else marry him to someone, for all our children are born with eyes as blue as his." ' In Granada King Philip's Inquisition too had by this time made itself well hated. To put the screws on a nominal Christian practising Islamic rites in secret was a profitable exercise, since a verdict of guilty left the Inquisitors legally free to confiscate all his property.

In 1564, Pope Pius IV had been obliged to rebuke King Philip for the unscrupulous way the Inquisition was being used against the Moriscos of Valencia. Like Archbishop Talavera – Ximenes' opponent in years gone by – the Pope was in favour of giving the Moriscos religious instruction in Arabic, so that they should not be obliged to go through the motions of a religion which meant nothing to them whatever.

On 1 January 1567 – the seventy-fifth anniversary of the conquest of Granada – the Moriscos discovered that by instalments over the next two years the Pragmatic was to be enforced. The King's minister, Cardinal Espinosa – soon to be his chief Inquisitor – had decided to reimpose this old law without consulting Iñigo Lopez de Mendoza, marqués de Mondéjar, and for twenty-five years Captain-General of Granada – the man on the spot.

Mondéjar at once sent warning that if the Pragmatic were enforced, there would be grave risk of an uprising. But to King Philip, with his passion for justice, it went against the grain not to enforce a valid royal law. The Pragmatic had been intended by his revered father Charles V to blot out those everyday differences between the Moriscos – potential traitors, perhaps – and his loyal Old Christian subjects in Granada. As for the marqués de Mondéjar – he like all his family, the Mendozas, local potentates in Andalusia, was apt to forget who was his king and master.

In the Morisco quarter of Granada, the destruction began of all the public baths – the *hammam* in that breathtaking architectural masterpiece the Alhambra suffering with the rest. The affront was all the more profound since, for the Moriscos, the *hammam* was something more than a bath house and meeting place. Unlike Christianity, Islam was a religion of ritual ablution. Cleanliness for them marked the radical difference between themselves and their conquerors – they liked to think they could smell a Christian coming.

The impression King Philip's policy over Malta had given them was of indecision, military weakness, a chronic shortage of galleys. Then, in the Low Countries, dissatisfaction with Spanish rule flared up into civil war – and 60,000 of Spain's best troops were sent there, under the Duke of Alva, to crush the Dutch. Thus by imposing the Pragmatic in stages over two years, Cardinal Espinosa had made a gross tactical error: he had given the Moriscos time to make up their minds to fight for survival. The rebuff the Turks underwent on Malta was judged by the Moriscos to be only a temporary setback. The corsairs – who had been landing on the Spanish coast with impunity – were just across the sea, and their great patrons, the Turks, had a reputation as winners.

The boldest spirits among the Moriscos began to store grain. They arranged with smugglers to buy arquebuses in North Africa, and formed dumps of weapons and gunpowder in mountain caves. For a reckless young Morisco buck it became the height of fashion to wear a Turkish turban. Appraising correctly these straws in the wind, Mondéjar thought it prudent to ask the royal government for reinforcements. These men when they arrived shed a glaring light on King Philip's present military weakness. To browbeat a potential enemy numbered in tens of thousands, the King had sent Mondéjar 150 horse and 150 foot.

Between the broad and fertile inland valley of Granada, irrigated abundantly by the melting snows of the Sierra Nevada, and the Spanish seacoast opposite Africa, there runs a strip of rough country, sixty miles or more wide and twenty deep, broken up by small rivers, cut into deep ravines; the Alpujarras. This terrain reaches out on one side towards the dry and impoverished borders of Murcia. In the Alpujarras, Morisco and Old Christian villagers lived uneasily cheek by jowl, cultivating patches of land along the river banks, and pasturing their sheep and goats on the uplands. Any Morisco who had a quarrel with the law would go up into the Alpujarras and live by smuggling or banditry. In the mountain caves up there, the malcontents of Granada had been hiding their stores of food and arms.

The marqués de Mondéjar, so feebly reinforced, was sure in his own mind that trouble was coming. His agents in the port of Almeria had intercepted a letter addressed to 'all the Moslem powers' and listing Morisco grievances. Fifty of his men out on patrol in the hills had been ambushed. But he could hardly have anticipated the farcical way in which the outbreak actually began.

On Christmas Day 1568 in Granada there was a fall of snow. Through an unguarded postern in the city wall a column of men trooped after dark, armed with yataghan and arquebus, and dressed like Turks. The man who led them through the postern and into the Moorish quarter was a wealthy Morisco dyer called Farax. Tonight all the Christians in Granada would be celebrating their fiesta – a good moment, therefore, to enter the city by surprise, and preach insurrection.

The 180 men wearing white Turkish turbans who stamped their way behind him through the snow were not in fact Turks, but 180 ne'er-do-wells, come down from the Alpujarras in fancy dress. Farax had arranged to meet his supporters living inside the city at midnight. He had promised them that he would be arriving with 8000 Turks at his back – but these 180 make-believe Turks were the best he could do. Even those in the Moorish quarter who sympathized with an uprising hung back, scenting a fiasco. Beyond killing a few guards who were warming themselves around a brazier, and sacking the shop of an apothecary popularly believed to be a spy, the handful of picturesque scallywags did little damage: they were a stage army. Nothing daunted, from a piece of high ground near the Alcazaba gate to the sound of horn and cymbal Farax formally proclaimed the Morisco rebellion. He then marched his men away, having picked up only a few volunteers, cursing the Moriscos of Granada for cowards and traitors. From a safe distance, as the 'Turks' withdrew into the hills, Mondéjar's men lobbed a few shots into them.

Yet this pantomime turned out to be all that was needed to set the Alpujarras ablaze. From village to village spread the word that a Turkish army had arrived. Moriscos scratching a hard living in mountain hamlets took up whatever improvised weapons they could lay hands on, and converged upon the nearest Old Christian village. Having slaked their rage – joined in the indelible fellowship of a bloody massacre – off they all went into the hills, to find and join this phantom Turkish army.

Upon the religion which for seventy-five years had been the ceremonial symbol of their defeat, the Moriscos took a thorough revenge. Jocosely they used madonnas for target practice, holy vessels for chamber pots. On the altar of the parish church they would slaughter a pig – a beastly animal eaten only by Christians. Priests came off badly. Some had ears, nose and tongue cut off, others were burned alive. One had his mouth filled with gunpowder and the top of his head blown off. Yet another parish priest, very much detested – perhaps on account of his blue eyes – was sewn up inside a pig, and roasted. They also got their own back on Christian women. In Guacijas, two cele-brated young beauties, sisters and Old Christians, were sent off to amuse the Sultan of Morocco. But first they were obliged to stand and watch as their father was chopped into small pieces. A few Old Christians escaped, making their way through the snow to Granada. Many more were marched down to the coast in long columns as prisoners, and bartered there to *contrabandistas* come in from Algiers, at the going rate of one slave to one arquebus. The women went to the harems of Algiers, their menfolk to the galleys.

There was at least one place in the Alpujarras where for some accidental reason – a strong personal friendship or perhaps a good priest – the local people declared from the start that they wanted to go on living as neighbours. There as in Granada many Morisco citizens were opposed to armed insurrection. But these well-intentioned minorities were to be allowed no say in the matter. As this cruel war further unfolded, there were to be no neutrals. All alike were made to suffer, the good neighbours along with the zealots and the torturers.

Having brought into existence more than perhaps he had bargained for, Farax had the acumen to resign soon after as the figurehead in the revolt, in favour of a handsome young man of twenty-two, with large melancholy eyes, the black sheep of a rich family, whose legal name was Hernandez de Valor. He had recently been in trouble with the law, and had fled to the Alpujarras taking with him a concubine and a black slave – but he was also descended lineally from the ancient Moorish kings of Cordoba, and this gave the insurrection a specious top dressing of legitimacy. Under his Islamic name of Mahomet ibn Umaiya the young man was proclaimed King of the Moriscos, Lord of Andalusia and Granada. Throned in state under an olive tree, he received his followers' homage.

Ibn Umaiya adopted a purple costume with a crimson shawl. He rode around the Alpujarras on a white Arab, and set himself up with a harem of the better-looking Christian girls not yet given away to friends abroad. From Granada, eager recruits made their way up into the mountains. A mosque was built, to replace the wrecked churches. The few Old Christian villages still holding out were besieged or blockaded. Bandits who had long since taken refuge in the Alpujarras began to teach hitherto law-abiding citizens the arts of guerrilla warfare. In this little corner of Andalusia, the ancient Moorish kingdoms had entered upon a revived though spectral existence. But how long would it all last?

By the New Year of 1569, Mondéjar had managed to scrape together about 3800 men, a sixth of them cavalry. The most gorgeously equipped were the Genoese merchants doing business in Granada, clever but unpopular foreigners, money men in the service of the King. Others too besides the Genoese saw this revolt in terms of commercial opportunity. After years of treating the hard-working and prosperous Moriscos as their natural inferiors, the Old Christians were out for plunder.

In a brush with a weaker Morisco force, advancing on them under the red and white pennants of this new little kingdom, Mondéjar's men were able to chase them back into the hills. All the Morisco civilians they came across they made prisoner, and sold for cash as slaves; every enemy village they passed through was stripped to the walls, and all they could grab, even cooking pots and mattresses, was promptly sold off, with a deduction of a fifth for the King, to the speculators who trailed in the army's rear. One or two beleaguered Old Christian villages were relieved. Then Mondéjar marched his men back to their winter quarters – before too many of them deserted.

A more sizable Old Christian force was coming down against the rebels from Murcia, led by the viceroy, the marqués de Los Velez, a great local landowner. Los Velez had levied his 5000 men and marched towards the Alpujarras without so much as a nod from King Philip. He lost no time from dread that the revolt might pass like an infection to his own Morisco labourers in Murcia, and thence into Valencia. Against a united Morisco rising 140,000 strong, no armed force King Philip could possibly call upon would make significant headway.

The marqués de Los Velez was a huge man, a celebrated horseman, insupportably proud, a grandee – one of those local magnates whose power King Philip had been trying to curtail. In his younger days, Los Velez had seen service under Charles V. When corsairs had the effrontery to land on the coast of Murcia, he had killed fifty of them with his own hand – the Moriscos nicknamed him Devil's Iron Head.

Los Velez did not keep his soldiers well in hand, so that if victory did not come to them quickly and easily, they were liable to fade away and go home. But in their first pitched battle, at Ohanez, they drove the rebels back decisively, killing 1000, enslaving many more, and rescuing thirty Christian maidens earmarked for the harem.

The day after the battle was the Feast of the Blessed Virgin Mary. The victorious *murcianos* all went in procession to church, with the liberated maidens wearing blue and white – the colours of the Immaculate Conception – and Los Velez and his officers marching at their heels in full armour, carrying tapers. His useful little victory dissuaded the Moriscos of Granada for the time being from carrying the revolt to their blood brothers living further north – and this in the end was a greater setback than might appear, since an insurrection which stands its ground and loses momentum is usually fated to fail.

By March 1569, this push by Mondéjar and Los Velez into opposite ends of the Alpujarras had petered out. Los Velez was picturesque, cruel, brave, larger than life, but an inefficient general. Mondéjar was the more competent professional soldier, and a decent man who did his best to check the troops' avaricious brutality. But though of the same rank and social class, the two generals were different in character, they detested one another, and this personal antipathy did the campaign no good. Some commander in chief of higher rank was called for, to bring these two opinionated aristocrats to heel and put their ill-conditioned armies under stricter discipline. The danger was too real for such personal rivalry, for so long as the little Morisco kingdom in the Alpujarras managed to hold out, the Turks would have a toehold here in Spain itself.

Ibn Umaiya, the Morisco king, had by this time about twice as many men under arms as Mondéjar and Los Velez. And every Morisco soldier fighting in the mountains had behind him two or three secret sympathizers down on the cultivated plain or inside the city. From Moriscos who to all appearances were peaceful civilians, trading or farming, the guerrillas in the hills procured their supplies, and such complete information that any move the Old Christians might make was known to them in advance. But though handsome, dignified and not stupid, ibn Umaiya lacked the force of character and, above all, the energetic audacity which marks the successful rebel leader. He might in better times have served well enough as a figurehead, but the help everyone had so confidently expected from abroad was not reaching the Moriscos. Ibn Umaiya had sent his brother,

Andalla, across to Algiers to plead their cause, but he managed to recruit there no more than a token contingent of Turkish and Algerine volunteers, some idealists, some adventurers. In the Alpujarras there were still no signs of that phantom Turkish army. The winter fighting petered out; after March came a lull.

In Constantinople, where Andalla went next, the lessons of Malta were still being digested. There was talk of a seaborne attack on some easier and more profitable objective, perhaps Cyprus. From Sokolli, now Grand Vizier, and the clearest political intelligence the Turks ever possessed, Andalla got the cold shoulder. Sokolli had identified the Morisco revolt in terms of power politics as a sideshow, which might turn into a trap if the Sultan got too deeply involved. Personally Sokolli sympathized with the Moriscos, but in Constantinople nowadays the network of intrigue was more intricate than ever. The rhetoric of Islamic solidarity counted for less among the Turks than once it had. Religious loyalty must yield to hard facts.

Madrid, however, appraised the danger as real. The papal nuncio, spokesman for the Vatican at King Philip's court, was confidentially informed, on 26 October 1569, that if the fighting in the Alpujarras went on for another winter, and spread to other regions, then the kingdom of Spain itself might fall.

Elizabeth de Valois, the fifteen-year-old French princess whom King Philip had married after the death of Mary Tudor, died eight years later, on 3 October 1568, in childbirth – at the time when the Morisco revolt, though simmering, had not yet boiled over. Don John came back from leading his naval patrol against the corsairs, and with the stink of the royal galleys still in his nostrils, just in time to attend her funeral. Elizabeth was the sprightly young queen who had teased him admiringly when as a youngster he dashed off to join in the fighting on Malta. She was the nearest Don John had ever known to an elder sister, just as his intelligent kinsman Alexander Farnese took the place for him of a younger brother. Elizabeth's funeral must have been for Don John a heart-rending occasion.

His half-brother, King Philip, had long ago decreed that Don John must never worship in church standing under the canopy that was the significant prerogative of the legitimate royal family. But at the Queen's funeral service, in the church of the Barefoot Carmelite nuns, Don John though just back from active service found that he had been allotted a place not only at a considerable distance from the royal canopy, but so out of the way as to be an obvious snub – another attempt by King Philip to put his half-brother in his place by the adroit use of etiquette. Philip was clever at using the nuances of court ceremonial to poultice the vanity of one courtier, or take another down a peg; the slur was not accidental.

What motive King Philip may have had for lacerating Don John's feelings at the funeral of the dead queen lies hidden, but may perhaps be guessed. Reports that the young man was conducting himself well at sea had reached Madrid – and at forty-one King Philip, though as monarch he could command the obedience of his fighting men, had never quite earned their respect. Moreover he could hardly forget Don Carlos, to whom this bastard half-brother had always been such a vivid contrast. And in the long run would Don John turn out to be as loyal as he looked? And had the King, when his girl-wife was alive, felt excluded by the sound of the young people's laughter?

The whispers and titters, the public snub, were too much for Don John's high temper. Without requesting the usual formal permission from the King, he left the royal court that same night, and made his way on horseback to the Franciscan convent of Santa María de Scala-Cocli, near Valladolid, where his foster mother Doña Magdalena was a frequent visitor. Don John had a friend there among the Franciscans – an austere but astute friar called Juan de Calahorra.

Fray Juan's influence over the perturbed young man was great, and for the next few months Don John stayed with the Franciscans, performing his religious duties earnestly, relishing the simplicity of the Franciscans' everyday life, their sympathy with the poor and their contempt for money, and talking seriously and at great length with Fray Juan de Calahorra, as if his first glimpse of the world and its ways – of naked galley slaves being flogged in the waist of the ship while gentlemen in perfumed gloves dallied on the poop – had disenchanted him. At court a rumour spread that Don John was having second thoughts about the religious vocation marked out for him by his father. Though did King Philip, the courtiers asked one another, wish to see this gifted and courageous half-brother of his move off the worldly scene, and pass his life among the Franciscans?

By this time Don John's presence as a figurehead of sufficiently high rank was urgently needed in Granada. To gain the willing consent of that well-intentioned old soldier, Mondéjar, and placate the resentful vanity of Los Velez, Don John would be just the man. He had once

talked of using his sword in the King's service. This was hardly the
moment to change his mind.

Fray Juan de Calahorra knew his man. Rather than poverty and
chastity he preached duty, and Don John's secretary, Quiroga, put
into words at last the argument which made up his master's mind: 'It
will make your name famous through all Europe'. Once the decision
was made to choose glory rather than renunciation, Don John wrote
to King Philip simply and loyally to accept the difficult command: 'I
can be trusted beyond most others, and no one will act more vigorously against these wretches than I'. Luis Quixada was to accom-
pany Don John on campaign, as his personal adviser. Requeséns,
having kept a fatherly eye on him when they went on patrol against
the corsairs, was to fetch over a contingent of regular soldiers by sea
from Italy to the Alpujarras, to give Don John's army a professional
backbone. The galleys thereafter were to blockade the enemy coast.
King Philip was planning to move the royal court, temporarily, to
Cordoba, so that Don John's orders should reach him with the least
delay.

Don John and Luis Quixada left the royal palace of Aranjuez on 6
April 1569. To cross La Mancha in the brief Castilian springtide and
traverse the mountains of Jaén took them six days. Outside Granada
they were met by the marqués de Mondéjar and his more important
subordinates, who escorted their singularly young commander in
chief deferentially towards the city. They were observed all to be
noticeably free in their use of the title *Excellency*, while scrupulously
avoiding the word *Highness* – the title usually accorded to a legitimate
prince. They were provincial aristocrats. If Don John in this war were
to be treated as a cut above them, on account of his birth, there was no
harm in continually reminding the young man that the royal family
itself was a cut above him.

Wearing full armour, with a crimson velvet mantle thrown neg-
ligently across one shoulder, and a plumed, polished and inlaid helmet
held in the crook of his arm, Don John walked his charger up and
down the lines of the 10,000 men – his reinforced army – drawn up
outside the city gates for his inspection. Then he rode under the gate-
way and through the tapestry-bedecked streets of Granada, where Old
Christian onlookers cheered him loudly. At his back, reiterated volleys broke from the guns, and from behind gloomy iron grilles in the
façades of great houses, the dark and glittering eyes of rich young
women glanced down at him. With any vows of chastity he may once

have contemplated put behind him, the young commander in chief was not long in finding himself a mistress – a beautiful and intelligent kinswoman of Mondéjar's called Margaret de Mendoza. (She bore him a girl child – Ana of Austria – who later became abbess of the royal monastery of Las Huelgas, in Burgos.)

The stalemate in the Morisco war – as in Don John's own life – was about to be resolved.

By this time the Morisco leaders had been made well aware that their Moslem brothers in Algiers and Constantinople, glad though they were to have Spain hamstrung by a revolt in the Alpujarras, proposed to send them only as much material aid as would keep the revolt on the flicker. To land an army from a fleet of galleys at the far end of the Mediterranean was an aggressive enterprise too large just at present for the Turks.

Hernando al Habaqui, later the Moriscos' commander in chief, and the best soldier to enter their service, had also pleaded their cause in Algiers with the governor, Ochiali, Dragut's old lieutenant, and since his death the dominant personality among the corsairs. With cruel complacency Ochiali told al Habaqui that he was 'more concerned to defend well his own state than to interfere in the concerns of others'. Ochiali, who controlled 4500 janissaries, soon made it clear to al Habaqui that he was not parting with any of them. In fact, he had plans for using them elsewhere to his own advantage. Nor would he let so much as a single arquebus leave the city's arsenal. But, since Moslem opinion in Algiers must be placated, Ochiali announced that anyone who possessed two weapons of his own would be allowed to deposit one at the mosque, for the Moriscos. Ochiali also gave permission for eight galleys to run the blockade, as a commercial speculation. He told al Habaqui that he was free to recruit 400 Algerines as arquebusiers; but then saw to it that these arquebusiers were all criminals, let out of gaol if they volunteered for service in the Alpujarras. On active service there, these Algerines made themselves notorious as rapists and looters: atrocities on both sides multiplied.

Ochiali, soon to prove himself the Sultan's best fighting seaman at a time of great crisis, figures in history less brightly than Barbarossa or Dragut, perhaps because his name is spelt in the records in so many different ways: Ali Pasha, Uluchali, El Louck Ali, Euldj'Ali, Ochiali. In chapter 39 of *Don Quixote*, Miguel Cervantes calls him Uchali.

There was a persistent rumour in his lifetime, plausible though unlikely, that he was a renegade Dominican – or perhaps a Dominican novice. To spell his name – arbitrarily – as Ochiali is at least a reminder that he was to all evidence born an Italian and a Catholic, in a poor village called Licastelli in Calabria. Before Ali Ahmed kidnapped him, as a youngster, and chained him to the oar of a galliot out of Algiers, Ochiali had been earning his living as a fisherman.

Ochiali must have been physically powerful, since his place of duty when a galley slave was the starboard bow oar, where the best rower would always have been chained, to set a good pace. Evidently he was disfigured with ringworm, since his nickname in the galleys was Scabbyhead. We know that his voice was so hoarse that from a few yards away what he had to say could scarcely be heard. The turning point in his life became an often repeated legend. One day this ugly, powerfully built, harsh-spoken Italian galley slave, bred up a Christian, was mortally insulted by a Moslem shipmate. Ochiali was a Calabrian, profoundly revengeful, and he hit on a way to get his own back.

Since Islam implies brotherhood, no Moslem could hold another as a slave. Ochiali formally repeated the words that signify conversion, so that though he tugged the same oar as before, from that moment on he was a volunteer, and free to defend his honour. He at once called out the man who had insulted him, and killed him in single combat, hand to hand. This violent and derisive action made Ochiali's name. He was promoted to bosun of a corsair galley – whipping instead of being whipped. With his prize money he bought a share in a galliot, and went on to make a rapid rise to corsair commander.

In the years when Dragut was making his terrific slave raids, Ochiali with his precise knowledge of the south Italian coast had served as his lieutenant. He behaved indeed almost as if he had by now a grudge against the country and faith of his boyhood – as if the violent drama compelling him to change his religion had transformed him inwardly. A fisherman born under Spanish rule in Catholic Italy, as Ochiali had been, could in those days expect to die a fisherman. Life held out no larger expectation for him, unless he entered the church and did well there (the new Pope, Pius V, had begun life as a shepherd boy). But any bold and lucky fellow in the Sultan's service, however mean his origin, might rise to the highest rank. The Ottoman Empire offered a poor man the only democratic opportunity available to him – with appalling risks but glittering prizes.

Ochiali never married, though he liked to call the corsairs who served under him his children. For his old patron, Dragut, he seems to have had some kind of passionate attachment. In March 1568 Ochiali had been named Governor of Algiers. Not long after came the first appeals from the rebels in the Alpujarras.

A man in Ochiali's position could climb even higher up the ladder only if he was able to guess what they might be thinking in Constantinople. Ochiali was perfectly clear in his own mind that after the débâcle he had witnessed on Malta, what the Turkish cause needed was not a small-scale Islamic insurrection within Spain itself, dangerous to dabble in since it might fail, but a cheap, spectacular and undoubted victory in some place everyone had heard of. The éclat of such a victory would refurbish the Sultan's reputation for invincibility. If only he could bring it off, Ochiali's own future would be bright.

The Spanish government had its own secret representation in Algiers, and King Philip's spokesman there bribed the new governor handsomely to deter him from helping the Moriscos. Ochiali took the bribe without hesitation – why not? He never intended to help them much anyway. But in consequence the Spaniards began to suppose that they had him in their pocket. Later, they took quite seriously a proposition to buy Ochiali off entirely, by making him a Spanish marqués. What better than that could an upstart Italian fisherman dream of ? Ochiali took their money and listened to their promises, and laughed up his sleeve.

In October 1569, when the corsairs' cruising season was over and no one was paying them particular attention, Ochiali took both the King of Spain and everyone else by surprise. Marching his corsairs and janissaries out of Algiers, together with ten light field guns, he led his little army overland, eastward, towards Tunis, the African city captured years before by Charles V in his one great Mediterranean victory. Tunis was still ruled by a king of the puppet dynasty Charles V had placed on the throne and lately he had made himself very unpopular.

Between Malta and Tunis ran the strait which gave the Turks access to the Western Mediterranean – both were controlled by allies of the Spanish King. Thus the Sultan's captains as they passed through these narrow seas were obliged to look over both shoulders at once. In Constantinople, the loss of Tunis still rankled.

The seaward approach to Tunis was protected by a strong outwork, the fortress of La Goletta, which had a Spanish garrison. But from landward, Tunis was open to attack, and very few of the subjects of

Above
Philip II by Titian
Below
Charles V at the battle of
Mühlberg by Titian

Right
Selim II by Titian
Below right
Soleiman the Magnificent,
circa 1560, signed by Nigari
Below
Francisco Borgia
by Juan Martinez Montañés

NAVALIS · PII · V · AVSPICIIS · DE · TVRCIS · AD · NAVPACTVM · PARTA · VICTORIA

PIVS · V · PAPA · ALEXANDRINVS · SEDIT · AN · VI · MENSIS · III · DIES · XXIII

Left
Pope Pius V
Below left
Don John of Austria
by an unknown painter
Below
William of Orange
by Antonio Moro

IOA · AVSTRI · CAR · V · FIL·

Above
Gianandrea Doria by Sebastiano del Piombo
Top
Ochiali

the present puppet king, Muley Hamid, would risk their lives for him. As Ochiali marched along the North African coast towards Tunis, over 1000 Berber irregulars came down from the mountains of Kabyle to join him. When he was two days' march from the city, the puppet king of Tunis threw his hand in, bolting to La Goletta with his treasure and a handful of followers. By January 1570, Ochiali had installed his own corsair garrison in Tunis, under the command of a renegade Sardinian who had adopted the Islamic name of Cayto Ramadan. In the Sultan's palace overlooking the Golden Horn, the news that Tunis had been recaptured was like a splendid clash of cymbals, behind which the far-off pleas of the Moriscos were drowned out.

Soon after war broke out in the Alpujarras, Mahomet ibn Umaiya had gone into hiding in the mountain village of Mecina-Bombaron, in the house of a sympathizer called ibn Abu. When Mondéjar's men came through the village looking for him, the young king managed to get away, but they caught his host, ibn Abu. The Old Christian interrogation of ibn Abu was brutal and prolonged, and when he stoutly refused to tell them where they could find the man they were looking for, the soldiers hung ibn Abu upside down from a branch of a mulberry tree in his garden, and castrated him. According to a Spanish historian who saw the Alpujarras war at first hand, the only answer they ever got out of ibn Abu was, 'May it please Allah that I die, so that my friends live.'

But now that the war was not being conducted with vigour, loyalties were changing, and ibn Abu found himself the leading conspirator in a plot to overthrow the young and pleasure-loving king on whose account he had been mutilated. A woman called Zahara, a singer in the royal harem, was his accomplice, and by a trick he won over to his side the ex-convicts from Algiers. One day when the king was revelling in his harem, and least expecting trouble, he was strangled with a bowstring, and his carcass thrown on a nearby dunghill. While the ex-convicts began an orgy with the women in the dead man's harem, ibn Abu publicly announced himself as the new king. His first act was to send Hussein, commanding the handful of Turkish volunteers who had managed to reach the Alpujarras, by sea to Constantinople with a large bribe for the Grand Mufti. If Turkish statesmen turned their backs on the Morisco cause, at least the good opinion of the religious leaders might be won.

Under their new king, the rebel Moriscos began to hit back. Taking the advice of their Turkish military engineers, they began to fortify strongpoints, particularly the little town of Galera, which blocked the best route from the city of Granada into the Alpujarras. Raiding parties sent out by ibn Abu pushed a long way into Murcia, where Los Velez's militia had by this time become too disorganized to hold such raiders in check. Ibn Abu himself led a bold thrust towards the coast, to capture a port and thereby improve his contact with the outside world.

But the attack on the seaport of Almeria failed. In an insane fury afterwards, ibn Abu seized those he supposed had cheated him of victory, buried them up to the neck, and used them as living targets. To the more discerning of his followers, this was a bad sign. Though he might call himself king, ibn Abu had no claim to legitimacy. His authority depended only on success. In defeat, he could not reasonably hope to command his people by terror.

The enemies of Spain were skilfully fishing in the troubled waters of the Alpujarras rebellion. The French ambassador in Constantinople reported on 14 March 1569 that William of Orange, who led the revolt against Spain in the Netherlands, had sent a personal agent to Joseph Micas, the richest member of the local Jewish community and a close friend of Selim's. William – to whom many of the Spanish Jews exiled to Antwerp were giving their support – wanted Joseph Micas to use his influence at court to embroil the Turks in the Alpujarras. This might oblige Spain to fetch home some of the troops now terrorizing the Low Countries. Three Jewish businessmen, sent to France by Micas to collect money owing him, set on foot in his name the alarming rumour that in 1570 the Turkish fleet would certainly sail to help the Moors in Granada. But a rumour was not an army. All King Philip's enemies were full of sympathy with the Moriscos – but few sent help, or came to join the fight.

From this time on, the Moriscos knew they must depend upon themselves. Murcia and Valencia had not risen to join them. The help they had anticipated from the Moriscos of Seville had also failed. But by August of 1569 they had 30,000 men under arms. On 18 October, King Philip, a sedentary man perhaps a little too prone to brood on cruelty as a cure-all, decreed for the Alpujarras 'a war of fire and blood'. That October he was holding the Cortes in Cordoba, near the

scene of action. For carrying on a 'war of fire and blood' there were to
be royal incentives. The pay of regular soldiers in the army was raised
to three crowns a month for pikemen, and four crowns for
arquebusiers. A soldier could sell his prisoner as a slave, and pocket all
the proceeds. Old Christian militiamen in the royal service might
from now on keep all their own plunder, without paying over the
customary fifth to the crown.

The winter campaign was launched on 19 January 1570, when Don
John and his foster father, Luis Quixada, led the larger part of the
Spanish army, now well-equipped and a little better disciplined,
towards the fortified township of Galera, held by a Morisco garrison
of 3000, of whom 200 were arquebusiers. Galera was built on a narrow
rock, rising between the rivers Huescar and Orce, and its name
derived from the resemblance between its high and rocky site, and a
war galley. Flat-roofed, limewashed dwellings rose one above the
other, like a heap of toy bricks, each roof a little higher than the last. As
Don John and Quixada approached Galera on horseback at the head of
their men, the turbans and robes and dark beards of Morisco sharpshooters could be seen, dotted across the flat roofs, aiming their
matchlocks.

The topmost building in Galera was a stone church, and in its belfry
the Moriscos had mounted a brass cannon. The town's main street
climbed up towards the church, but had been blocked at every fifty
feet by a barricade. Doors and window shutters were loopholed, and
party walls had been broken open so that defenders could move from
one end of a street to the other without exposing themselves to fire.
Conspicuous among the defenders of Galera were the long-haired
volunteers of the Women's Battalion. The certainty of rape followed
by enslavement if their menfolk were defeated had brought Moslem
women out from behind the iron grille and locked door of the harem.
The defenders of Galera had too few firearms, and powder was short,
but since the little town blocked the Spanish army's way into the
Alpujarras, Turkish military engineers had made it as thorny as a
porcupine.

Don John – not yet twenty-three years of age – had received from
King Philip the strictest orders not to expose himself in action. 'You
must keep yourself,' the King insisted as the campaign opened, 'and I
must keep you, for greater things.' What the King had in mind was for
his half-brother to be a figurehead, while the decisions were taken for
him by expert military advisers. Don John's own riposte to this royal

command had been respectful but cool: 'I see that Your Majesty's interest requires that when there is any call to arms, or any enterprise, the soldiers should find me in front of them.'

Requeséns's galley squadron, patrolling offshore, had fetched in siege artillery from Cartagena. The heavy guns were dragged by mule team up to Galera, entrenchments dug for three batteries, and the systematic bombardment of the town wall begun. But even when the Spanish artillerymen had succeeded in making a practicable breach – a hole in the wall, with a sloping heap of debris filling the ditch, so that infantrymen could clamber up and force a way into the town – they would still have to fight through Galera bloodily, house by house.

The sniping of the Morisco arquebusiers up on the rooftops was so uncomfortably accurate that the communication trench linking the batteries needed to be protected by gabions – faggots of broom cut on a neighbouring hill, which as it happened was also in the snipers' field of fire. Don John not only led the work party there and back again under a hail of bullets, but he cut and carried his own faggot, which greatly heartened his men, but was hardly what King Philip had in mind for him.

The recommendation of Don John's advisers was to push only 4000 of his infantrymen through the breach the guns were making, thence to fight their way dangerously upward house by house, but to put his chief trust in a mine being excavated higher up, beneath the town wall at the point where it merged with the rocky crest. Through the second breach that the mine would blow, the bulk of his men could then move down into Galera from above, and take the Morisco defenders in the rear.

The huge charge of gunpowder buried by the engineers in the shoulder of the rocky hill did indeed explode, but the wrong way, leaving the upper wall intact. Don Pedro Zapata led the forlorn hope into the breach – the small advance guard which planted a flag there and cut a way through for the rest to follow. But the men who swarmed up behind him were driven back – to their shame and anger – by a force of Morisco women. Led by Don John in person, the 4000 infantry, though unsupported by the hoped-for crossfire from above, then made two successive attacks into the town. Don John was knocked over – but only bruised – by an arquebus ball which struck his breastplate. Both attacks failed. The Spaniards left behind them 400 dead, of whom fifteen were officers, as well as 500 wounded.

Surrounding Don John at his council of war that night were men of much greater military experience, some of them pulling long faces. The King himself was waiting, uncomfortably near, at Cordoba, for news of a victory. When he got to hear of this day's work, some of their careers might come to an abrupt end. Perhaps because he was less in awe than others round the table of the royal wrath, Don John found a way to encourage them. 'If we use the diligence we ought to use,' he is reported as saying, 'the news of our success will reach His Majesty as soon as the tidings of today's misfortune.'

If to blow another hole in Galera's upper wall the Spaniards needed many more barrels of gunpowder, their ships and mule trains could fetch them in. But in that first day of defiance the Moriscos must have blown away much of their powder. Tomorrow some of the enemy would be relying on bow and arrow. A fortress, strategically considered, is an elaborate delaying device. The garrison in Galera could have only one real hope   that the Morisco army would march in and relieve them; otherwise, sooner or later, any fortified town must fall. But was the Morisco commander in chief likely to march to their help, when all the advantage in a pitched battle under the walls of Galera would so clearly be on the side of the Spanish regular troops? Don John's bold opinion was evidently the right one, and his advisers took heart from it. The right move was to renew the attack with no loss of time.

When the miners were sent back to their pickaxe work, two hundred Moriscos armed with pike and sword sallied forth to interfere, but their brave sortie failed. On 10 February Don John was told that the second gunpowder charge was ready. He had brought his twenty guns closer in, and was opening up a concentrated fire on the little town. The mine once again achieved less than was hoped from it, but even so the Spanish infantry managed to force their way into Galera from two sides at once. In this assault everyone noticed that Don John, as if putting snipers at defiance, was wearing even more conspicuous armour, inlaid with gold, burnished, and with a plume in his casque. The panache was good for morale. Both by his discernment in council and his conduct on the battlefield, the young man was escaping from the tutelage of his advisers. He intended – as he had told the King – to lead his men from the front.

Orders to Don John from the King in Cordoba were to give no quarter, and to destroy Galera utterly. During a nine-hour battle, Galera's defenders went down one by one, the women of the Amazons' battalion screaming insults to the last, and hurling down stones from the rooftops. The royal command that everyone inside the walls should be killed disgruntled the rank and file: they had hoped to take prisoners and sell them off as slaves. Aware of their monarch's present bloody-mindedness, the military advisers tried to enforce his orders. But Don John, though repeating what King Philip had commanded in a way that was frightening enough, appears when battle began to have interpreted his orders on the side of humanity. For instance he saw to it that the 4200 noncombatant women and children of Galera were spared. The victors found a vast plunder of gold, silver and silk, and enough barley to have fed the garrison for two years. In obedience to King Philip, the little fortress town was razed flat, stone by stone, and the terraced fields around it sown with salt. Nothing, so the King intended, was ever to grow there again – but, by this time, nobody lived there, either.

Old Luis Quixada had meanwhile gone off to reconnoitre on Don John's behalf the Sierra de Seron, where the Moriscos were massing. In a brush with them he was hit in the armpit by an arquebus bullet. An incompetent surgeon made five successive incisions with his probe, but failed to find the ball. Doña Magdalena rode posthaste into the Alpujarras, and reached Don Luis in time to close his eye. 'Our best consolation,' wrote King Philip to Don John, when informed by him of Luis Quixada's mortal wound, 'is that we are sure he must be in a better place, seeing how he lived and died.' Don Luis, in his will, had asked Doña Magdalena, as they had no children, to unite their property, and use the proceeds to found a monastery. Doña Magdalena put their joint fortune at Father Francisco's disposal. In 1572 the newly founded Jesuit collegiate church at Villagarcia held a nine-day service for Don John's foster father. The battered remains of the old soldier lie buried there beneath the high altar.

Told of the risks Don John was taking, King Philip sent him a sharp reproof. He was to remember 'how important your life is, seeing you are my brother, and that you are not to risk it, as you have hitherto been wont to do.' Swallowing the rebuke, Don John wrote, privately, to Ruy Gomez, the King's chief minister, saying simply: 'Had you been in my place and circumstances, you would have done as I did.'

The losses at Galera had shaken his soldiers' morale. When first sent into attack at Seron, the Spanish infantry ran. In the second attack, the able general on the other side, Hernando al Habaqui, led 80 horse and 700 men in a furious charge against them, hoping to sweep their demoralized line into confusion. With the two generals in this affair almost face to face, the outcome depended on their individual speed of decision. Don John quickly ordered his field guns to break up the Morisco attack and, wheeling his cavalry, made an unexpected attack on al Habaqui from the rear.

The duel had been brilliantly managed on both sides. Don John's helmet was struck by a bullet, but once again he emerged unscathed. Two of the Spanish soldiers who had shown cowardice were hanged out of hand, as an object lesson to the army, and four others marched off to the galleys. There could be little doubt henceforward of Don John's courage and judgement as a commander in the field; he could hardly be treated any longer as a convenient figurehead.

Left without a confidant after Luis Quixada's death, Don John was mortified by the way his men had behaved. They 'had not the least sense of honour among them,' he reported, 'and they cared for nothing but plunder and an easy life. The officers,' he went on, 'are much to blame. The chief cause which makes the men so ill-disposed and so weak of courage is, I well know, their dissolute ways, their carelessness about their souls, and their easy consciences. If they are not humoured and pampered, nothing can be done with them.'

Don John was beginning to realize that much of the chivalry inculcated in him since boyhood by Luis Quixada was a noble illusion, the creed of a few. Compared with the Knights of Malta – courageous and magnanimous – the men now fighting a similar battle for King Philip in the Alpujarras were mercenary and self-centred. Yet what but magnanimity – greatness of soul – could make headway against an enemy who fought, as did both Turks and Moriscos, at least in part from a religious motive?

Here in the mountains the soldiers of the King of Spain, whatever their other deficiencies, had weight of metal and weight of numbers on their side: their advance into the little Morisco kingdom was implacable. Seron was taken, and on 21 March Don John prepared to besiege the stronghold of Tijola, garrisoned with over 1000 men, of whom 300 were arquebusiers and forty Turkish volunteers. One last pathetic appeal had been sent by the rebel leaders to Algiers and Constantinople: if the cause of the True Faith should perish in Spain, the Moriscos warned, a strict account would be required of the Sultan on the last day.

Hernando al Habaqui, commanding the Morisco army, knew that if a stronghold as expertly fortified as Galera should fall to Don John, Tijola was doomed, and the Morisco kingdom with it. Rather than drown the Alpujarras in blood, and sacrifice the lives of the Turkish and Algerine volunteers under his command, al Habaqui opened up secret negotiations for a truce. The terms offered him by King Philip were less than generous, but they were enough to break the back of Morisco resistance. Any rebel soldier between fifteen and fifty who came in within twenty days, carrying his weapon, could exempt himself and two other persons from slavery. Once this offer had expired, any male Morisco in the Alpujarras over fourteen would be shot on sight. Thirty thousand laid down their arms, leaving only a couple of thousand guerrillas with the Morisco king up in the mountains.

On 19 May, Hernando al Habaqui was seen approaching Granada, at the head of 300 Morisco arquebusiers, marching in files of five. From the tip of the leading rider's lance, ibn Abu's royal banner, red and white, trailed in the dust. Martial music blared out, and the Spanish guns fired solemn volleys. The discarded banner was flung at Don John's feet. Al Habaqui rendered up his own damascened scimitar, and knelt to kiss his young opponent's hand. Don John, who always performed well on such ceremonial occasions, raised up Hernando al Habaqui in brotherly fashion, and giving the Morisco general back his scimitar, told him to use it henceforth in the service of King Philip. After the ceremony of surrender, he 'conversed with him affably'.

Under the surrender agreement, Turkish and Algerine volunteers were to get passage home in Spanish vessels, but were to defray the cost of it by giving up half their plunder. But as they left, another 200 Turks arrived, surreptitiously, and joined ibn Abu. The mutilated Morisco king was a man of a more obstinate temper than his commander in chief. 'If he were left alone in the Alpujarras,' so a Turkish envoy reported him as saying, 'with only a shirt to his back, he would rather die a Moor than enjoy all the favours King Philip has to bestow.' Ibn Abu is known to have kept up the spirits of his few thousand bitter-enders with continual predictions about more help coming from the Sultan. And all was not yet lost. As guerrillas, passively supported by tens of thousands of civilian sympathizers, the irreconcilables could hold out for a long time to come. 'The Moors who surrendered, and those of the lowlands,' wrote the Tuscan ambassador in Madrid to the Grand Duke in Florence, 'were keeping the war alive, for it was they who secretly provided the rebels with food.' On 14 August, Don John was reluctantly compelled to admit that, despite the advantageous bargain struck with al Habaqui, there would never be peace until all those Moriscos who had pretended to submit, and yet went on helping the rebels, were forcibly removed from Granada.

How much ibn Abu was whistling in the dark about more help coming – how much it was a settled Turkish policy to keep at least a guerrilla war alight in the Alpujarras – is never quite clear. Some assert and others quite strongly deny that for example Sokolli, the most powerful man in Constantinople after the Sultan himself, had a well-concealed but real sympathy with the Moriscos – and perhaps saw a political advantage in letting their war linger on for as long as a handful of Moriscos were willing to fight. But King Philip, whose political instincts were hardly less acute, ruthlessly crushed out this last spark of revolt.

He gave orders for a punitive expedition to go into the Alpujarras and burn and destroy without mercy. The harvest that year had been so bad that some Moriscos came down from the mountains and sold themselves into slavery, merely to eat. On 2 September, Requeséns marched from Granada into the mountains with a force 5000 strong. As his men went by, every house, fence, fruit tree or vine that they passed was either cut down or burned to the ground. All Morisco women encountered were made slaves. Every man they caught was shot or hanged. Those who tried to hide in mountain caves were smoked out. Only the lives of those Moriscos who, though they had failed to come in, could prove they had helped the royal cause, were spared; they were marched off as galley slaves. One thousand five hundred men were slaughtered in cold blood, 3000 women and children enslaved. Within six weeks the Alpujarras had been devastated from end to end.

The Spaniards began building forts in the mountains, penning in the last handful of rebels like wild beasts – and the guerrilla war quickly degenerated into banditry. During their war for independence, 21,000 Moriscos lost their lives. On 1 November – All Saints' Day – the last of them remaining alive in the province of Granada, whether or not they had taken part in the rising, were marched away north into exile. Such was the overplus of Morisco slaves that some were actually exported to Italy. The brilliant Arab civilization of Andalusia was a lost memory. Of the little Morisco principality, nothing remained but a handful of men following ibn Abu from one hiding place to another across a ruined landscape.

Don John himself left Granada in November 1570, and was not

sorry to go. Four months later, when ibn Abu was hiding in a cave, one of his band called el Senix, bribed with the offer of a free pardon, came up behind ibn Abu and smashed in his head with the butt of an arquebus. Next day, with the corpse of the last Morisco king slung across the back of his mule, el Senix came into Granada. He was carrying ibn Abu's weapons, as trophies, and in the Plaza Vivarambla the traitor was publicly accorded his free pardon. He came to a bad end, though, a few years later, in Guadalajara, when the royal justice impaled and quartered him, as a highway robber.

With the Morisco war petering out, speculators descended on Granada like blowflies, and an orgy of profiteering began. The property of exiled Moriscos could be bought for a song, and was sold off to newcomers from other parts of Spain at bargain prices. According to the Venetian envoy, Donato, King Philip was still receiving 125,000 gold crowns annually, in royal dues from confiscated Morisco goods and lands, as late as the year 1573.

The calculated brutality used to crush the Moriscos of Granada out of existence, and the mediocre performance – despite Don John's victories – of the royal soldiers there, did King Philip's reputation abroad little good. Don John himself had at least once opposed the policy of deportation in council, only to find himself in a minority. On 5 November, as the bulk of the Morisco civilians, innocent and culpable alike, were being marched off, and he himself was just about to leave Granada, Don John wrote to Ruy Gomez, describing their appearance as 'the saddest sight in the world, for at the moment of departure there was so much rain, wind and snow that the poor folk clung together, lamenting. One cannot deny that the spectacle of the depopulation of a kingdom is the most pitiful anyone can imagine.' He added, in a curt and uncourtly Spanish phrase as if between clenched teeth, *al fin, señor, es hecho*: at last, my lord, it's done and done with. Made aware at last of his own capacity, the young man went on to confide in Ruy Gomez, 'I should be glad to serve His Majesty on some business of importance. I would that he would understand that I am no longer a boy.' But after this sordid campaign in the Alpujarras, he would rather, he said, enhance his good name 'in a war that concerned all Christendom.'

Don John may already have heard rumours that the new Pope, Pius V, was making valiant efforts to form a league 'for the destruction and ruin of the Turk' among those countries which the Sultan directly menaced. There was no greater belief among practical men than there had ever been that his pious intention would ever amount to very much. The essential political obstacle was still there. The two great Christian naval powers in the Mediterranean were Spain and Venice. With the help of enormous cash subsidies recently granted him by Pius V, and paid over by the Spanish church, King Philip was building many more war galleys, but the Turkish fleet was still so immensely preponderant that Spain would never catch up. The Venetian fleet was as large as the Spanish, and added together they could confront the Turks on fairly even terms – but until now the interests of Spain and Venice had never coincided. Indeed, they were chronically at odds. Venice lived off the trade of the Ottoman empire, much as did her rival Genoa off the trade and finance of the Spanish empire. The Venetians would swallow almost anything, rather than quarrel with the Turks.

But the new Pope, a powerful personality and a profound mystic, had convinced himself that a Holy League could be conjured into being. He had followed the campaign in the Alpujarras attentively. From the confidential account rendered him of the fighting at Galera and elsewhere, Pope Pius V had almost made up his mind that young Don John, with his romantic piety, his humane scruples, his courage physical and moral, and the Emperor's blood in his veins, might be the God-given man to lead the Holy League in action – if that far-fetched dream of his could ever be made a reality.

8

Pope and Sultan

Sancho cried out, 'I said it was a sin to set them at liberty. For they
were all going to the galleys because they were very great villains.'
'Blockhead!' broke in Don Quixote. 'It is no concern or duty of
knights errant to investigate whether the distressed, chained and
oppressed persons they meet on the roads are brought to that pass,
or suffer that anguish, for their crimes or for their whims. Their
only task is to succour them because they are in distress, taking
account of their sufferings, and not of their villainies. I met some
mournful, miserable wretches strung together like beads on a
rosary, and did for them what my duty requires.
The rest is no affair of mine.'
MIGUEL CERVANTES: *Don Quixote*, Part I, Chapter 30

'All skin and bone,' was how one ambassador in Rome described this
new pope. Sumptuous papal banquets were a thing of the past – Pius V
dined off an egg and a plate of vegetables. He owned two coarse
woollen shirts – one to wash and one to wear – and had such a dislike of
money that he could hardly bring himself to discuss it.

A sixteenth-century pope had usually been someone of a Renaissance cast of mind, often a man from an important Italian family who
had accepted a career in the church for what it had to offer, and once
elected pope was only too ready to plunge into complicated politics.
But Pius V was the son of an Italian muleteer called Ghislieri, who
shipped corn across the Alps.

Young Michele Ghislieri joined the Dominicans at the improperly
early age of fourteen, to become in due course a professor of theology,
and then an inquisitor. Even after he had been promoted bishop and
cardinal, Ghislieri preferred to go up and down Italy on foot, in a
shabby robe, with a knapsack over one shoulder. There was nothing
about him of a prince of the church. A Dominican, as he saw it, should
be poor.

Though profoundly learned, Pius V still had traces about him of the
awkward, angular simplicity of a poor but pious man, convinced that
the particular faith in which he happened to have been bred up must be
right, and all the others wrong. 'There has always been on earth only

one true religion,' Pius V declared after he had been elected pope, 'and there can be only one, which is the religion the Apostles preached, handed down from the time of the Apostle Peter by means of his successors.'

The ascetic appearance of Pius when elected at the age of sixty-two to the throne of St Peter marked him out from the more self-indulgent cardinals of the college: a long, haggard face, a huge nose like a hooked beak, a white beard falling to his chest, a bald head and small, bright eyes. Though naturally hot-tempered, he had trained himself to contain his rage, never to go angry to bed, never to hold a grudge. He was often in great pain from stone in the bladder, yet did his best never to show it. 'The man who once told him a lie,' said the Venetian ambassador – and ambassadors from Venice were expert prevaricators, 'lost his favour for ever.'

In Pius V, intellect and sanctity were linked to a character of iron, which in practical matters could carry all before it. His formidable personality had been noted at the last Council of Trent. His election to the throne of St Peter over the heads of better-placed cardinals of good family and great influence had been a signal to the world at large that the impulse to reform inside the Roman Catholic church had reached zenith. Some wondered what would come next. On the day of the Pope's election, 7 January 1566, in London where Henry VIII's theoretically illegitimate daughter by Anne Boleyn, young Elizabeth, held her throne by what was as yet a precarious tenure, two comets with large and bloody tails were to be seen, following the midday sun.

King Philip was told by his envoy in Rome that the Pope with whom he would now have to deal was 'a good man of exemplary life and great religious zeal'. In the ambassador's opinion, 'the church had not had a better head for 300 years'. All the diplomats agreed that Pius V was a man who in matters of church reform might be highly effective. But how he would perform on the European scene was anybody's guess. He might be impulsive, he might be wrong-headed.

Pius V regarded himself as having been entrusted by the Holy Spirit with one overriding duty – to renew the church by putting into full effect the decisions taken at Trent. The church as he saw it must also face up to its two enemies, the Turk and the Protestant. Anyone living in Italy in those days felt almost physically menaced by the Turk. Had not Rome itself been indicated by the Sultan as a military objective – the Red Apple? Were not the Turks openly boasting of turning St Peter's one day very soon into a mosque? When he was a cardinal, Pius

V had once lost his baggage – little as it may have been – to a corsair. His nephew Paolo Ghislieri was a slave in Algiers. (Pius V promptly ransomed him. But the young man turned out to be too 'luxurious and immoral' to make a success of his promotion as captain in the papal bodyguard: his uncle gave him ten days to get out of Rome.)

The Turks were the nearer and more blatant threat. But Pius V's unrelenting attitude towards Protestants, particularly when they were Calvinists, needs a little more accounting for in a generation like our own, which until a short while ago looked upon 'wars of religion' with a certain incredulity.

From its base in Geneva, Calvinism had by this time become a force in several other parts of Europe. John Knox's Calvinists held most of Scotland; the Huguenots controlled much of France. In the rebellious provinces of the Low Countries, Calvinist volunteers, some of them French, Scots, English and German, were to become William the Silent's best soldiers. John Calvin and Ignatius Loyola had in their day been fellow students at the Sorbonne, where they had the same teacher as Erasmus and Rabelais. As men they typify some of the radical contentions of the time. Loyola was a nobleman, a wounded soldier, a Spanish mystic; Calvin the intellectually gifted son of a French attorney concerned with church property. In 1559, when the first Huguenot synod in France was held, only fifteen churches were represented. But Calvin's star was in the ascendant. Though by training a theologian and canon lawyer, he was in another sense the first French intellectual of the modern revolutionary type, and the clarity and penetration of his mind, the exquisite precision of his style, quickly won him a hearing.

A Roman Catholic church in France, controlled by the royal family and farmed out by them to their courtiers as though it were a private estate, was arousing disgust among the French provincial middle classes. At the synod of 1561, only two years later, the number of Huguenot churches represented was 2150. By 1562 a civil war had broken out between those loyal to France's traditional religion, confused and corrupt though it might be, and these new zealots. Desultory war between them was to pull the kingdom of France first one way then another for the next forty years, reducing royal authority to a shadow.

It thus began to appear, particularly to Spaniards and Italians, as if the danger in the Calvinist heresy lay not so much in its challenge to orthodoxy as in its threat to law and order. There were by this time in southern and western France a great many ruined churches, with crucifixes broken and sacred images defaced. Everyday life there after the Huguenot upsurge had become unsafe for all but Huguenots. In France between 1560 and 1580, of the Franciscan order alone, 200 friars were martyred.

For Catholics in Italy – and most Italians were profoundly Catholic – a current nightmare was that these logical and disciplined revolutionaries would cross the mountains and make a bridgehead for their new version of Christianity by force of arms. The morbid fear of such a religious war, though not justified by events, was vivid both in Italy and Spain – countries where Catholic belief was the cement holding society together. And as had lately been made evident in the Alpujarras, even a small and localized anti-Catholic uprising near the Mediterranean coast might give the Turks their chance.

As a former inquisitor, Pius V had taken a hand in the game of keeping John Calvin's dangerous opinions out of Italy. The Grisons in neighbouring Switzerland had been under Protestant influence since about 1543. Copies of Calvin's *Catechism* and *Institutes* were frequently concealed by Swiss traders in bales of merchandise and smuggled into Italy. Merchants in Lyons found similar roundabout ways of sending intellectual contraband to their business correspondents in Genoa, Lucca and Venice. With its emphasis on lay control of the church and its legalistic bias, Calvinism appealed very much to businessmen and bankers, who were chagrined in those days by the unprofitable way the Catholic church handled its landed property, and resentful of the poor opinion it held of usury – by which so many of them lived.

As early as 1550, the newly promoted inquisitor, Michele Ghislieri, had managed to seize twelve bales full of such books, which the Swiss had smuggled by boat across Lake Como, and planned to send on to Cremona, Vicenza and Modena. The Roman Catholic bishop of Bergamo – a man with a taste for intellectual novelties – was keeping two trunkfuls of heretical books hidden in his villa. Ghislieri did not hesitate to cite him for heresy. Promoted to Rome, the plebeian inquisitor was not afraid even to call the Pope himself to account – though for this he was rapped across the knuckles. But he got his own back. One of Pius V's first acts after his election had been to send Pope Paul IV's worldly and embezzling treasurer, Minale, to the galleys for life.

Though not so corrupt nor so violent as in the time of the Borgias, the city of Rome still set the Christian world a bad example. Pius V began by trying to clear out the tribe of harlots who infested the Borgo – the suburb through which pilgrims must pass on their way to the Vatican. They were plying their trade almost on the Pope's doorstep. Pius V decreed that unless they married or entered the Order of the Penitenti they were to be expelled from Rome. Forty substantial citizens came on a deputation to persuade the Pope that abolishing prostitution in Rome would be bad for trade. The ambassadors of Portugal, Spain and Florence spoke up as one man for the girls in the Borgo. Some of them, having fled the city at the first threat, had been given a bad time by bandits up in the hills, so the Pope relented. They were to be confined henceforth to the Ripetta – which after 1569 was walled in, so that it resembled the ghetto. Suitable sermons would be preached to the women there, and any wishing to take up a different way of life would be given money and the chance to make a fresh start.

Pius V was no respecter of persons. In December 1568 he had one of Rome's richest bankers, de Vecchi, whipped in the open street for adultery. He did his best to stop bullfighting in Catholic countries – though in Spain the bishops were by this time so much under King Philip's thumb that they dare not read the Pope's condemnation of bullfighting from the pulpit. The Pope insisted that Indians in King Philip's American dominions be treated with humanity. But most vigorously of all, he attacked scandals in the church itself.

Castel San' Angelo was soon crammed with delinquent priests and bishops. There was even one imprisoned cardinal – accused of rape – but having looked closely at this man's case Pius V let him go, declaring that he should never have been made a cardinal in the first place. An Index of prohibited books was compiled and enforced – hundreds of Italian printers fled to Switzerland and Germany. Monasteries were obliged to live according to rule, and guilty monks were sent to the galleys, as were the very few Italian Protestants and religious dissenters whom the Inquisition managed to ferret out. Cosimo dei Medici in Florence had been tactfully persuaded no longer to tolerate the presence there of Italian Protestants – two years later he was confirmed by the Pope in the title he coveted, of Grand Duke.

In April 1566, three months after Pius V was elected, there was panic in Rome among the dissolute nobles there. The Pope had publicly ordered that all those guilty of sodomy ('that terrible sin, on account of which the judgement of God burned all the cities that were infected with it') should be taken out and burned alive. Any persons charged with 'crimes against nature' were also, he said, to be held on suspicion of infidelity and heresy as a matter of course. (Who can tell what ugly experience as a boy in some unreformed monastery years before may have left the Pope with this particular merciless rancour?)

But at the same time as persecuting deviants, Pius V was doing much for the Roman poor. He abolished the tax on wine, put an end to speculation in the price of bread, improved the water supply, drained the marshes, fortified the city against the raids of corsairs. The papal household had been reduced in numbers from 1062 to 601, and there was to be no more lingering and sniggering in the Borgo after dark: everyone was obliged to be indoors by nightfall. 'The Apostolic Palace,' reported one ambassador, 'was like a monastery. There were no longer any traces of the old court life.'

Pius V disliked poets – ever a disrespectful crew – and to crowned heads who might enjoy sculpture more than he did he gave away those embarrassingly naked classical statues so lovingly accumulated by his predecessors. Yet when cracks appeared in the ceiling of the Sistine Chapel he at once had it repaired. Art and architecture – as for instance in Rome's spectacular new Jesuit church, the Gesù – might in his view be used even theatrically in the service of religion. But he laid it down that church music was not to provoke sensuality.

Francisco Borgia, a man after Pius V's own heart, had been General of the Jesuits since 1565. The reforming Pope depended on the Jesuits from the first as his moral commandos: whenever a town in Europe was retaken from the Protestants, the Jesuits were to move in on the heels of the troops, and by their impassioned preaching and systematic control of education win back souls. When the plague arrived in Rome, in 1566, the Jesuits contended with it on the Pope's behalf, dividing up the threatened city into fifteen areas, each with a Jesuit in charge of relief, and sending the sick to an improvised hospital, where forty Jesuits acted as nurses. In the seven years that Father Francisco was General of his Order, thirty-six Jesuits died fighting epidemics.

A strong-willed pope, observers decided, might well succeed in cleaning up Rome. But abroad, would not this reforming Pope's inexperience, his simplicity, his imprudence lead him astray? The French Catholics in their armed struggle with the Huguenots were hard pressed for money. Pius V imposed a special tax on the Papal States. From the proceeds he raised 500 papal cavalry and 4000 infantry in time to reinforce Henri de Valois at the battle of Jarnac, where on

13 March 1569 the Huguenots received such a drubbing that afterwards Italians became much less worried that foreign heretics might invade.

Henri de Valois, who in 1574 was to become King of France, though he defeated the Huguenots both at Jarnac and at Montcontour, was hardly such a model of Catholic chivalry as would warm the heart of Pius V. He lavished his affection on marmosets and lapdogs, loved sweetmeats, painted his face, and whenever he knew himself observed would pose his long and slender hands to advantage. Even after he had become King he would sometimes dance at court balls dressed as a maid of honour. But Henri too was tormented by intense fits of that same violent and poignant emotion as had once afflicted Father Francisco. Turning his back on his lapdogs, the epicene royal prince would spend days and nights on his knees with the Capuchins in the rue St Honoré, fasting and scourging his sinful flesh. Always at the tormented young man's shoulder was his power-hungry mother, Catherine de' Medici. She might be glad enough to accept all the help the Pope saw fit to send her, for use against the enemies of the Catholic faith. But, as the papal nuncio succinctly reported to Rome, 'the Queen does not believe in God.'

The Queen who 'did not believe in God', though she might toy at times with the notion of allying France with the Sultan, had a strong family reason for remaining at least nominally Catholic. Any pope who might want to reform the Catholic church in France would face one enormous obstacle. Under an agreement extracted from Rome in the days when the papacy was decadent, a king of France could dispose of church patronage. Because of this – wrote a statistically-minded Venetian ambassador in 1569 – the French king had 106 bishoprics, seventeen archbishoprics and between 600 and 700 abbeys with which 'to pay his debts, reward his grandees and dower his daughters.' A few of these benefices fell into the hands of good men inclined to take their duty seriously; most did not, and this had been more than the Huguenots were prepared to tolerate. At the French court, the ambassador remarked, 'they dealt in bishoprics and abbeys as elsewhere in pepper and cinnamon.'

In the Pale around Dublin, sustaining an English political presence there, was a force of English soldiers, but traditionally Ireland was a papal fief. In 1569, when victory in the Alpujarras was almost won, a scheme was set on foot which might well have made Don John of Austria King of Ireland.

A leading spirit in the enterprise was a forty-nine-year-old military adventurer called Thomas Stukeley, generally believed to be an illegitimate son of Henry VIII's by Jane Stukeley, who had been a matron of honour at court and Henry's mistress just before he took up, in turn, with the sisters Boleyn. Tom Stukeley's motto in life was, 'I would rather be king of a molehill than subject to a mountain.' His career as a soldier of fortune, living by his wits and getting into one scrape after another, is very much what Don John's own life might have been, had his half-brother King Philip decided not to acknowledge him.

Six years earlier, on 14 March 1563, Queen Elizabeth of England, chaffingly addressed by Tom Stukeley as 'my loving sister', had sent him to sea in command of five ships and a pinnace. Publicly, the expedition was given out as being for 'peopling Florida', and Elizabeth's own royal investment in the venture had included guns and powder to the value of £120. But Tom Stukeley had in fact set out with his little squadron to make money for the Queen by piracy, operating from a base in Ireland, and using her Lord Deputy there as his agent in disposing of the plunder.

Apart from any royal blood that may have coursed through his veins, Tom Stukeley had family connections with that cousinage of gentry in Devonshire, many of whom after doing particularly well from the share-out of monastic lands, were now engaged, like Stukeley himself, in piracy – under one pretext or another and always with a Protestant tincture – against either the King of France or Philip of Spain. Some were eventually to officer the Queen's ships in the Armada fight: the last thing any of them wanted was the restoration of Catholicism, since it might mean kissing their estates goodbye. One of Stukeley's uncles, for instance, Sir Hugh Paulet, had been supervisor on the crown's behalf of the lands and manors of the deposed Abbot of Glastonbury. Another uncle, Richard Pollard, was one of the three commissioners sent down to Glastonbury on Henry VIII's behalf to discover hidden treasure. Families like this would support Henry VIII's Protestant daughter, Queen Elizabeth, through thick and thin. But since the Irish at about the same time were finding in the purified Catholicism of the Counter-Reformation the very essence of their own nationhood, a clash was bound to come.

Tom Stukeley found Ireland congenial to him. His swashbuckling, larger than life character went down well with the Irish aristocracy, and he made himself popular with the English troops by his personal courage and by what was described as his 'royalty to men-at-arms'. From Ireland he successfully plundered both French and Spanish shipping, until diplomatic protests became too loud to ignore, and Queen Elizabeth had to go through the motions of throwing him over. Nor at the end of the account had she been very pleased with him. Stukeley had perhaps treated himself and his own followers a little too royally; the Queen thought her own share too small.

After wavering in his religion for many years, shifting his loyalties according to the fortunes of war, when in Ireland Tom Stukeley came down firmly on the Catholic side. In letters to the Queen he even flaunted his new loyalty by marking the head of the paper with the inked cross which was the sign manual at the time of Catholic fidelity. Since the Queen's chief minister, Sir Robert Cecil, soon to be Lord Burghley, was immovably pro-Calvinist, this was hardly what an ambitious man with an eye to his own career would have done. Stukeley's belated conviction was real, and governed the rest of his life.

Tom Stukeley having quit the sea announced his intention of settling down in Ireland. But any attempt he made there to better himself was in some underhand way or other blocked. The man trying to chivvy him out of Ireland was undoubtedly Burghley – a minister too sagacious to allow an experienced soldier with distant claims to the blood royal and, by now, strong Catholic affiliations to take up residence in an Ireland simmering on the brink of rebellion. In 1569, by means of an unconvincing accusation, Tom Stukeley was taken up and locked away in Dublin Castle.

There Stukeley found himself in good company. A memorial had lately been signed by Maurice O'Gibbon, Archbishop of Cashel, together with four other archbishops, eight bishops and twenty-five Irish nobles, petitioning that a non-English monarch be sent to Ireland, under the protection of the Pope and the King of Spain, so that Ireland might 'be entirely separated and freed from the crown and unstable government of England, and to have no other connection with the English but that of Christian charity.' Some of the more important signatories were locked up in Dublin Castle at the same time as Stukeley, and the prince they evidently had their eye on was Don John. Here was the first whisper of a hinted promise that was to bedevil the chivalrous young man for the rest of his life: the promise of a throne.

Thomas Stukeley made common cause while in gaol with his Irish fellow prisoners, and this made him guilty of what the Queen's spy master, Sir Francis Walsingham, was later to define, subtly, as 'secret treasons of the mind and heart.' The prisoners shared the same faith, but Stukeley had what the others lacked and needed: military skill. He also had enough influence at the English court to wangle himself a pardon. Once free, Stukeley bought and victualled a ship at Waterford – everyone supposed it would be going on some private piratical venture. He took on board a hand-picked crew, among them two master mariners, both Catholic, who had served their time with Hawkins and Frobisher. Taking with him his eight-year-old son, he set sail southward. Stukeley's plan had been confided to the Spanish ambassador in London, who sent word thus to Madrid: 'Thomas Stukeley an English Catholic residing in Ireland whom in consequence of being Catholic the Queen hath deprived pretends that with his friends he is ready to give that Island to Your Majesty or another Catholic prince.'

Ireland was then a little-known place on the very edge of Europe, where feuding cattle-herdsmen lived in a wild countryside. The far-off days when Ireland's saints and scholars had helped to civilize a barbarous Europe were a vanished memory. The entire English presence in Ireland then numbered only 1500. Pope and Spanish King between them, if they had responded with only moderate vigour to the Irish petition, had a chance to topple English power in Ireland which would not recur for several centuries. But with her reign only beginning, Philip had a marked sympathy with his sister-in-law Elizabeth – and she skilfully fostered certain of his illusions about her private religious beliefs and real political stance. King Philip never liked to fight until war was forced upon him, and he was already bogged down by the revolt against his authority in the Netherlands. He would rather keep England neutral than put a king of his own house on the throne of Ireland. It was a chance it was not in his nature to take.

Even so, Tom Stukeley impressed him as a man who might have his uses. Between 1570 and 1574, Philip of Spain – never a man to part pointlessly with money – paid over to Stukeley and his followers, most of them English Catholic exiles, the large retainer of 27,576 ducats. He appears to have raised Stukeley to knighthood in the half military, half religious and wholly aristocratic Order of Calavera, thus putting him on a par with many of the most important men at the royal court.

Sir Thomas Stukeley was full of good ideas. Dutch, Huguenot and English pirates were preying upon Spanish merchantmen on their way from Biscay to the Netherlands. He offered to police the Channel, making full use of his own experience in those waters as a pirate. He proposed seizing the Scilly Isles as a naval base convenient for his Channel patrol, but from which both England and Ireland could at need be overawed. But in the end the principal service he did King Philip was in the fight against the Turks.

As so often with men at odds with their own government in a matter of principle, most of our knowledge about Stukeley at this time comes from his enemies – from the verbatim reports of the spies Walsingham set upon him in Spain (*'They say I am a traitor to Her Majesty – 'tis they are traitors that say so. I will ever accept her as my Queen'*) as well as from a fictitious biographical account later concocted and put about in London by Burghley to blacken his character. But Puritans in England – even in London – were altogether too respectable to have much following as yet among the poor. Tom Stukeley struck the popular imagination. He was the hero both of street ballads, and of George Peele's *Battle of Alcazar* – where he was portrayed as a man a little grandiose, living with that eloquent and violent energy which always appealed to Elizabethans. They saw him as a man capable of marrying a city heiress and running through her fortune at the rate – then enormous – of a hundred pounds a day, yet ready to go to his death with calm mind, at the head of his men, on crusade.

The choice confronting Tom Stukeley, once he felt obliged to affirm his Catholicism even if it meant sacrificing his military career, had to be faced by many other Englishmen at the time. Some went into exile, rather than submit to the ingenious religious compromise put forward by Queen Elizabeth, from which the Church of England emerged: a Catholic-sounding liturgy, and Calvinistic articles of faith. Their dilemma was once expressed by a Catholic country gentleman, who when being cross-questioned told Lord Burghley bluntly, 'I ought rather to believe in the doctrine of the Church than an Act of Parliament.'

Queen Elizabeth's bold attempt to bring into being a national church, acceptable to the largest possible number of her subjects, so that only extremists on both sides would feel out of it, suited the English temperament very well. But this was not the rigorous mood then dominant in the Rome of Pius V. English exiles in Rome, hoping to put the clock back to Mary Tudor's time, gave the Pope optimistically erroneous information about the likelihood of Catholicism being yet again restored in England. Under their influence, Pope Pius V issued a Bull excommunicating Elizabeth and releasing her subjects from their allegiance: his greatest blunder.

From his knowledge of England gained when he was Mary Tudor's husband, Philip of Spain did his best to hold the Pope in check. A Bull so intransigent – he warned – would do English Catholics nothing but harm. But to Pius V, Elizabeth was the woman who 'pretended to be Queen of England.' She was, as his Bull put it, 'a slave of wickedness, monstrously usurping the place of the supreme head of the church in all England.' She had 'prohibited the exercise of the true religion which Mary lawful queen of famous memory had by the help of this see restored after it had been overthrown by Henry VIII'. She had 'oppressed those who embraced the catholic faith, abolished the sacrifice of the mass, prayers, fasting, unmarried life and the catholic rites.' Then came the hammer blow, which in England for centuries after was to make the Pope of Rome a bogeyman. 'We declare the aforementioned Elizabeth a heretic. We do declare her to be deprived of the pretended title to the kingdom, all who have in any manner sworn to her to be forever absolved of any such oaths and all kinds of duty, fidelity and obedience.' John Calvin, too, released his followers from their loyalty to all monarchs except such as 'provided for true religion among subjects', in this way sanctioning treason, though the fact is not often remembered against him. In those days religion and the nation-state were often rival contenders for any serious-minded man's allegiance; nor were those on either side who 'preferred their religion to an Act of Parliament' always the worst of men.

A temerarious London Catholic, John Felton, nailed a copy of Pius V's Bull to the door of the bishop's palace in Fulham, and was hanged for his pains. Apart from that one day's sport round the gallows, the damning document created little stir. Its value to Walsingham and Burghley was that it gave them a pretext whenever they needed one for condemning automatically any Catholic Englishman as a traitor. Under their resolutely Protestant government, spying, fines, torture at the rack and arbitrary imprisonment so wore away Roman Catholicism that a dozen years later, when missionaries trained abroad began to arrive in England clandestinely, to celebrate Mass – made illegal – at the risk of their own necks, they found their harassed flock, not long since a majority in the land, reduced to perhaps only 100,000. The essential predicament of English Catholics after Pius V had issued his Bull had been put into blunt words by Thomas Stukeley, when he told Walsingham's spy so unmistakably that he still regarded Elizabeth as his Queen. If the Pope could cancel fealty – if all oaths made in the name of the Queen of England were null and void at the stroke of a pen in the papal chancery – what was to become of England as such? What else would hold together a land which for the previous seven hundred years had been united and represented by its monarch? The throne, men felt in those days, was the keystone. Loosen it, and all fell down.

The French Huguenots had been defeated at Jarnac (where young Walter Raleigh from Devonshire claimed to have fought as a Protestant volunteer). All but a brave handful of Italian Protestants had been despatched to the galleys or the stake. Elizabeth Tudor had been disposed of by a resonant if ineffectual blast of words. The immediate threat from heresy began to fade from the fervent mind of Pius V, the intenser danger being as he now saw it from Turkish aggression. He took the first steps towards forming a Holy League of the threatened Christian powers.

But first the internal enemy must be held in check. In the Pope's ears, the antisemitic utterances of the Inquisition still echoed. Jews in Italy had until now looked upon Rome and Venice as fairly hospitable places. About a thousand Jews lived in the high and crowded buildings of Venice's ghetto – the very word is Venetian – and were well entrenched in the silk, woollen, spice and wheat trades. They did business with co-religionists in Constantinople who were often their relatives. Half the Italian Jewish population lived in the Papal States, and had been settled there since the early Middle Ages; their business connections with the Ottoman Empire were less in evidence. Though stringent laws against the Jews existed in Rome, they had been allowed to lapse.

To a veteran inquisitor, like the Pope, Jews were likely to be guilty not only of usury – theoretically forbidden all Christians, though enthusiastically practised by Italian bankers, thanks to theological hairsplitting. By the Inquisition they were also suspected of procuring women, of 'divination, conjuring, magic arts and witchcraft', of making people believe they could foretell the future, trace thieves and find buried treasure. Yet though living under the suspicion of possessing such disconcerting powers, the Jews in Rome but for rare lapses had hitherto been left alone – so that the measures taken against them by Pius V in 1567 had overtones of persecution. The Roman ghetto was to be walled around as strictly as the Ripetta. Only Jews of 'good character' – and the less likely, presumably, in the Pope's eyes, to tell fortunes and pimp girls – were to be granted so much as a pedlar's licence. All practising Jews were under pressure to accept baptism, and some of those who remained staunch were sent to the gallows.

On 26 February 1567, all Jews were formally expelled from the Papal States. Those who stayed on, said the decree, would lose their possessions and become the serfs of the Roman church, but those living in the port of Ancona and in Rome itself got a stay of execution, since their sudden departure would have disrupted economic life. The threat was so atrocious that the new law was often eluded. But the hearts of all Italian Jews – pedlars, craftsmen, international traders, pawnbrokers, bankers – had been gripped by a paralysing fear. And this fear – as the persecutors must have hoped – would make them think twice about giving the Sultan any kind of helping hand. They had been reduced to the same plight as the tiny and extraordinarily brave remnant of Italian Protestants, living clandestinely, and passing on with great caution the illegal books which taught their faith, sometimes disguised as wandering merchants, sometimes even as Catholic priests.

For unrepentant Protestants as for obstinately pious Jews, for immoral monks, clerical embezzlers, captured bandits, defeated Moriscos, sexual deviants and men so poor that they had to sell themselves to eat, the war galleys that King and Pope alike would henceforth launch year after year were the great repository. Into the galleys went all the rebels and misfits and dissenters of Christendom, the criminal, the nonconformist, the unlucky. The galleys did indeed create another hell, as a shocked churchman was heard to remark, when he saw and smelled for the first time in his life these naked, shaven-headed men, chained to the bench and living amid their own ordure, on a galley moored in the Tiber near St Peter's. A parallel hell – a hell on earth.

On 1 May 1566, with the previous year's setback on Malta still bitter in his mind, Soleiman the Magnificent set out from Constantinople in his carriage to fight his thirteenth and last campaign. Once his huge army converged it would number 300,000 men – a court poet had already predicted that 'cypress branches would wave him on to victory'. At the same time as his armies marched westward overland, a squadron of Turkish war galleys raided Ancona, the Adriatic port serving the Papal States, to give Mediterranean Europe in general and particularly Pope Pius V a sharp reminder that they were by no means forgotten.

This year's army was controlled from day to day by Sokolli, not long since promoted Grand Vizier, and an old campaigner in the Balkans. Before being swept up in the *devşirme*, the Grand Vizier had spent his boyhood at Sokolic in Bosnia – the Eagle's Nest – where his father was the Orthodox priest. Soleiman's carriage took forty-three days to reach Belgrade. Bandits had come down from the mountains to raid ration wagons and cut off stragglers – a sure sign that in the Sultan's Balkan dominions where the peasants had once welcomed Turkish troops as liberators, poverty and resentment were beginning to grow. The bandits were remorselessly hunted down, and their bodies hanged from one gibbet after another for miles along the road.

The Sultan in the course of his journey had picked up Sigismund Zápolya, a candidate for the throne of Hungary whom the Turks supported, and a serviceable pretext, if one were ever needed on that turbulent frontier, for threatening the Emperor with war. The Emperor Maximilian II was a half-hearted Catholic – on his deathbed he refused the last rites. Many Hungarian nobles, with their eye on church lands, had been toying with Lutheranism, and even though Maximilian would often come to tolerant local arrangements with Lutherans this religious split between Austria and Hungary was judged by the Turks to be a useful source of weakness. Sigismund the pretender had recently changed his own religion from Catholic to Protestant, and subtle-minded Sokolli had hopes of playing on the religious quarrel so as to confuse the ranks of the Sultan's enemies. Sultan Soleiman himself stoutly declared that he would not lay down arms until the iron crown of Hungary had been placed on Sigismund's brow. The French – Soleiman's tacit allies in the Christian West – were happy to see the Turks making trouble like this for the Emperor. Guillaume d'Aube, the French ambassador, had come into camp to offer his congratulations as the army headed towards Hungary.

Count Miklós Zrinyi, commanding an outlying imperial fortress at Szigetvár, made a successful foray on a Turkish encampment, and rode off with a booty of 17,000 ducats. Soleiman was exasperated by the impudence of the raid. Turkish rule required instant obedience imposed by fear – he altered his plan of campaign. A large part of his army was diverted to go and obliterate Szigetvár at once. There would still be plenty of time in hand to march on to Budapest, and impose on the Hungarians their new puppet king.

To concentrate an army at Szigetvár meant extravagant preparations. A bridge of 118 pontoons – got ready in seventeen days – was flung across the river Drava. A flotilla of war galleys had been rowed up the Danube. By 19 July the Turkish army had been carried across the great river, and on 5 August the Sultan himself arrived at Szigetvár in his carriage. Sokolli had already blockaded town and fortress with 90,000 men, and was hammering the walls from a vantage point on a nearby hill with 300 guns. To greet the Sultan on his arrival Count Miklós Zrinyi raised a large crucifix in the midst of his fortress, where all the Turks could see it. He then fired off, politely, the correct formal salute for an Ottoman Sultan from his own guns.

Szigetvár itself was strongly placed – a 'town of islands' covered on two sides by a tributary of the Drava. Occupying the town itself, on its three islands connected by bridges, would involve the Turks in hard fighting. Afterwards they would need to contend with the brick-built castle defended by its five earth bastions, and last of all the inner citadel. To rub this fact home to them, Count Miklós Zrinyi had hung lengths of scarlet cloth along the outer ramparts like pledges of defiance, and from the citadel's tower he was dangling large sheets of tin, which glittered and shook in the sun.

There was method as well as high spirits in the swagger with which Zrinyi accosted the Turks. His garrison were outnumbered by perhaps as many as a hundred to one, so they needed every encouragement. Though the town could be carried by sheer numbers, fortress and citadel were more defensible, and might hold the Turks up for long enough to spoil the momentum of the Sultan's summer campaign. His great army was already encamped in a low-lying place, with a bad reputation for fever. Last year on Malta was repeating itself: a fortified position obstinately held, and fever in the besiegers' camp. Count Zrinyi, with the example of the Knights well in mind, was avid for glory and aware that his turn had come. This year the eyes of all Christendom would be upon him.

By overwhelming force the Turks after fifteen days had occupied the town of Szigetvár. When the houses around the fortress could no longer be held, Count Zrinyi gave orders to set them on fire. Into their ruins the Turks hauled siege guns by long teams of water buffalo, and from point-blank range continued their bombardment of the fortress walls.

To cut short Count Zrinyi's foolhardy resistance, and free the Turkish army for its march on Budapest, a different tactic was also being tried. Sokolli knew that the garrison inside the fortress of Szigetvár included men of several races and more than one faith. Propaganda letters playing on these differences, and written in German, Hungarian and Croat, were shot by arrow into the castle to sow division. As Sokolli saw it, the Catholics were always his more resolute enemies; the Protestants might be won over. Sultan Soleiman then made a secret personal offer to Count Zrinyi – he could be governor of all Croatia if only he would yield up Szigetvár. Count Zrinyi used the offer to play for time – but when it became clear that the garrison were still obstinately united, the castle was put to assault. To the Turks' astonishment, the first attack en masse was thrown back.

The second onslaught, three days later, on 29 August, the anniversary of Soleiman's great victory at Mohacs, was yet another humiliation for the Turks. From his tent, where he was sick with dysentery, Soleiman wrote chidingly to his Grand Vizier, 'This chimney still burns, and the big drum of conquest has yet to be heard.' On 5 September, a huge Turkish mine blew out the grand bastion, leaving Count Zrinyi's final stronghold, the citadel, wide open to assault. But that same night, in his tent, Soleiman the Magnificent died.

Sokolli quickly took a grip on the perilous situation. He must extricate the tens of thousands of Turkish soldiers bogged down here at Szigetvár, but it must be by means of a victory. Everyone was well aware that the janissaries, for their next sultan, would have preferred their dead hero, Mustafa, to the actual heir apparent, Selim the Sot. Men were already beginning to say that if only Prince Mustafa had led the troops last year into Malta, the Turks would have won. If the news arrived that their legendarily invincible Sultan was dead, and Count Zrinyi still defiant inside the walls of Szigetvár, that might tilt the janissaries all over the Ottoman Empire into mutiny. Selim needed time to win Constantinople to his side, and this could only be done in Soleiman's name, for in the army as in Constantinople and throughout the Empire, the Sultan's authority was absolute.

Apart from the doctor in attendance on Soleiman at the time he died, so far only his secretary and his swordbearer were aware of the dangerous secret. Sokolli saw how, with their help, he could decide the fate of the Empire. The doctor he strangled at once. With the secretary's connivance he went on to concoct orders to the army, in Soleiman's name and as if he were still alive. They were detailed orders for the immediate capture of Szigetvár. Sokolli had the swordbearer send urgent word to Prince Selim that same night by a breakneck rider, advising the heir apparent first to make Constantinople secure, then to join the army at Belgrade in person – since only if the army, the ultimate source of all power in the Ottoman Empire, could be persuaded to accept him would his sultanate be secure. Nothing could be worse than a civil war for the succession to the throne, at a time when the Turks had enemies on all their frontiers.

By 8 September – and with Sultan Soleiman to all appearance still keeping to his tent and nursing his dysentery, yet watching over his army – the Turks besieging Szigetvár by following out Sokolli's forged orders had destroyed the citadel's outer works. Only the inner tower and the powder magazine were still held by Count Miklós Zrinyi. Having imposed on the huge Turkish army a delay long enough to have ruined their campaign, the Count made up his mind to die in style. On that last morning he wore a silk surtout. Around his neck he had hung a gold chain. His hat was black, embroidered with gold thread, and with a panache of heron's plumes, and a diamond brooch. Raising up his gold-inlaid sword, Count Zrinyi declared to the 600 men who had consented to make this last sortie with him, and die fighting rather than surrender, 'With this sword I earned my first honour and glory, and I want to appear with it once more before the eternal throne, to hear my judgement.'

Outside the gate of the innermost tower was a drawbridge, then a defensive ditch. Behind the closed gate, a mortar charged to the brim with scrap iron, as if it were a blunderbuss, had been trundled up. The gate opened suddenly. The mortar fired into the living mass of Turks, crowding on the far side of the moat. As they flinched, the drawbridge was lowered, and under cover of gunsmoke Count Zrinyi and his 600 made their last charge. It was not to last long, though they all went down fighting.

Two arquebus balls struck Count Zrinyi in the breast, and his skull was pierced with an arrow – he had gone into action without helmet or breastplate, to put himself on an equal footing with his least well-

furnished man-at-arms. But he was still alive. The Turks spreadeagled
Count Zrinyi on a gun carriage, and cut off his head. The severed head
still wore its bediamonded hat and gold chain when it was put into
Sokolli's hands that day as a trophy. To placate the Turkish army's
sense of frustration – since this had been a long, hot summer with no
sacking of cities – Sokolli gave orders for every Christian survivor in
Szigetvár to be killed out of hand. Nothing relieved their feelings
better than a massacre.

On the long and painful journey to Szigetvár, Sultan Soleiman had
hardly ever left his carriage. For him not to attend a divan in person,
even when on campaign, had become by this time not at all unusual.
So it was not impossibly difficult when the Turkish cabinet met, eight
days later, for Sokolli so to manage matters that the Sultan's death
continued to remain a secret.

The fact was that Count Zrinyi's tiny force, in holding up the
Turkish army for over a month, had disrupted all their plans. But all
the viziers agreed with Sokolli when he urged the importance of
presenting Szigetvár to the outside world as a victory. Triumphant
letters were sent to every Ottoman governor, and to every ally. Extra
pay was awarded to the thwarted troops – who can hardly have been
unaware that the 'victory' was specious. An order forged in Soleiman's name commanded that a mosque be erected at Szigetvár. The
fortress there was to be rebuilt, and held for Islam.

Sokolli explained the Sultan's invisibility by pretending that his
dysentery had been followed by a crippling attack of gout. The secret
was kept until enough time had passed for Selim to have made sure of
Constantinople. After being attended to the city gate there by his
intimate friend Joseph Micas and by the ambassadors of France and
Venice, Selim was in fact on his way to army headquarters in Belgrade. He was reported to have reached Sofia on 8 October. Ten days
later he galloped into Belgrade. His dead father's last summer of
warfare had been most unprofitable; war was no longer a good speculation for the Turks. Selim was unenthusiastically proclaimed Sultan
by an army which had been cleverly distracted from its private discon-
tents by yet another payday.

Though so expertly handled, the death of Soleiman the Magnificent
began to have political repercussions. In the Morea the Greeks of the
Mani rose in a gallant but ill-starred insurrection against Turkish rule,

only to be bloodily repressed by a force landed by Piale Pasha from fifteen galleys. The twenty thousand janissaries, having begun to feel their power as kingmakers, openly showed their displeasure with this new Sultan – not a patch on his famous father, not to mention the legendary Mustafa. Only by profuse bribery did Sokolli hold them back from open revolt. Since the janissaries' esprit de corps made them politically dangerous, their ranks from 1569 onwards were watered down by recruiting Armenians and Jews. By implanting religious and racial bickering into their ranks, the janissaries' solidarity was impaired, but so, of course, was their fighting efficiency. Times were no longer what they had been.

Sultan Selim generously promoted his old tutor, the conspirator Lala Mustafa, to be vizier next in rank to Sokolli himself – though Selim was at first afraid, or ashamed, to tell the indispensable Sokolli what he had done. In 1569 another revolt against Turkish rule broke out, this time in the Yemen. Sokolli sent Lala Mustafa there to put it down – quite expecting him to fail, and thus to vanish from the scene. Sokolli succeeded, to the extent that the former tutor disgraced himself before he ever got to the Yemen. But he failed, in the sense that when Lala Mustafa was put under arrest for his shortcomings, the Sultan had him released. In years gone by that sort of failure would have cost a vizier his head.

In June 1567, the ambassadors from Vienna who had been sent to Constantinople to negotiate a peace on behalf of Maximilian II made their first move in accordance with their secret instructions by giving 2000 ducats to Joseph Micas, and offering Sokolli as Grand Vizier an ongoing bribe of 2000 ducats a year. Sokolli though a man of clear mind and immense ability was insatiably avaricious. He was already said to be taking a million ducats a year in bribes. The great days of conquest in the Ottoman Empire left only their afterglow. With Selim II as Sultan, favouritism, harem intrigue and bizarre corruption were what signified.

9

The Fire in the Arsenal

I offered him my hand in greeting, but he would not take it,
since it was not a bribe.

Turkish poet

Selim II was forty-two when he became Sultan. He was haughty,
unimpressive, cunning, unwarlike – a small, sharp-featured man with
a high complexion from winebibbing, a sparse beard dyed black, eyes
habitually smudged with kohl. The man with the greatest personal
influence over him was not in fact Sokolli, the Grand Vizier, who
had taken such trouble to hoist him to the throne, but Joseph Micas,
'the Great Jew', described as 'a large person with a trimmed black
beard.' Selim had promptly named Joseph Micas as Duke of Naxos – a
little principality of Aegean islands – in return for past services. The
former Duke of Naxos, an Italian called Giacomo Crispi, now lived in
Rome, nursing his revenge.

The first coffee shop in Constantinople opened in 1554, and became
so popular that the owner made 5000 ducats from it in three years.
Even so, some purists continued to wonder if drinking coffee might
be compatible with the teachings of the Koran. Though his father had
reminded him that, for the Prophet, wine was 'the mother of vices,'
Selim stuck to the bottle, and Joseph Micas kept him supplied. At the
height of the struggle among Soleiman's sons for succession to his
throne, Selim had developed a morbid fear of being poisoned by his
rivals. Joseph Micas put his mind at rest by sending him every week a
sealed hamper of food and fruit which could be eaten without fear. At
the decisive moment in the struggle for the throne, Micas like his great
rival Sokolli had had the foresight to back the outsider – the drunken
poet Selim – and had openly joined him in his palace in Asia with a
useful supply of treasure, clothes, arms and horses. He had thus
become the one man Selim trusted.

At the shoulder of the Great Jew stood two women. One, a stunningly beautiful Jewess called Esther Kyra, manoeuvred the harem in his interest. The other was his famous aunt, called with affectionate respect La Señora Ha-Gevereth – the Lady – by Jews all the way from Lisbon to the Red Sea. In 1492, as a young girl, she had fled from persecution in Spain to Portugal. But persecution followed her, and five years later, greatly against her will, she had been compelled to accept baptism. She took the name of Beatrice de Luna, and married another converted Jew, a spice broker and banker named Francisco Mendes, who had large business connexions in Antwerp.

By 1536 she was established in the Low Countries, a widow, with a thriving bank under her control. She divided her time between international banking and arranging the flight to the Sultan's more tolerant domains of those who like herself had had conversion forced upon them. In 1545, La Señora decided to make the ghetto of Venice, with its crowded seven-storey houses and its animated and prosperous community, the base for her work, since Venice was halfway to Constantinople, and trade with the Ottoman Empire was brisk.

She was eventually denounced as a Judaizer (in fact, by her own sister) and had to move in a hurry to tolerant Ferrara, where Father Francisco's Borgia cousin and his wife were still able to shield both Protestants and Jews. But, with the Inquisition putting on the pressure, La Señora shifted her ground yet again. In 1553 she reached Constantinople.

The man of the family was by this time her unmarried nephew Joseph, whose father, Samuel, when converted under duress, had adopted the name of Miguez, eventually simplified to Micas. Since it was easier for a Jewish physician to observe the Sabbath without arousing suspicion simply by not seeing any patients on that day – Joseph's father had taken up medicine. Though they might have to masquerade as Christians, Jews like Samuel Miguez went on practising their ancestral faith in secret, as had the Moriscos: it was notorious in Spain that on Saturdays not a puff of smoke could be seen from their chimneys.

Joseph's father had moved to the Low Countries, there to become court physician to Charles V. His son Joseph was in due course baptized, and he was sent to Mass, but the boy would come back afterwards to his father's house and there practise austerities to atone for what had been forced upon him. At the cosmopolitan, easy-going court of Charles V young Joseph was made welcome, as much for his personal accomplishments as for his aunt's prodigious wealth. He played cards and shook dice with Maximilian, then Charles's nephew, and now Emperor. Joseph was famous at jousting, and on a visit to Antwerp, Charles V dubbed him knight.

When La Señora left Antwerp for Venice, she entrusted the Mendes banking business to Joseph, and as a financier he became internationally celebrated, travelling widely – even to England, from which practising Jews had by law been excluded since the time of Edward I. He made large loans to the French crown. In the course of transacting business face to face with men of importance, Joseph Micas acquired an insight into the realities of European politics. He developed a wide circle of correspondents with a background like his own – men who whether openly professing to be Protestant or Catholic could not forget their ancestry and had at heart the plight of the Jews. The private intelligence service available to Joseph Micas has been compared with that of the Rothschilds, the great bankers of the nineteenth century.

In Constantinople his aunt had reverted openly to Judaism and begun once again using the name of which baptism in childhood had deprived her: Gracia Nasi. She sent word to Joseph to cut his losses and join her. Described by intimates as 'a gentleman, expert in arms, well read, and a friend to his friends', Joseph made no secret of his journey, but crossed the Balkans in state, with twenty servants in livery and a bodyguard of two janissaries. In April 1554, at Galata in the old Jewish quarter on the far side of the Golden Horn, he was circumcised. He then married his cousin Reyna – Gracia Nasi's daughter – the uncharitable said, so as to keep her dowry of 90,000 ducats in the family. On their wedding day, d'Aramon the French ambassador crossed the Golden Horn to Belvedere, Gracia Nasi's palace, to congratulate bride and groom. From the moment he arrived in Constantinople there was no mistaking Joseph Micas's importance.

Soleiman the Magnificent had been particularly well served by his network of spies – usually renegades indistinguishable from their countrymen – whom the Turks had planted everywhere, even in the shadow of St Peter's. But though he never quite mastered Turkish, and had to rely on an interpreter, Joseph Micas was soon recognized as a man better informed about Western Europe than even the Sultan. (Some of the difficulties the Turks laboured under are hinted at in the way one of their agents accounted for the sacrifice of the Mass: 'they kill a Lamb and drink the Blood '. Micas would have known better.)

Apart from the reliable appraisal he could usually make of what was otherwise inexplicable in the West, Micas was also valuable to the Turks as a financier. Islamic law not only condemned usury, but formally forbade any official post being given to a practising Jew (though in the past a Jew called Sinan had successfully commanded the Sultan's fleet). Through the Mendes bank the Sultan's government had access at last to a modern banking system. Hitherto there had been no money market in Constantinople. There were no bills of exchange, not even with Venice, the Turks' most important trading partner, so that all transactions had of necessity to be settled in cash. But by making use of Joseph's correspondents, the house of Mendes could draw bills on other banks in a network extending from Salonika, Valona and Venice to Seville, Lisbon and Antwerp – then the great financial centre of northern Europe – thus linking the Ottoman Empire in a more businesslike way with its source of manufactures and its market for silk and spices.

Having recently conquered several Greek islands with thriving vineyards, the Sultan's government in view of Koranic prohibitions found it convenient to grant Joseph Micas a monopoly of dealing in the delectable but forbidden fluid. He also made large sums – though at the expense of his popularity – by farming the taxes, that is, by advancing the Sultan's government its just due at once, out of his pocket, and getting his own back, but at a profit and in course of time, from the hapless taxpayers. Joseph Micas soon became a man of such power in Constantinople that foreign ambassadors on arrival there would wait on him with gifts as a matter of course. When they found themselves short of funds he might even oblige them with an interest-free loan. The Franco-Turkish commercial treaty of 1569 was drawn up, significantly enough, not in French or in Turkish but in Hebrew. But to Joseph Micas, as to his aunt, and Esther Kyra, and all his other secret helpers, all this profit and power were but a means to a greater and more worthwhile end.

In 1516, Sultan Selim the Grim had taken Palestine from the Egyptian mamelukes. A few of the many Jews fleeing inhospitable Western Europe had decided to settle there, under Ottoman rule, on the soil of their ancestors. Gracia Nasi was in touch with a coterie of Jewish mystics, scholars and cabbalists, whose retreat was at Safed in northern Palestine, near the ruined city of Tiberias. She offered the Turkish authorities a rent of 1000 ducats a year for Tiberias, and from Sultan Soleiman Joseph obtained in 1561 a grant both of the ruined city and of the seven Arab villages nearby. Tiberias was to become a city of refuge.

Arabs living in the neighbourhood were spoken of as being hostile to newcomers. The first need therefore was to enclose Tiberias in a squared-off defensive wall, 500 yards long. The derelict hot baths there were put into working order. Mulberry trees were planted to nourish tomorrow's silkworms. To the first of her settlers, La Señora shipped in looms and Spanish wool of high quality. She sent them patterns, and they began weaving clever imitations of the imported Venetian textiles that sold best in the Ottoman market. By the time the Jews in Rome and Venice were being placed in jeopardy, Tiberias was ready to receive them.

We know that in 1567, when Pius V was making their lives unbearable, 300 Jews left Rome for Tiberias, and there must have been numerous others. Letters originating in Constantinople went covertly from hand to hand, urging Jews harassed by the Pope to migrate to the new Jewish settlement in the Holy Land, where an early and rudimentary Zionist movement was being organized for their relief. Textile workers would be particularly welcome, and ships sent by Jewish merchants living under the Sultan would soon arrive at Ancona to convey them.

Yet these early forbears of the Zionists never struck root. The reasons may only be surmised. Perhaps La Señora and her influential nephew were trying too hard to implant a capitalist economy, artificially, in a hostile economic desert. Perhaps Tiberias was too paternalist – to establish a city of refuge may have called for not merely skilled weavers but pioneers resolute in their use of both spade and sword. Some immigrants were poor and unskilled and lacking in self-reliance. Some were scholars unwilling to do physical work for their benefactors. Islamic society might in theory tolerate immigrant Jews, but they could never in practice be better than second-class citizens. The local Arabs, fearful of being elbowed out, continued hostile; the rabbinical casuists already settled at Safed were soon at odds with the newcomers. By the end of the century the Tiberias scheme was petering out, and fifty years later no Jew was to be found living there.

Sokolli and Micas were political rivals. Sokolli despite his notorious avarice was a man of the old school. Though he took harem intrigue into account – no one could survive otherwise – he acted whenever he could on principle. Sokolli's unique fidelity was to his Sultan; he would never openly oppose the Sultan's wishes: 'if ordered to fit out 10,000 galleys he would never say it could not be done.' He was tall, thin, quiet, cold, impassive, impenetrable, and though a morbid passion for accumulating treasure disfigured him, it must also be said that, as the 'Sultan's slave', everything Sokolli possessed in the world was legally at the Sultan's instant disposal, except for what he might have salted away in a religious endowment. Thus Sokolli's fortune like his rank of Grand Vizier was held on the most precarious of tenures. To judge by the policies he followed, his private hope must have been somehow to organize a rational peace by means of Ottoman power. He was the first Ottoman leader to grasp that war no longer paid a dividend.

Joseph Micas was less single-minded. Though he served the Sultan he also felt responsibility for the Jews. There were times when he used his great influence at court for private revenge. Simply to recover an old debt of 150,000 ducats – which the French had cleverly repudiated on the grounds that Micas was now openly a Jew, and Jews were forbidden by law to live or traffic in France – he put an unnecessary strain on the politically useful friendship between the Sultan and the King of France. Some of his wife's property in Venice had been sequestered. To visit the city and settle the matter – in view of his status as the Sultan's closest friend – might also have helped protect the Jews in Venice from the blows now being aimed at their heads. The Venetian Senate would usually go to great lengths to curry favour with the Sultan, but they were having none of Joseph Micas. Pocketing the curt letter of refusal sent him by the Doge, Micas is said to have decided that one day Venice should pay for it.

Selim II was not single-minded, either. He was physically unappetizing but he knew how to impress when he had to, sitting on the throne with a diamond half an inch square on his thumb, and surrounded by his comical but sinister bodyguard of 100 dwarfs, large of head and stunted of leg, clad in cloth of gold and all carrying murderous little scimitars. But though he could manage the ceremonial, Selim had no great gift for decision. When he insisted on having his own way he was likely to blunder.

In the first years of his reign the covert rivalry between Sokolli and Micas could sometimes bring a note of hesitation into Turkish policy. Sokolli favoured the traditional understanding with France; Joseph

Micas, though sedulously courted by the French ambassador, was of the opinion that the Huguenot uprisings had left France hamstrung. He inclined towards the Protestant powers. He found it difficult to forget that the French still owed him money. He liked to play a personal role on the international stage. After he had negotiated a 150,000 ducat loan in 1570 for the King of Poland, Turkish policy in Poland was for a while all of his own making. The Imperial ambassador wrote home that had it not just then suited Micas's book, personally, to favour the King of Spain – his old acquaintance at the court of Charles V – Sokolli might well have sent more help to the Moriscos.

Inconspicuously, Sokolli began patronizing the rich Greeks – Orthodox Christians thriving under Ottoman sway – using them as a financial counterpoise to the Jews, until at last his wealthy protégé Michael Cantacuzenos ousted Micas as government financier. Sokolli had served years before as admiral in chief, and therefore had a better grasp than most on the realities of naval warfare in the Mediterranean. He knew better than anyone that the preponderance of the Turkish fleet could never be challenged unless Spain and Venice joined forces. An unwavering principle of Sokolli's foreign policy was therefore to keep Spain and Venice on bad terms. Micas, efficiently exploiting his island dukedom of Naxos, was by this time casting his eye covetously on other islands, and the nearest, largest and most profitable of them, Cyprus, belonged to Venice. The Venetians had only a shaky legal title to Cyprus, and lately, by letting the galleys of the Knights of Malta take shelter in Cypriot ports after their raids, they had been giving needless provocation.

Each newly enthroned Ottoman sultan was expected to use the plunder from his first victory in the field to build a mosque. But in the first three years of Selim II's reign, the fortunes of war went against him. The 30,000 ducats extracted from the Emperor Maximilian II by the treaty of Adrianople, 'a present of honour' which in fact was the price of a truce, did not even pay the cost of the siege of Szigetvár. The war along the frontier against the Shia heretics governing Persia had been totally profitless. Arab revolts in Syria and the Yemen had disrupted the trade routes along which silk and spices came to Alexandria and Constantinople – this was costing the Sultan 2,000,000 gold ducats a year. Not surprisingly, at a little urging from Micas the rich and vulnerable island of Cyprus off the shores of Asia Minor began to bulk large as a temptation. On Cyprus there were plantations of sugar and cotton, and the wines were famous.

The Venetians were paying the Sultan 236,000 ducats a year for their commercial privileges – elsewhere in Christendom Venice was referred to, scathingly, as 'the harlot who slept with the Turk'. But this financial consideration did not deflect Selim, nor did the possible effect that any war with Venice might have on the balance of naval power. Having come to the throne of a state traditionally financed by war plunder, and needing money for his mosque, Selim was ready to ignore Sokolli and listen to Joseph Micas. In a tipsily expansive moment he seems even to have dropped the hint that he might if all went well promote his old friend to be King of Cyprus. To be duke of what must have been the smallest dukedom in the Mediterranean was much, to be King of Cyprus – an ancient title – even more. Micas was taken in, at least to the extent of experimenting with the addition of the blazon of Cyprus to his present coat of arms. He is said to have sketched out a plan for populating the island when it was his with skilful, industrious and grateful Jewish refugees. Sokolli, though his rule was to put all his strength and intelligence into carrying out whatever the Sultan decreed, must have had grave misgivings. He used his talents to limit the damage.

Built on a cluster of islands off the estuary of the river Po, with canals in lieu of roads, Venice was a city like no other. The Venetians had a foothold ashore, on the Italian mainland and the Dalmatian coast, but their island city looked out to sea. Their empire too was a chain of islands – Corfu, Crete, Cyprus – which took them like stepping stones from the northern end of the Adriatic to the profitable markets of the Levant.

Between Venice's imperial system then, in the sixteenth century, and Britain's in the later nineteenth, there are clear resemblances. With so many of her people at work in manufactures – particularly of textiles and glass – Venice like Britain had to make a living by banking or trade, and buy food with the proceeds. Her greatest outlet was the Ottoman Empire – just as India had been Britain's. Ever since the first treaty between Venice and Byzantium was sealed in AD 992, trade with Asia Minor had been vital for the Venetians. They sold their manufactures there, acquired silk and spices with the proceeds, and bought corn. Each day as a solemn duty, the Doge verified the Republic's stocks of grain; to buy bread for her people, Venice every year had to earn and spend millions. *Pane in piazza, giustizia in palazzo* – bread and justice – defined Venetian policy at home.

In her foreign policy, Venice knew that she was always in the middle, between hammer and anvil – between the King of Spain, with his viceroys in Sicily, Naples, Milan, Lombardy, Sardinia, and the systematically aggressive Turks, ever moving closer. The diplomacy of the republic had therefore to be subtle. A Venetian statesman once described his city's diplomatic method as being 'to play with a ball of glass, which must be kept in the air by light and skilful touches, and would be broken either by a fall or a violent blow.' Since joining a Christian League against Soleiman the Magnificent, organized by Charles V and Pope Pius III thirty years before, and being expensively defeated, Venice had somehow contrived to remain at peace with the Turks, however much others might get involved. This peace – the keystone of her foreign policy – cost Venice annually a fortune in tribute, while enabling the city, though in slow decline, to survive as a trading and financial centre, and even as a ramshackle empire.

Fortification was an expensive business – the sixteenth century built fortresses as earlier centuries had built cathedrals. Espionage and diplomacy were cheaper. During the thirty years of this chancy peace between Venice and the Turks, most of the fortified strongpoints of outlying Venetian islands had become run down and out of date. Venice considered her real defence to be not castles or soldiers, but the silent yet ever-present threat of her famous galley fleet. Like the British Empire in its last century of existence, Venice relied for her survival on her reputation as a sea power.

The Turkish Arsenal of Kasim Pasha, on the Galata shore beyond the Golden Horn, with its 'hundred vaulted arches, each long enough for a galley to be built under cover', was one of the two great manufacturing centres in the known world. The building of war galleys for the Sultan was carried on there principally by renegades who had served their time as shipwrights in Venice or Naples. The methods of construction in daily use at the Arsenal of Kasim Pasha were sedulously copied – just as the Turkish fleet itself had been copied, detail by detail – from Venice. The world's other great industrial centre at that time, where all those methods had been invented and perfected, was the Arsenal at Venice. The Arsenal occupied an outlying island three miles in circumference. By 1570, nearly all the techniques of standardization, flow production and line assembly which later were to make famous the name of Detroit had already been developed there, in embryo.

The shipwrights of Venice, if they put their backs into it, could lay down a keel at the outset of their working day, and by using their production-line methods launch a new galley hull by nightfall. In May 1570 – for by then, Selim II's threat to Venice was becoming unmistakable – the workers at the Arsenal launched twenty-five new galleys in less than a month.

In times of peace, Venice kept thirty of her war galleys, with their distinctive gilded prows, out on patrol. They policed the mouth of the Adriatic, chasing Turkish pirates who, from little ports on the Balkan shore like Valona and Durazzo, continually preyed on Christian shipping. They maintained imperial communications from one island stepping stone to the next. Though the physical presence of the Venetian navy at sea was never flaunted, everyone was well aware that on the slipways around the great saltwater basins of the Arsenal, the 100 hulls of her reserve fleet were always poised like a silent threat.

The hull of a war galley comprised less than half her cost. To the bare hull – the 'chassis' – once launched down the slipway and towed along a sequence of canals as down a conveyor belt, would be added, in an orderly fashion, one by one, the standardized masts, spars, rigging, ironwork, sails, oars, guns, shot, casks of powder, water and biscuit – until the ship of war needed only a crew to take her to sea. Of the entire annual revenue of the Venetian Republic – 7,000,000 gold ducats – the sum of 500,000 ducats was always set aside for the needs of the Arsenal. The rapid launching of the Venetian battle fleet was a feat of organization no other power could match.

In the sail loft of the Arsenal, 400 women sat cross-legged, sewing triangular galley sails. There was a ropewalk over 100 yards long. A hundred blacksmiths worked day after day at twelve forges. There were three foundries, and a huge timberyard of seasoned wood. Eight hundred ship's guns were stored in readiness, and enough weapons to arm 50,000 men. Standing orders laid down that at the first alert, eighty-five galleys were to be launched, one after another, each ready for combat – thus transforming, at a simple word of command, the balance of naval power in the Mediterranean.

Venice had at one time used her heavy galleys, of up to 250 tons burthen, for carrying high-cost cargoes of spices, silk or malmsey wine as far as the English Channel or the North Sea. But nowadays cheaper spices – of inferior flavour – came in bulk round the Cape of

Good Hope to Portugal, using the route pioneered by Vasco da Gama. Through the last thirty years of Venice's costly yet still profitable peace with the Turks, her own spice trade had been in slow decline. Venetian trading voyages were shorter, the game of juggling with the glass ball – on which her existence depended – was every year trickier. And compared with the vast territorial empires of Philip II or Selim II, the population of Venice was small.

Each war galley needed up to a hundred men at the oar, so that to keep even the thirty vessels of Venice's patrol squadron at sea called for 3000 rowers, apart from soldiers and crew. The islands and shore bases of her scattered empire needed perhaps as many as 30,000 men for garrison duties alone. Her brilliantly organized Arsenal might have the secret of launching a large fleet at the drop of a handkerchief. But could the city of Venice still man them?

Venice had been ruled for many centuries by an aristocratic merchant oligarchy, in some ways not unlike Britain's Whigs. 'We are the slaves of our laws,' the Venetians boasted, 'and in this our liberty consists.' Though Venetian law was strict in all vital essentials, when censorship both religious and political had become irksome elsewhere, Venice was still by far the freest city in Italy and a great European publishing centre: printed books were a valuable export. For such a people to have the war galleys which maintained their freedom rowed by enemies chained as slaves to the bench somehow went against the grain. When it came to a sea fight, they would rather have volunteer oarsmen with some kind of loyalty, however slight, to the republic. Not only could rowers of such a stamp be trusted with weapons; fewer soldiers would be needed to keep an eye on them than if they were slaves.

Until halfway through the century, enough poor men had still been procurable in the Venetian empire, willing to pull an oar for the sake of the rations. But from then on, crews became harder to find. As a second best, able-bodied Venetian convicts were sent to work out their sentences at sea. To meet the threat from Sultan Selim, two thousand men from Venice's mainland possessions were conscripted for galley service. Foreign mercenaries were hired. Banished Venetian citizens were told that they could earn a pardon at the oar, and afterwards come back home. Peasants from Veneto if willing to volunteer were let off four years' taxes. But the bottom of the barrel was soon reached. Some of the galleys had been on the slipway for thirty years. Since there were probably not enough men to pull all the oars, was the threat of Venice's great seagoing fleet any more than a nostalgic bluff?

The English crusader king, Richard Cœur-de-Lion, had conquered the island of Cyprus from the Moslems as long ago as 1191. When the little Latin kingdoms on the mainland fell to the Saracens one by one, the island became the crusaders' last refuge. Since those days, though the island had gone from hand to hand for 400 years, the Crescent had never replaced the Cross there. The Turks were now saying that Cyprus was legally theirs, and their argument ran as follows: in 1426, a man making a bid for power on Cyprus had sought help from Egypt in exchange for fealty. But Selim the Grim had long since conquered Egypt – it was now incorporated in the Ottoman Empire. Logically therefore the paramount rights on Cyprus had been inherited by the present Sultan Selim II.

In 1479 the Venetians had elbowed out their rivals, the Genoese. Though the Venetians were in actual possession, their real right to the island was dubious. The Duke of Savoy probably had a better hereditary claim – and a few years earlier, Sokolli had craftily prompted him to invoke his right there, so as to divide opinion and isolate Venice. The population of Cyprus in 1570 was 180,000, of whom 90,000 were serfs.

The Turks like all true believers preferred to be scrupulous in legal matters. When an attack on Cyprus was first proposed, certain misgivings had been expressed. The long-standing peace with Venice had been renewed only a couple of years before, in 1567. The Venetians had faithfully paid their heavy annual tribute – and had not the Prophet said, 'O true believers, perform your contracts'? An opinion was therefore sought from the Mufti, the highest authority on Koranic interpretation. He managed after profound reflection to find a form of words which would gratify Sultan Selim II, yet be compatible with doctrine. He issued a *fetva* declaring it lawful to recover by force any lands which had been Moslem in years gone by. The definition applied to Cyprus; it also applied to Sicily, and for that matter to Spain itself.

Venetian businessmen had been exploiting Cyprus with their usual thoroughness. They were cultivating crops which in the West had a ready sale at a high price – sugar, cotton, wine – using plantation labour. Their workpeople were Orthodox Christians – the island's Greek inhabitants. Over the past ninety years the Greeks had learned to hate their Venetian taskmasters: hard-faced men who though calling themselves Catholic yet insisted heartlessly on the exact discharge of every petty feudal right; money-grubbers who worked their serfs with bourgeois efficiency. The rulers were Catholic, the serfs Orthodox – a social conflict in religious terms which Sokolli knew precisely how to exploit, here as in the Balkans. Among poorer people in the Mediterranean, the Turks still had a reputation for being easy-going masters. In places where they ruled, class distinction between serf and free was ironed out, since all were but subjects of the omnipotent Sultan. Not many poor Cypriots were likely to risk their skins for Venice.

Not only had the Venetians succeeded in making themselves unloved by their plantation labourers on Cyprus. Almost everywhere else in Christendom, they were mistrusted for their habit of seeing state policy very dispassionately in terms of commercial advantage. In recent years they had courted the Turks, their best customers, perhaps a little too ardently. When everyone, even Elizabeth of England, was sending help or at least eloquent good wishes to the heroic Knights on Malta, Venice had hung back and stayed dumb – even poured a little scorn.

Since the Venetians were almost the only Italians he could not somehow control, Philip of Spain had a marked dislike for them. The city was too free for his liking – indeed, almost the last refuge for Catholic thinkers who elsewhere might be in danger from the Inquisition. The Venetians for their part frustrated Philip politically whenever it was safe to do so; they particularly affronted him by treating the Adriatic as though it were their private lake. Luckily for Venice, as her moment of danger approached, the moral climate changed. The proud, efficient, calculating, businesslike island-city might be relatively friendless, but the Turks were hated – and this popular hatred was growing hot, as a revivified Roman Catholic church began preaching united resistance to Islamic aggression.

In September 1569 came the news that the Arsenal of Venice, the key to her power, had been destroyed by fire and explosion. The word spread through Europe with such orchestrated unanimity as to suggest a whispering campaign.

Joseph Micas himself brought the glad news to Sultan Selim, and from then on to persuade Selim that Venice still counted as a naval power was out of the question. He had set his heart on Cyprus, and now found it easy to convince himself that the Venetians lacked the means to oppose a landing there.

During the night of 13 September, all Venice had been deafened by a big bang. The huge powder magazine in the Arsenal had blown up, the woodyard was afire. Out from their palaces along the Grand Canal tumbled the nobles, fully armed. An ever increasing throng of citizens crowded the Piazza San Marco, their anxious faces lit by a sinister glow as flames rose downstream, from the Arsenal. All were looking for someone to blame, and through Venice spread the glib rumour that this was the work of the Jews. Of the thousand Jews in Venice, must not at least some be working in the interest of the Grand Turk? After so many years of being pro-Turkish themselves, the Venetians no doubt found relief in unloading upon the Jews their growing sense of guilt.

The evidence about the part Joseph Micas may have played was not even circumstantial but only guesswork – a suspicion in men's minds. There could in the nature of the case be no proof that the Arsenal fire was lit at his prompting – nor even that through his network of correspondents he had a hand in the prompt diffusion of the bad news throughout Europe. The damage – though the enemies of Venice were hardly likely to credit the fact – was not so bad as at first had been feared. Four nearby churches were knocked down by the violence of the explosion. The loss of seasoned wood was serious, but the fire had been brought under control so quickly that only four galleys were destroyed on the slipway: a week's steady work would make them good.

But even if Joseph Micas's hands were clean, the rumours of destruction in the Arsenal could hardly have come at a better moment for his ambitions. In fact the half promise that Micas might become king on Cyprus was never to be fulfilled. The 'Great Jew' had made himself a little too prominent. His use of influence for personal ends had been too blatant. His unpopularity was rubbing off on the Sultan, and Sokolli was intriguing against him with masterly skill. The explosion of 13 September 1569 may have resonated in Joseph Micas's ears like a prediction of triumph, but the invasion of Cyprus marked the beginning of his decline.

September 1569 in Venice had been a month for bad news. The Italian corn harvest had yet again failed – which meant in effect that the city would be almost wholly dependent next year on corn bought from the Turks for *pane in piazza* – her citizens' daily bread. The Venetians were still convincing themselves that any threat to Cyprus could be countered somehow by skilful parleying. For all their ability as diplomats they were living in the past. Soleiman the Magnificent, with whom they had dealt for a quarter of a century, had been honourable and large-minded, a man of his word. Selim evidently meant to break the treaty of peace, and no argument.

Knowing how awkward the Turks usually found it – since their centre of decision was the Sultan himself – to conduct a war on two fronts simultaneously, the Venetians had done their best to embroil them once again with Persia, and had even tried to provoke trouble for them with the King of Poland. Accustomed to Sokolli's apparent goodwill, and perhaps relying on it a little too much, the Venetians expected to go on being treated in Constantinople as they had been for thirty years past: if not with special favour, at least with respect. They were now being harassed. Venetian merchants living in Galata were arbitrarily and unjustly arrested; they were hostages. Venetian ships at anchor in the Golden Horn were commandeered, and, adding insult to injury, were taken as troopships for the Cyprus landing.

The fervid appeals of Pope Pius V in favour of a Holy League had so far left the Venetian Senate coldly unimpressed. Here was a pope with his head in the clouds, a man who notoriously had no interest in money. Any Holy League to which he gave his blessing must mean for Venice an alliance with Philip of Spain – the oppressor of Italy. Joining such a League would also involve making common cause with those aristocratic pirates, the Knights of Malta, men recklessly indiscriminate in their raids on Levantine commerce. The Pope's little galley flotilla had been lost off Djerba, and never replaced. Venetian galleys in the Adriatic would be expected to defend the Papal States. So at first the Venetians dragged their feet, though not rejecting outright the option of a Holy League. They still put their trust in the diligent manoeuvres of their diplomacy. Day after day they turned out new war galleys, from their reorganized Arsenal. Any able-bodied young Jew who might presume to wander outside the ghetto was picked up and sent to pull his weight on a galley oar for the duration of the emergency. Bandits were offered a safe-conduct if only they would come in as volunteer oarsmen. There had been bad news so far, but the wind might change.

Late in the afternoon of 15 March 1570, the arrival offshore was signalled to Pietro Loredano, the aged Doge of Venice, of a ship flying the Turkish flag. The Sultan had sent an ambassador to the Doge with an ultimatum: Cyprus or war.

Pietro Loredano, a man of eighty-five and near the end of his term of office as Doge, began by refusing the Sultan's ambassador permission to land – a calculated snub, which put him in his place. The Turkish envoy was obliged to pass the moonlit night nursing his chagrin in the fairway offshore, yet within clear sight of this marvellous seaborne city of floating domes, towers and palaces, in certain details resembling Constantinople yet more magical, and with endless hammering from the Arsenal nearby ominously loud in his ears.

Files of Venetian soldiers were drawn up next morning on the stone quayside, to conduct the ambassador under armed escort to the Signoria – a vast chamber, designed with its gilt mouldings and panelling and magnificent wall paintings to inspire awe. At the far end, on a dais, the old Doge sat in dignity under a canopy. There was no negotiation, and no argument; the meeting lasted fifteen minutes. The Venetian Senate had already considered Cyprus, and decided on its policy by the close vote of 220 to 199: if necessary, war. The ambassador delivered his threat: since Cyprus rightly belonged to Selim, as Lord of Egypt and Jerusalem, then Venice must give the island up. 'In cold and dignified terms' Pietro Loredano refused. 'The Republic would defend itself against attack, trusting in the justice of God, and would defend Cyprus, its lawful possession, by force of arms.'

To Venice, hitherto proudly going her own way, her Catholic neighbours now that war was imminent made some unexpected gestures. Savoy offered ships, Florence and Urbino troops. Opposition to the Turk had for Pius V become a religious duty incandescent in its clarity. He used all his influence with Philip of Spain to allow the Venetians to buy the corn they urgently needed in Sicily, Spain's own source of supply. Philip responded well; he had always mistrusted Venice but he did not want to face the Turks alone. The precious Sicilian galley squadron, never risked even in Malta's worst days, was ordered to work alongside the Venetians in the defence of Cyprus. The Pope himself declared that he would bear the cost of fitting out twelve galleys as a papal squadron, if only Venice would supply the hulls. (Never for a moment losing sight of even the smallest commercial advantage, the Venetians towed down the Adriatic for the use of the Pope a dozen of their shoddier hulls.)

In early spring of 1570, a large Turkish fleet was reported out at sea, and cruising – but the Venetians by June that year had 127 galleys in service. Most were undermanned, some were reported to have typhus and dysentery on board: galleys were dirty places. The hard-headed men who governed the Republic of Venice had a reputation for looking facts in the face, and naval predominance was a matter of arithmetic. The Holy League, preached week after week by enthusiastic priests even in the churches of Venice, might prove to have more solid advantages for the Republic than might at first have been supposed.

After its menacing spring cruise, the Turkish fleet concentrated in June at Rhodes. In the Sultan's cause, Sokolli that consummate organizer had managed to mass 100,000 men on the inaccessible Turkish shore near Cyprus at precisely the right time. Sokolli was making himself an indispensable agent for the conquest of Cyprus, without becoming identified personally with the campaign. Joseph Micas's enthusiasm for the landing on Cyprus was bound to be suspect, since he had hopes of the throne there. Anyway, his star was no longer in the ascendant: malcontents in the bazaar were beginning to mutter, seditiously, that Selim was not the rightful heir, but 'the son of a Jewess'. Of the other conspirators who had come together to put Selim on the throne, the Sultan's other son-in-law, Piale Pasha, had tried in 1566 to redeem his failure on Malta by plundering Genoa's last privileged commercial outpost in the Levant – the wealthy Genoese merchant corporation in Chios off Smyrna. But he had since become suspected of illicitly pocketing some of the plunder. His conduct on Cyprus would be closely watched. The fourth conspirator, the ex-tutor Lala Mustafa, having botched his task in the Yemen before it ever began, was to share the command on Cyprus with Piale – with luck it might ruin him. Sokolli was evidently content to step back temporarily into the shadows and wait while his rivals made trouble for themselves.

In July the Turkish fleet loaded on board the vast force concentrated on the coast by Sokolli, and landed them at Limassol, unopposed. There were 50,000 regular infantry and 2500 of the Sultan's superb cavalry, the rest were feudal levies. Once ashore, the Turkish army converged on the Cypriot capital of Nicosia – its garrison, of 10,000, was outnumbered by ten to one. The fortifications of Nicosia were antiquated. Moreover, Nicolas Dandolo, the civil governor, convinced to the last that Venetian diplomacy would somehow fudge up a peace, had not even victualled the city to stand a siege.

10
Famagusta

. . . the inmost sea of all the world is shaken with his ships
They have dared the white republics up the capes of Italy,
They have dashed the Adriatic round the Lion of the Sea
And the Pope has cast his arms abroad for agony and loss.
And called the kings of Christendom for Swords about the Cross.
The cold queen of England is looking in the glass;
The shadow of the Valois is yawning at the Mass;
From evening isles fantastical rings faint the Spanish gun
And the Lord upon the Golden Horn is laughing in the sun.

G. K. CHESTERTON: *Lepanto*

In Rome that year, in the month of June, negotiations for a Holy
League had officially begun. Philip of Spain was represented by Car-
dinal Granvelle, more politician than cleric, by Don Juan de Zuñiga, a
diplomat, and by a Spanish churchman with aristocratic connexions,
Francisco Pacheco y Toledo, Archbishop of Burgos. The Pope
appointed seven cardinals to argue his case. Spokesman for the
Republic of Venice was her ambassador in Rome, Michele Suriano.
They all met in the house of the Pope's nephew and confidant,
Cardinal Alessandrino who had started life as a tailor's apprentice.

Venice now urgently needed – though only for so long as it might
suit her – an immediate offensive to save Cyprus if possible, and if not,
at least to defend the rest of her island empire. Spain with the Morisco
revolt subdued was not in immediate danger. King Philip would
rather have a long-term defensive league, to keep the Turk out of the
Western Mediterranean, and perhaps recapture one or other of Spain's
North African outposts, lost to the corsairs in years gone by. But now
as ever, Philip was apprehensive of what the cunning Venetians might
have in mind. Suppose they committed Spain to an all-out war against
the Turks, then withdrew, and left the others in the alliance to take the
brunt? At present, to withstand the Sultan's fleet, Spain and Venice
both needed one another's help, but for contradictory motives.

The negotiations dragged on, with Spain showing no signs of
urgency and Venice becoming impatient – until it was known that
the Turkish galleys had landed their invasion army on Cyprus

unopposed. But if a fleet could be sent to the far end of the Mediterranean soon enough, perhaps the enemy ships supplying the army could be threatened – better than nothing – or even brought to battle.

On 20 August 1570, the Sicilian squadron of forty-nine war galleys, led on the King of Spain's behalf by Gianandrea Doria, kept a rendezvous at Otranto on the heel of Italy with a dozen rather mediocre galleys of Venetian provenance which by this time were flying the banner of the Papal States. Twelve of the galleys arriving from Sicily were Gianandrea Doria's private property. They sailed in company for Crete, there to join up with the Venetians.

Doria, at thirty-one, was unprepossessing – sunken-eyed, meagre, ungraceful and with a pendulous under lip – 'more like a corsair than a Genoese gentleman.' But he was shrewd and strong-willed. He bore a great name, and had King Philip's confidence. Genoese merchant prince and Spanish monarch were indeed men of a similar cast of mind – cold, cautious, self-interested, clever, and not afraid to cut their losses.

At Candia on the northern coast of Crete, the arrival on 31 August of the Sicilian and papal contingents was greeted by a double line of Venetian war galleys, red with gilt beaks, fifty-four in all, drawn up near the shore under their admiral, Hieronimo Zanne. Overall command had been given to the admiral of the twelve papal galleys, an Italian nobleman of thirty-five called Marcantonio Colonna, tall, fresh-complexioned, baldheaded, with little side whiskers. No one doubted that Colonna's heart was in the right place. He was unremittingly courteous, and devoted to the cause. The only trouble with the appointment of Colonna was that he would be giving orders, in action, to squadrons much larger than his own, commanded by two admirals, Zanne and Doria, of greater seagoing experience, and from city states, Genoa and Venice, which detested each other.

The rivalries in the heterogeneous fleet Colonna had been given to command were so intense that all his qualities of tact and moral courage were to be kept at full stretch. Marcantonio Colonna himself – and this had no doubt been in the Pope's mind when sponsoring him as commander in chief – could hardly be identified with any one side. As hereditary Grand Constable of Naples he was a feudal vassal there of Philip of Spain, and had led three galleys of his own in a Spanish attack on a corsair base in Africa. Yet by inheritance he was also a Venetian nobleman – and a Roman magnate into the bargain, as titular head of the great house of Colonna. But when the fleet was drawn up at Candia for review, the squadron he led in the Pope's name was by far the smallest, and that counted against him.

Including supply ships, the fleet at Candia numbered 205. Off Cyprus, the Turks under Piale Pasha were stronger as a fighting force, but even so, Marcantonio Colonna declared his willingness to bring them to battle. Gianandrea Doria, however, had no such intention. Doria's critics in the fleet were already gossiping sourly about his unwillingness to put at risk the 6000 ducats a year he was paid in hire for each of his twelve galleys serving in the fleet. Others whispered that since the Tripoli fiasco, Doria had never got his nerve back. The better-informed and better-natured surmised that Doria might well have in his pocket secret orders from King Philip, warning him not to imperil Sicily, and thereby Spain's corn supply, by overdoing any help he might ostensibly offer Venice.

In public, Doria's argument, which he developed at Candia with great skill and scorn, was that the fifty-four Venetian galleys were simply in no condition to fight. There was something in it. In Venice's policy towards the Turks there had for far too long been an element of bluff. As the Venetian diplomat, Cavalli, phrased it in 1560, 'Clearly we must not go to war with them, but they should not be allowed to suppose that we cannot go to war.'

Doria sarcastically pointed out that the day the Sicilian squadron arrived, the fifty-four galleys from Venice had been drawn up for review across Suda Bay with poops to landward – the poop being high, the prow low – so as to mask the pitiable state of their crews. And during the inspection, Venetian officers had moved men on the sly from one galley to the next in line, so as to mask their real condition. Even if hulls launched recently at the Arsenal after thirty years on a slipway were fit for combat, their crews were so feeble that a stiff breeze from northward this very morning, said Doria, would lay them all flat on their faces.

The Venetians made the best they could of their usual argument – that the fighting strength of their galleys was not to be estimated by counting heads, since their rowers were not Moslem prisoners but free men, most of them, and Christians, willing to fight for Venice – men who could be trusted with arms. But Colonna himself was well aware that the galleys Venice had obligingly sent to the Pope were not in good condition, either. He found it difficult, therefore, to impose his will on this running argument – which wasted seventeen precious days at the height of the campaigning season. Obviously some offensive gesture had to be made in what was left of the good weather – so at last Gianandrea Doria was overborne. On 17 September 1570 the combined Christian fleet, carrying 16,000 troops, moved eastward from Candia, halfheartedly, with the modest intention of at least disconcerting Piale Pasha by attacking his base on Rhodes.

On 9 September, Nicosia, the capital of Cyprus, had fallen to the Turks – but the news did not reach Colonna until 23 September, when the combined fleet had already put to sea. The assault on the city had been launched by Lala Mustafa, the former royal tutor, and Ali, son of the muezzin in the mosque nearest the Sultan's seraglio – commanding land and sea forces respectively. In their final attack on Nicosia, they had accepted a risk which shows their low opinion of the Christian fleet. From each of their own warships anchored offshore they took a hundred fighting men to enlarge the assault force hurled against the walls of Nicosia. The gamble came off brilliantly – but had the Christian galleys made better time and their leaders been more re-solute, the entire Turkish fleet during the twenty-four hours it was stripped of soldiers would have been at Colonna's mercy.

Now that the Cypriot capital was in Turkish hands, any proposi-tion that the allies had previously discussed at Candia of making trouble for the Turks by attacking Rhodes – or threatening the south coast of Asia Minor, or raiding the Dardanelles – appeared futile. Galleys were flimsier than the round–bellied sailing ships which came up in their wake with supplies – and by late September there is always a risk that the good cruising weather in the Mediterranean might break.

Gianandrea Doria openly enjoyed his commander in chief's dis-comfiture. 'Marcantonio thought he would gain glory in Cyprus at my expense,' he gloated, 'but he was mistaken.' For Doria, nothing now was more important than to shepherd his galleys back safely to their base in Sicily. He refused to winter them any closer to the enemy, so as to make an earlier start next spring. 'If we are going back,' he told Zanne and Colonna cynically, 'why stop halfway?' Yet even so, Doria lost four of his galleys from bad weather on his way home. The hulls of Colonna's second-hand galleys were so unseaworthy that he brought only three of them back intact, after undergoing shipwreck himself.

Despite his advantages of birth, candour and courage, Marcantonio Colonna would hardly do, another time, as commander in chief. Nor for that matter would his rival, Gianandrea Doria. He was admittedly lukewarm, and already the Pope was taking him to task for it. As Pacheco, Archbishop of Burgos, observed scornfully in Rome, King Philip 'would never be well-served, while his fleet was commanded by a ship-owner.'

Lala Mustafa's fleet commander during the siege of Nicosia was Ali – young, ambitious, overconfident, and the darling of the harem. While intoning prayers on his father's behalf from the minaret nearest the seraglio – where nothing more reviving was usually to be heard than the twitter of eunuchs – the masculine resonance of his voice had melted the hearts of the Sultan's favourites. His promotion from then on had been rapid and assured.

Ali in fact had valuable qualities as a leader in war. He liked to be well thought of, and this could prompt him to be generous – for instance, he treated his galley slaves well. He was evidently a romantic, doing his best to behave as an ever victorious Turk of the old school might have done. The Ottoman state was still strong in the armed men and the empire it had inherited from the days of Soleiman the Magnificent; stronger still, perhaps, was the legend the Turks had set on foot about themselves. But power corrupts most quickly those who when they have attained the top of the greasy pole have dirty or bloody hands to show for it. Neither Lala Mustafa nor Ali could be proud of the way they had risen in the world, and on Cyprus the degenerate trend began to show.

Lala Mustafa's capture of Nicosia was marked by unwonted treachery, and ended in a programme of brutality meant to strike terrified obedience into the hearts of the islanders. To an enemy garrison yielding on terms, the custom of war accorded their lives. When after forty-six days of siege only the governor's palace in Nicosia held out, a Greek monk was sent in by the Turks to discover if Nicolas Dandolo would make terms. There were only five hundred Italians left in the palace. After the surrender had been agreed, Turkish soldiers broke in and cut them down in cold blood. Then in the city itself, Lala Mustafa's soldiers were let off the leash, and the twenty thousand inhabitants were massacred, many in such bizarre ways that those merely put to the sword were lucky. The houses were sacked to the bare walls; the Sultan needed plunder for his mosque. 'All that cruelty, brutality and avarice could commit,' said an eyewitness, 'were wreaked on men, women and children.' To elude rape, women first stabbed their daughters and then themselves, or else they leaped from housetops. Two thousand of the prettier boys and girls were spared – to be shipped off as sexual provender to the slave markets of Constantinople. Yet even in the departing Turkish ships, the resistance went on. A young woman called Amalda de Rocas struck the last blow. As a prisoner in a ship belonging to Sokolli, with 800 slaves aboard and much plunder, she put a flame to the powder magazine and blew them all up.

There was one other place on the island capable of putting up a fight, the old crusader castle and port of Famagusta. Turkish cavalry rode the thirty miles across country to the walls of Famagusta with the severed heads of Nicolas Dandolo and other dignitaries from Nicosia stuck like toffee-apples on their lances, only to find the port and town fortified against them. Famagusta had by no means been intimidated. On 1 September, Lala Mustafa mounted his first battery of siege guns outside the little town's earth ramparts. But it was too late in the year to begin on a siege in due form. Forty war galleys were left in Cypriot waters on blockade duties, the rest of the Turkish fleet dispersed to winter bases. Cyprus was not yet quite Turkish – the summer's campaign had come to an untidy end.

In January 1571, Marcantonio Quirini from Crete ran the Turkish blockade with sixteen of his best galleys and three supply ships. From beleaguered Famagusta he took off civilians and stiffened the little garrison there with munitions, rations and 1600 men. To Sultan Selim's fury, the Turks would be held up around Famagusta, not only all that winter but well into the next summer.

Piale Pasha though the Sultan's son-in-law was blamed for not bringing Colonna's fleet to battle and he was blamed, too, for the way the land fighting still dragged on: Malta, Chios, and now this. Sultan Selim was impatient for a triumph; Piale Pasha, Sokolli's rival, was ignominiously sacked.

Patiently following his strategy of dividing Venice from Spain, Sokolli the Grand Vizier let the Venetians know privately that a separate peace might always be possible, even though Famagusta was still holding out. A large minority in the Venetian Senate had been unwilling to go to war over Cyprus. Evidently this was the influential group upon whose pressure Sokolli relied.

The Venetians had at first been more eager than Spain for a Holy

League. That winter they began to drag their feet. Spaniards were always slow to make up their minds, but at last they saw that to entrust their future to a combined fleet as ineffectual as Colonna had led out last year might mean delivering Christendom to the Turk. The Pope was sure in his own mind that unless the Holy League had been made effective by the spring of 1571, the present chance of rebuffing Turkish aggression would be lost. Combining acts of financial generosity with words of passionate conviction, he laboured all winter to bring Spain and Venice closer – or, at least, to prevent their flying apart.

At the conference table in Rome, the Venetian ambassador had begun to procrastinate. He quibbled for instance over the share Venice might have to pay towards the League's running costs – though Pius V had by now saddled the church itself with the lion's share of the expense. Among other benefactions, the Pope allowed Philip II the concession known in Spain as the *cruzada* – money made available to the King for a crusade. According to one estimate, a hundred galleys of the Spanish fleet were in the end to be paid for out of church funds. In Venice the church authorities had conceded to the Doge, at the Pope's bidding, an impost worth 100,000 gold scudi, to help in the defence of Cyprus. Yet in Rome, the Venetian ambassador went on making greedy noises.

To place limits on the bickering between Venice and Spain, the Pope had done his best to involve other powers, not always with success. Having at last been recognized with the Pope's help as Grand Duke of Tuscany, Cosimo dei Medici showed his gratitude by patronizing a Tuscan Order of St Stephen, to fight the Turks at sea: that would mean a dozen more war galleys. But when appealed to for help by the Pope in a personal letter, King Charles IX of France sent a cold, brief and negative reply. To offset this, the Knights of Malta – so many of whom were Frenchmen – were in the League heart and soul.

Geographically France of all the Mediterranean powers was the least menaced by Turkish aggression, and had seized the opportunity of trading with some of the markets in the Levant temporarily lost to Venice. The Sultan's principal European enemies – Spain and the Empire – were the two of France's neighbours which she thought of as standing in the way of her territorial expansion. The Spanish ambassador in Paris sent a warning to King Philip that 'here in France, everyone is doing his best to prevent the League from taking place. I would not be surprised if next year they do not offer Toulon to the Turks.'

The boy king of Portugal, blue-eyed, red-haired Sebastian, was at heart a passionate crusader. His teacher had indeed been rebuked for feeding the boy's mind exclusively on romances of chivalry. His little kingdom's Atlantic coastline was under constant attack both from Moroccan corsairs and from Huguenots out of La Rochelle, cruising as pirates in the name of religion. Since Sebastian had only ten galleys to patrol his coast, there were none to spare for the Holy League. But earlier there had been fighting between Portuguese and Turks in the Red Sea. Unable to spare galleys, young Sebastian promised that 'next year' he would make a diversion, by attacking the eastern marches of the Ottoman Empire with ships sent out from the Portuguese trading posts in India.

Since 1561, Poland and Lithuania had been united as one country with an elected king. Though culturally these were Poland's golden years, militarily the country then as now was weak, with no natural frontiers and enemies on all sides. Calvinism had made headway in Poland in the past twenty years, and there were Polish nobles with an eye on church lands who had succumbed to the Lutheran temptation. But Calvinists and Lutherans in Poland were by now so violently at odds with each other that Jesuit missionaries had slipped into the gap between them – in the past five years the Jesuits had been having an amazing success in recovering Poland to the Roman church. Perhaps it was logical that Poland, threatened by Orthodox Russians on one side and Lutheran Germans on the other, with Ottoman Turks to the south, should find the fervent Catholicism of the Counter-Reformation answer best.

As well as living in a country so hard to defend, the Poles relied for their material prosperity on the tens of thousands of beef cattle they sold on the hoof every year to feed Constantinople. The Turks not only dominated their economy but even took a hand in their royal elections. For the Poles to join a crusade against the Sultan – whatever moral support they might otherwise give – would be national suicide.

The Emperor Maximilian II was lukewarm, and glad of the eight-year truce he had bought, after Szigetvár. Indeed he actually paid over his 'gift of honour' as the Turks were moving against Cyprus. The Pope had even gone so far as to seek help – of course, in vain – from Ivan the Terrible. Once criticized in whispers by the cool-headed clerical politicians of Rome as an impractical mystic, the old man disconcerted them that winter by the urgency and effectiveness with which he spoke and acted: a Holy League by next year! A Holy League

– impossible but essential. Yet all through the winter of 1570, the two powers with most at stake, Venice and Spain, scored debating points and made rhetorical speeches at each other's impassive faces. And Venice, of course, was playing a double game.

When the first flowers of the Roman spring were embellishing the ancient city, the Venetian ambassador was still making blank-faced denials to the slightest suggestion that his government might be having second thoughts. Venice, he let it be supposed, was still deeply interested in a Holy League – if the terms were right. Look at the evidence. Was she not still launching new galleys one after another from her Arsenal? Still recruiting soldiers? Yet the small and deadly fact was that Ragazzoni, secretary of the Venetian Senate, had been in Constantinople since the previous January, and there with the help of Barbaro the republic's ambassador he was trying hard to come to terms with Sokolli. Selim II could not decently lay claim to the first fruits of victory, as custom decreed, to spend on a mosque which would bear his name, until all Cyprus was Turkish. The Venetian negotiators were making use of the heroically prolonged defence of Famagusta as a diplomatic lever.

Had Selim II been as unimpassioned and clear-sighted as his own Grand Vizier, a bargain convenient to both sides but fatal to Europe might well have been struck. 'Peace is better for you than war,' Sokolli reminded the Venetians paternally. 'You cannot cope with the Sultan, who will take from you not only Cyprus alone, but other dependencies. As for your Christian League, we know full well how little love the Christian princes bear you. If you would but hold by the Sultan's robe, you might do what you want in Europe, and enjoy perpetual peace.'

The heads of a possible agreement between Venice and the Sultan were established. Venetian merchants arbitrarily imprisoned in Constantinople were to be set free, and trade between Venice and the Ottoman Empire restored. Sokolli was even ready to let the garrison of Famagusta march out with all the honours of war. If Venice were to survive, Venetians must be realists. The defence of Famagusta was no more than a brilliant delaying action. Cyprus was lost, and last year's craven performance by the Christian fleet under Zanne, Doria and Colonna hardly encouraged Venice to entrust her destiny to any kind of alliance.

Yet even as they played their hidden game, the Venetians kept in mind another variation. Sokolli favoured them – and so he should, they paid him enough. Or gave every appearance of favouring them – Sokolli was deep, too. But Sokolli's master, Selim II, was notoriously under the personal influence of Joseph Micas, the Great Jew – a man hostile to Venice. And Selim was neither stable nor rational – not a man to be trusted. Suppose by an abrupt twist of fate – some petulant impulse on the Sultan's part, or one bribe too many, perhaps – Sokolli tumbled from power. He would not be the first Grand Vizier reduced to nothing overnight. If the Sultan refused to sanction the peace Sokolli had arranged on his behalf, what was there to stop the Turks gobbling up not only Cyprus but every other Eastern Mediterranean island flying the banner of St Mark? The Venetians could not, any more than the Spaniards, fight the Turks alone. This was the fearful knowledge that kept them together, when intrigue and material interest tugged them apart. So Venice kept her other option open. If Turkish aggression intensified, a Holy League could be their last hope.

Nothing was known for certain in Rome about Venetian confidential parleys with Sokolli, but no one at the conference table entirely trusted Venice. King Philip might be a man who moved circumspectly towards any great decision, but his essential quality of mind was his Catholic faith. The Pope's single-minded fervour had won him over to a disinterestedness he was never to show again. All that would hold back the Turk from a rampage into Europe – King Philip was by now convinced – would be a huge confrontation of galley fleets somewhere on the smooth Mediterranean late next summer. Philip tried conscientiously to avoid war – but let it come if it must. Knowing that their King had at last made up his mind, the Spanish representatives in Rome got vigorously down to business. By March 1571, the terms of a treaty were clearly established.

The cost of the Holy League would be defrayed – and plunder, if any, shared – in a simple proportion of Spain 3, Venice 2, Pope 1. Each signatory would be allowed to buy corn in the others' markets. The League was aimed against both the Sultan and his dangerous auxiliaries the North African corsairs. It was to be 'perpetual'. By April of 1571 – and for every year thereafter – the allies would pledge themselves to send out 200 galleys and 100 supply ships, manned by 50,000 infantry. The thorniest problem of all was solved when the Pope carried his own audacious proposal for a supreme commander, capable from his rank and character of rising above the jealousies which last year had bedevilled Colonna's fleet, a war leader competent to win what no Christian admiral had ever yet won: a great sea battle against the Turks. At the age of twenty-four, the late Emperor Charles V's bastard son, Don John of Austria, had the fate of the civilized world placed in his hands, 'in a war that concerned all Christendom'.

Some in Rome had heard well of his conduct against the Moriscos in the Alpujarras. But that had been a minor campaign in a remote Spanish province, with only a few thousand fighting men involved. Many thought that as commander in chief he would never amount to more than a dignified figurehead – a nominal leader, congenial to Spain, acceptable to Venice and admired by the Pope. The professionals, they supposed, would do the real fighting.

On 7 March 1571 – the Feast of St Thomas Aquinas – the representatives of Spain and Venice, after attending Mass in Santa Maria sopra Minerva, the Dominican church in Rome, were formally to sign the treaty on behalf of their governments. After the Mass, King Philip's chief spokesman, Cardinal Granvelle, turned to the Pope and coldly informed him that whatever the treaty might say, Spain could not possibly get her fleet to the rendezvous at Messina by April. (He was right, of course. In such practical matters Spain was lamentably slow – but the idea of a Holy League had never made Granvelle's blood beat faster. He had held to a policy of only helping Venice when her plight was desperate, until overruled by the other cardinals.)

All through these frustrating months of negotiation Pius V had kept his temper under control, in a way to make those who knew him marvel. Now his violently passionate nature broke out. Rounding on Granvelle furiously, he drove him from the room. When Cardinal Granvelle had been thus disposed of, the Venetian ambassador announced that he too had something to say. Venice – unlike Spain – could perfectly well meet all the terms of the treaty. But the Republic of Venice would not sign. The ambassador gave no explanation; he was evidently repeating his instructions. So long as the faintest likelihood remained of striking an advantageous bargain with Sokolli – until the very last moment in 1571 at which a naval campaign could feasibly be launched – Venice would keep her hands free.

After the Mass at Santa Maria sopra Minerva, Pius V went back to the Vatican, alone. The Roman crowd, which misses nothing, did not fail to observe that the haggard old man's eyes were red with weeping.

★   ★   ★

The small harbour of Famagusta was formed by an offshore reef and shoal where shipping could ride at anchor under the guns of the citadel. The harbour could be closed against an enemy by an iron chain. To the north was the protective headland of Cape Saint Andrea, to the west, Cape Greca. The town itself was defended by a parapet only four feet high along a square earth rampart, each wall being half a mile long, and protected at intervals by small defensive towers. The garrison numbered 7000. The civil governor of Famagusta, Marcantonio Bragadino, and his military commander, Astor Baglione, had made good use of those forty-nine unmolested days while Nicosia was still holding out. The suburbs had been levelled so as to give the guns in the bastions a clear field of fire. The two leaders had begun to move out idle mouths – during the course of the siege, 8000 civilians were taken away to safety. Several hundred Orthodox Greeks had by now formed the opinion that on Cyprus the Turks might well be worse than their hated Venetian taskmasters. These 'peasants and bourgeois' were recruited as volunteers in the city's defence. When the first Turkish horsemen from Nicosia galloped up, triumphant, with identifiable heads stuck on their lances, they came up against men confidently led, and not easy to frighten – men not unlike those who had confronted the Turks at Szigetvár and on Malta. The little coastal city was to hold them at bay for ten months.

The Turkish troops left behind that winter on blockade pitched camp on Cape Greca, between the city and the setting sun. Against Famagusta's insubstantial city wall their artillerymen mounted twenty-five guns, and began to hammer away. A patrol of seven galleys cruised offshore. Meanwhile, the bulk of the Sultan's fleet made its way through equinoctial seas that were particularly rough that year, to winter bases in the Dardanelles, and at Rhodes, Chios and Negropont.

All winter the Turkish soldiers blockading Famagusta were given a lively time; there was no hibernating. The brothers Rondacchi led out their handful of cavalry on impudent sallies from the ramparts. Venetian raiding-parties attacked the Turkish batteries with hand grenades. The Turks dug a mine through the rock in the hope of breaching the wall. The Venetians, led by Nestor Martinengo, Famagusta's enterprising sapper and gunner, riposted according to the book with a countermine dug even deeper, from which they listened intently while the Turks in the tunnel overhead placed their barrels of gunpowder in readiness for the explosion. Famagusta was running short of gunpowder. Up through a hole came the Venetians, from their countermine underfoot, and carried off the Turkish powder barrels before they could be exploded. All winter long the Venetians kept a Greek work force toiling, to thicken and improve Famagusta's outermost defence – the city wall. And even if the wall were taken by assault, they could withdraw, here as at Nicosia, to an inner strongplace, the citadel, and hold out a little longer.

On 26 January 1571, a fine winter's day, the seven galleys of the Turkish blockade patrol were anchored in Constanza Bay close inshore under cover of an army battery – one account less favourable to the Turks says that they were beached. When the Turks looked up, they saw sixteen scarlet and gilt galleys from the Venetian base at Candia, walking the sea on their long oars, escorting three armed merchantmen stuffed with food and munitions. These blockade-runners had made the passage from Candia to Famagusta in eight days. Pinned between ship and shore – taken at a mortal disadvantage – the Turkish galley patrol slipped their cables and ran out to sea, with Marcantonio Quirini and his Venetian galleys hotly after them. Quirini sank three, the rest got away under cover of darkness. Having replenished Famagusta and taken off wounded, sick and noncombatants, Quirini then led his galleys on a cruise around the shores of Turkish-occupied Cyprus. With a cheerful audacity that put new heart into the garrison of Famagusta, he burned Turkish watchtowers, and sent armed parties ashore to make a hash of enemy communications. He captured and sank two large Turkish supply ships, and before he left had added 1600 fresh troops to the city's garrison. Later that winter, another contingent of 800 soldiers under Onorio Scotto arrived in a blockade runner from Venice itself, bearing a letter of encouragement from the Senate, addressed to 'our most dear and faithful city of Famagusta'.

The Venetians maintaining the walls of Famagusta felt that the republic had not forgotten them, and indeed they were right. In their peace negotiations with Sokolli the Venetian spokesmen though yielding much had insisted upon honourable treatment for the garrison of Famagusta. This Sokolli had said he was willing to grant. That winter the sonorous word *Famagusta* became a symbol through all Christendom. The garrison told one another that when the Turks tried to come back in force, next spring, a Venetian galley fleet would surely intercept them and bring them to battle. Bragadino and his men had as yet no clear idea of the scale upon which the Turks planned to operate, in 1571, against the small city that was still defying them.

Had it been left to a combative and angry old man called Sebastian Veniero, the governor of Crete, all ninety-seven of the galleys at his disposal would have gone off to tackle the returning Turks, without waiting for the battle fleet. Veniero last year had been governor of Corfu. Over seventy, with ragged hair and a snow-white beard, he was another of those fierce and proud veterans who seemed to incarnate Venice's glorious past, and never to be discouraged by her present weakness. When a Turkish expeditionary force attacked Corfu, old Veniero had defended the island with irregular light horse, dispersed and poised so as to interrupt a Turkish landing at any point along the island's shore. He had at the same time carried the war to the enemy with an audacious attack on the coast of Turkish-held Albania.

Veniero would cheerfully have risked all his galleys off Famagusta and gone down fighting, but his senior naval officers overruled him. Their intelligence was of a Turkish arrival at Cyprus in such force that opposing them would be throwing galleys away.

Irate that the conquest of Cyprus should have dragged on through the winter when his military advisers last year had presented it as a walkover, Sultan Selim II had told the divan that there were to be no other military enterprises anywhere whatever until Cyprus was disposed of. Bragadino and his men in Famagusta had thus set back for half a year at least the Turkish programme in the Aegean and the Adriatic, and in Italy itself. The taking of Famagusta in 1571 had therefore been planned as a stunning public demonstration of Turkish might – a preliminary to all-out war on other Venetian possessions.

The first Turkish war galleys were through the Dardanelles that year before March. They had a rendezvous with galleys from Rhodes and Chios, and were joined by an important galley squadron sent north from Turkish Egypt by its governor Mahomet (whom the Italians called Mahomet Scirocco – from the south – to distinguish him from another Mahomet who commanded the advanced Turkish naval base at Negropont, as well as from all the other Mahomets in the Turkish service). When brought together the fleet intended for Cyprus numbered 200 sail. By an ostentatious and perhaps unnecessary display of force, the Sultan was making it clear that he still held command of the sea. Piale's place as admiral had been given to that same Ali whose voice from the minaret had once so titillatingly informed the ladies of the harem that 'prayer is better than sleep'.

In April Ali with seventy galleys of the Turkish vanguard arrived off Cyprus. A few days later, men on duty along the walls of

Famagusta could watch newly landed janissaries pitch row after row of their green tents along the shore of Costanza Bay. More troops came in from one day to the next, until the mass of men crowded around the little city was hard to credit. In all there were possibly a quarter of a million. Lala Mustafa their commander in chief boasted that if each of his soldiers threw only one sandal ahead of him, they would together make a mound so high that from the top of it the walls of Famagusta could be dominated and stormed. His actual frontline fighting men probably numbered about 100,000. The assault troops were outnumbered by the pioneers – forced labour under military discipline – who in April began to drive trenches through rock towards the city wall. In six weeks their trenches were so deep that when cavalry rode into them the tips of their lances became invisible.

The winter blockade had worn the garrison of Famagusta down to about 4000 men, but they were combative. Turkish sappers digging entrenchments and establishing batteries were continuously attacked by Venetian grenadiers. When the Turks drove their first mines the Venetians countermined and this time blew them skyhigh. But inevitably the Turkish grip on Famagusta began to close. By the end of May, Lala Mustafa had seventy-four guns in ten batteries hammering at weak places in the makeshift earth rampart, four of them being basilisks – huge brass siege guns throwing a 200-pound ball. Breaches appeared in the wall, but each hole made by the guns was rapidly filled up from inside the city with sandbags. The Venetian commanders lived day and night in dugouts under the wall, at the actual point of danger. The deep trenches their pioneers had dug in the rock enabled the Turks to establish a bombproof gun emplacement point-blank, under the very ramparts. The Venetians blew it up. In provocative scorn, the Turks were flying a Venetian banner – the Lion of St Mark's – which they had captured at Nicosia. Astor Baglione, the city's military commander, led out a sally, and took back the flag with his own hand.

The Turks at last managed to blow a hole in the city wall too big to be patched up, by exploding a mine under a demilune near Famagusta's arsenal. The city was at last opened to assault. The first attack lasted five hours, but was beaten back. A second breach made in the walls was attacked by Turks in mass formation for six hours, yet again the Venetians managed to hold them. Turkish losses by now were discouragingly high, but since the Mufti had defined the invasion of Cyprus as a holy war, the assailants were encouraged by the reminder that their dead went straight to paradise.

Lala Mustafa – already suffering in his reputation – ordered a simultaneous and sustained attack on every breach so far made in the wall, from all sides at once. The defenders were meanwhile to be smoked out – choked and blinded by smudge fires. When his third mass attack on 9 July was flung back, the Turks were maddened. A fourth attack on 31 July also failed. By this time the city wall had been breached in five or six places, and of the 4000 defenders, only 1800 were left alive. There could be no more dashing cavalry sorties because nearly all the horses had been eaten. The flour was almost gone. The defenders were down to their last seven kegs of powder. Marcantonio Bragadino as civil governor, aware that the city's power of resistance was almost at an end, yielded at last to those who urged upon him the tactic of a parley with Lala Mustafa.

Bragadino as a Venetian Senator had inherited a tradition eight hundred years old for making the best of a bargain. He knew that Lala Mustafa – that old intriguer – must be under increasing political pressure from his rivals around the throne to bring the long-drawn-out struggle to a victorious end. Famagusta had cost the Turks dear. They had for instance shot off 150,000 cannonballs – on one single day, 8 July, the eve of the third assault, they fired 5000 shot in twenty-four hours. The lives of at least 52,000 – some say more, but at least half Lala Mustafa's fighting force – had so far been lost outside the city walls. For all the Turks knew otherwise, Bragadino still had the option of retiring into the citadel, and holding out even longer.

The Senate in its wisdom had obviously decided not to risk galleys in a hot-headed dash to raise the siege – but the Turks were not to know this. They might even suppose that Famagusta's resistance – which was putting the Sultan in such a rage – had been so confidently prolonged in the knowledge that help would arrive. Thus Bragadino had several good cards in his hand.

The laws of war granted their lives to the garrison of a besieged city who after parleying agreed to yield. The houses would not be pillaged, the citizens were saved from rape and enslavement, and the garrison were usually allowed to march out with their weapons as free men. A shrewdly negotiated capitulation might therefore save the Greek citizens of Famagusta from the horrors of a second Nicosia massacre.

On 1 August 1571, terms having been secretly agreed with Lala Mustafa, the Venetians yielded up the city. Marcantonio Bragadino had managed to strike not a bad bargain. Lala Mustafa expressed

Fore and aft views
of the war galley
Real

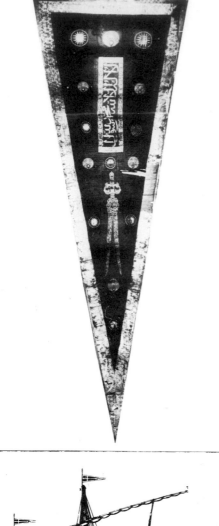

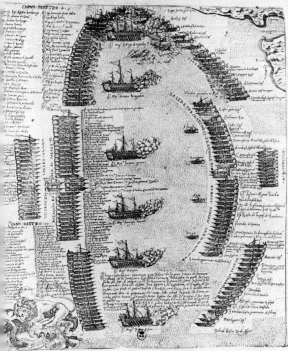

Opposite page

Above
The Ottoman standard
captured at Lepanto, which can
still be seen at the Doge's
Palace in Venice
Below
Galleys from Furtenbach's
Architectura Navalis

This page

Above
The battle of Lepanto
by an unknown artist
Left
A plan of the battle of Lepanto
from an original document held
in the Bibliothèque
Nationale

Allegory of the battle of Lepanto
by Paolo Veronese

himself as willing to grant life and liberty to all those inside the city walls. Citizens of Famagusta might go or stay as they chose. Those who opted to live under Turkish rule could retain their property, and were to be allowed the free exercise of their religion. Soldiers of the garrison might keep their arms. They could march out with five pieces of artillery, and with their three principal commanders mounted on horseback. The entire Venetian garrison was then to be shipped across in forty designated Turkish galleys, to join their fellow countrymen on Crete. By 1 August – the day the agreement was signed – the sick and wounded had in fact already been moved aboard the galleys. The terms of the capitulation were slightly more advantageous than those in the draft peace treaty made in Constantinople between Sokolli and the secret Venetian mission there. Bragadino had done his best.

On 4 August Lala Mustafa called the principal Venetian officers to his tent. For four days, the capitulation had been implemented fairly smoothly – there was no reason to anticipate trouble. Marcantonio Bragadino came out from the battered city in his usual dignified fashion, on horseback at the head of his fellow commanders, with a guard of forty arquebusiers. He wore his purple robe as a Venetian Senator, and his squire as he rode held over his head the scarlet parasol that was the indication of his rank. An eyewitness later recounted how he led the little procession 'towards Mustafa's tent, serenely, without fear or pride'. At the outset of the parley, Lala Mustafa was affable, seating the Venetians near him. But he soon began displaying the artificial anger of a man who has decided to regret his bargain.

He opened by accusing Bragadino of having killed Turkish prisoners during the period of truce. He went on to demand guarantees for the return of the forty Turkish galleys now waiting to carry Venetian soldiers over to Crete. Marcantonio Bragadino, calm and alert, pointed out to him that all this would have been better said before the treaty was signed. Bragadino, to judge by his manner, evidently grasped at once that the Turkish commander in chief was seeking to provoke him – though he could hardly have guessed at the particular atrocity Lala Mustafa had in mind. Bragadino's reasonable answers – his absence of all outward signs of fear – began to vex the Turk, who seems next to have searched his mind for some particularly insulting provocation which the Venetian Senator would be bound in honour to resent.

Antonio Quirini, a good-looking boy whose father had been an officer in Nicosia, after serving well throughout the siege here at

Famagusta, had been chosen that morning to act as Bragadino's page. Any other boy from Nicosia as handsome as young Antonio had already been rounded up and shipped off by the Turks to the pleasure markets of Constantinople, but this one had escaped. Lala Mustafa said that he would take, for a start, Bragadino's page as a hostage for the return of the forty galleys. His leer can be envisaged. Bragadino repeated coolly that nothing in their treaty had been said about hostages. Then, at a covert signal from Lala Mustafa, argument ended and violence broke out.

Lala Mustafa's guard forced all Bragadino's companions out into the open air. Marcantonio Bragadino himself was put in chains, and compelled to watch while Baglione and the others who had marched out with him from Famagusta that morning were hacked to pieces. One or two of the youngsters, however, to whom the Turks had taken a fancy, were led off prisoner, and could later recount what happened. The blood of Bragadino's companions, they said afterwards, ran across the ground until it reached his feet. The Turks then decided to play a practical joke. Three times they forced Bragadino's head down upon the executioner's block 'in order to test his courage'. But instead of chopping off his head, they contented themselves for the time being with cutting off his ears and nose.

With Bragadino and the others away, a subordinate called Tiepolo was commanding inside Famagusta. He had no idea what was happening, and saw no reason but to confide in the treaty the Turks had made. He marched all the soldiers from Famagusta down to the shore, as agreed, and up gangplanks into the waiting line of Turkish galleys, where they were dispersed into their prearranged places. Turkish soldiers then seized them, stripped them to the skin and chained them to the oar. Tiepolo himself was taken out and hanged.

The Turks cauterized the wounds with which they had disfigured Bragadino. Their purpose was to let him live a little longer. On Friday 17 August – the Moslem Sabbath – the mutilated man was put in a harness, and led on his hands and knees around the circuit of the Turkish batteries, ass panniers filled with earth having been slung across his back. Each time he was dragged by his bridle past Lala Mustafa's tent, he was forced to kiss the ground.

The galleys in which the Venetian soldiers had been stripped and chained were then towed around to a place from which they could watch what the inventive Turks next intended. Lala Mustafa's troops were also lined up as spectators. Wrapped in chains, Marcantonio

Bragadino was tied in a bosun's chair, hauled to the high end of a galley's spar, and hung up there with no ears and nose for everyone to recognize. He was then lowered, dragged to the market place inside the city, and exposed in the pillory so that Greek citizens too could be made aware of his plight. Those standing near said afterwards that they could hear him muttering a Latin prayer. Then, 'to the sound of drums and trumpets' – and with Lala Mustafa himself watching intently, with his back leaning against the marble wall of what until lately had been Bragadino's palace – the Venetian Senator was flayed alive. He died before all the skin was stripped off him, when the executioner's knife had reached 'the height of his navel'.

This macabre pantomime – intended to humiliate Bragadino, and, in his person, Venice – went on ridiculously long after death. Bragadino's skin was stuffed with straw and paraded through Famagusta under the red parasol of a Venetian Senator. The stuffed dummy was then swung from the yardarm of Lala Mustafa's galley, together with the decapitated heads of two of his fellow commanders, Luigi Martinengo (who had led the men brought in by the blockade runner from Candia) and Giovanni Antonio Quirini. The trophies were shipped thus to Constantinople. After being paraded through the streets in triumph, Bragadino's effigy was sent to symbolic confinement in the slave prison.

All through their imperial history, the Ottoman Turks had used cruelty as an implement of dominion: there was nothing in their religion to forbid it. There may be just wars but there are no innocent armies: Christian armies too could be despicably cruel, as they were in the Alpujarras. The ministrations of the Spanish Inquisition were not gentle, either. But bloody deeds done by nominal Christians went contrary to the utterances of the founder of their religion. Some of those concerned must have been aware at the back of their minds that what they did was wrong. In an accumulation of time, from this friction between doctrine and practice might come a change for the better. Perhaps this is the reason why the Christian West has never stagnated.

The Turks, however, when they emerged from Central Asia to get away from their singularly cruel enemies, the Mongols, became converts to a religion which though admirable in its law-abiding and philanthropic aspects had been based from the start on victory in war and the pleasures of the flesh as a reward thereafter. For some – for more than one might suppose – cruelty too is a pleasure.

The banner flown by the Holy League recalled to mind, by intention, a Man-God voluntarily submitting to the death by torture inflicted on a rebel slave. The Cross was a symbol the Turks found incomprehensible – much as if they were being subjected to some kind of ludicrous confidence trick. Their own Turkish flag had in the early days been green, like the Prophet's. But now it was red, to signify a river which after an early Turkish victory had actually run with blood. In this river of blood the Turks had seen reflected a symbol of their religion: the crescent moon. These images give a clue to the conflicting states of mind. Islam as the Ottoman Turks had promoted it at sword point was extravagantly virile, a religion for men of violent action, and its tenets (whether honoured in the breach or the observance) were not forgiveness and loving-kindness but brotherhood in war, comradeship, the subjection of womankind, with ultimate rewards in the form of pleasure and power.

But clearly these doctrinal differences do not entirely account for the treatment meted out to Bragadino. Soleiman the Magnificent could be spectacularly cruel – as after his victory at Mohacs – but he would not have broken his pledged word. Half Lala Mustafa's fighting force had met death around the walls of Famagusta – gone, as they believed, to extremities of carnal pleasure in paradise. The survivors may have craved a bloody compensation, and their commander in chief provided it, like a raree show. But this explanation too is only partial.

The atrocity had also been an act of deep policy – a stumbling block placed by Lala Mustafa in the way of his great rival, Sokolli. War served Lala Mustafa's ambition; he intended to make the rumoured peace with Venice difficult if not impossible. Had Sultan Selim come to Cyprus himself and led his army in person, as did all his predecessors, the Sultan's word pledged to a treaty similar to that his father had granted to the Knights years before on Rhodes might well have been honoured – if only from motives of pride. But Sultan Selim was the first of his dynasty to prefer the amenities of the harem to the discomforts of active service. The cruelty like the decadence of the Turks may eventually be traced back, perhaps, to the human relationships which the nature of their empire forced upon them – and particularly to their strange and artificial sexual relations.

★   ★   ★

As it turned out, Lala Mustafa's clever perfidy had less effect in Venice than he might have intended, because by the time news came to them of Bragadino's fate, Doge and Senate had already committed themselves to fight.

Delays in the arrival of news often introduce a blundering note into the politics of the time. The fall of Nicosia, for example, was known in Constantinople by 24 September 1570, but the bad news did not reach Venice until a month later, and King Philip in Madrid got to hear only on 19 December. A courier riding hell for leather could carry a despatch from Venice to Madrid in forty days, though usually he could not start back again until King Philip himself had decided on the right answer. Small wonder that Spain in these years was so often slow off the mark and tardy at the rendezvous.

Those who governed Venice now saw clearly that with Selim II continuing his aggressive war into its second year, the east coast of Italy had become the front line in a war between not merely two great empires but two world religions. In such a war, the islands of Venice's endangered stepping-stone empire would merely be outposts.

One of Ochiali's corsair captains, Kara Hodja, raided and pillaged that spring into the bay of Venice itself, almost within gunshot of St Mark's. The city had hitherto been protected by treaty against this kind of molestation – now there would be no end to it. As if intending to have the entire Adriatic for himself, the Sultan had made Lepanto on the Gulf of Patras his advanced naval base. A Turkish fleet operating from Lepanto unchallenged could land an army anywhere it chose along Italy's eastern coastline. Venice's protective lagoon no longer ensured the city's safety. If Turkish cavalry were landed near Ancona, Rome itself was only a hard day's ride over the Apennines. Turkish spies of Italian descent – renegades who could melt into the background – had already been unmasked actually inside Rome. How long, wondered the pessimists, before St Peter's – like Constantinople's Santa Sophia, the great shrine of Orthodox Christianity – would be transformed into a mosque?

But Sultan Selim could land an army within striking distance of Rome only if he had command of the sea. This is exactly what his attack on Cyprus – as Sokolli saw more clearly than anyone else – had put at issue. By prolonging the war he was giving the Christians time to unite and discover their strength. The 'destruction' of the Arsenal though a dramatic way of swaying the Sultan's mind had been politically inept – a mere bluff. What mattered politically were hard facts.

Last autumn a scratch Christian fleet, huddled together, ill-found and badly led, had dismally failed to challenge the Turkish landing on Cyprus. But every week since then, Venice's Arsenal had turned out half a dozen galleys, apart from those somewhat more robust warships slowly being built by King Philip. The next fleet sent out to defend Christendom would obviously be more seaworthy and better manned. How it performed therefore would depend largely on its morale and the character of its commander.

The sagacious mercantile aristocrats who for centuries had held power in Venice began to discount the inevitable risks that would be run this year by their commerce and their island possessions. As Kara Hodja's guns from the lagoon resonated against the narrow windows of their marble palaces, they brought their minds to bear upon this simple piece of arithmetic (it was also in the forefront of Sokolli's mind). The galleys of the Venetian Republic plus the galleys of the King of Spain, adding also into the account the nautical oddments deriving from Tuscany, Savoy, the Papal States and Malta, would equal and might even outnumber the entire Turkish battle fleet. If both sides were thus well-matched in material strength, the deciding factor would be the kind of moral ascendancy shown of late at Malta, Szigetvár and Famagusta.

Thus when Pius V declared, 'I am taking up arms against the Turks, but the only thing that can help me is the prayers of priests of pure life,' for once he was not uttering a clerical platitude, but putting his finger on a new value unbalancing so many political equations of the time. Priests of notoriously impure life, culminating in the Borgia Pope, had been the scandal which gave the Protestant reformers their unanswerable justification. But the chaplains already preaching to those who in 1571 would take the brunt of the fighting were men of a new type. Their integrity and their readiness for self-sacrifice were beginning to earn the fighting man's respect. Even in cool and calculating Venice this high-minded and at times exalted religious mood was invisibly at work.

Jacopo Ragazzoni, the secretary of the Senate who had been striking a bargain with Sokolli, started back to Venice on 18 June 1571 – before the débâcle on Famagusta. He felt pretty sure of securing ratification of the draft peace treaty he carried (which included, ironically enough, the honours of war for the defenders of Famagusta). But by this time the mood in Venice had altered. Since both sides this year were likely to be equally matched in naval strength, the shrewd Venetians had begun to believe that morale (or as they chose to express it, God's will) would tip the balance. After jibbing at the papal Mass in the month of March, and coldly refusing to sign the Pope's treaty, Venice on 25 May 1571 had formally joined the Holy League – solemnly proclaimed that day at Rome in the basilica of St Peter's.

11

Go and Seek Them Out

Let me be nothing if within the compass of myself
I do not find the battail of Lepanto, Passion against
Reason, Reason against Faith, Faith against the
Devil and my Conscience against All.

SIR THOMAS BROWNE

In spring of 1571 – the year of decision – all Venice had crowded to the Lenten sermons of Father Benedetto Palmio, a Jesuit of great eloquence; there were preachers sounding the same note, as to a tuning fork, in every country of the Holy League. Conflicts of interest among the great and powerful were not dissolved by the signature of the treaty on 25 May, but the cause was popular, the groundswell had begun.

To win over opinion, Pius V was relying very much on the Jesuits. Francisco Borgia, their General, was in bad health, but influential behind the scenes. By a clumsy turn of phrase, King Philip had managed to affront Marcantonio Colonna (who technically owed fealty to the King of Spain, and loyalty to Venice as well). 'They are going to make me "do my duty",' Colonna exploded, 'as if this were something new to my House and me!' Father Francisco, another man of aristocratic origin who had suffered, like the Pope's admiral, from the authoritarian quirks of the Prudent King, managed to smooth things over.

Pius V was sending his kinsman and trusted agent, Cardinal Alessandro, to visit Spain and keep King Philip up to the mark. Francisco Borgia had great influence there, he had better go too, and then on to Portugal, and use his influence with the boy king, Sebastian. Father Polanco SJ pointed out to Pius V that ordering their General to Spain in his present state of health was probably a sentence of death. But the Pope insisted, and Francisco himself seems not to have been unwilling – he had a duty of obedience, and this was a year when many other lives besides his own would be put at risk in the cause.

Father Francisco entered Barcelona 'with a belt from which hung a rosary of seeds strung on a violin string.' He was so gaunt and shabby that few who had known him in his days as viceroy could recognize him. Marcos, the lay brother who had been given authority over the General in everyday matters, accepted on his behalf a new suit of clothes and new riding boots, pressed on him by Francisco's heir, Duke Carlos, who apparently was scandalized. In this unaccustomed attire, and riding at King Philip's left hand, Francisco entered Madrid – the city from which not many years before he had fled for his life. The Grand Inquisitor, as if conceding defeat at last, had ordered the publication of Francisco Borgia's theological writings, hitherto censored. Francisco for months to come travelled in atrocious discomfort up and down the peninsula, talking earnestly with influential friends, knitting up the invisible web of private commitment which held together, at least for the present, this uneasy alliance against the Turks. Though the treaty of the Holy League had been signed by the chief naval powers, they had signed belatedly, with secret misgivings, like men driven into a corner by popular pressure and common danger.

Chaplains for the allied fleet were being drawn from the religious orders which had been given a new impulse by the Council of Trent – Capuchins, Jesuits, Theatines, Dominicans. A Capuchin and a Jesuit were the chaplains aboard Don John's flagship, the galley *Real*. Cristobal Rodriguez, the Jesuit, had earlier led a mission among the Calabrian bandits, as well as nursing several hundred plague victims in an infirmary. Don John himself, formed in piety by the saintly Magdalena, in courage by her husband Luis Quixada, was accepted by these zealots in the fleet as personifying in action the cause they were preaching. Hard-headed men in high places might have private reservations about entrusting the fate of Christendom to a royal bastard aged twenty-four. But to ordinary people, taking their cue from priest, monk or friar, Don John was their man.

The rendezvous for the Holy League's battle fleet was in the straits of Messina, between Sicily and the toe of Italy. After saying prayers at the Catalan shrine of Montserrat, Don John joined his squadron at Barcelona. At sea he opened his sealed orders, and was galled to read that though acknowledging him as commander in chief, King Philip had laid it down that he was never to issue an order without the countersignature of Luis de Requeséns – the man once chosen by King Philip to be Don John's mentor in seamanship, and of late his naval commander in the Morisco war. This was a precaution which would do nothing for the unity of the fleet; Requeséns' countersignature on every order would remind the allies that the King, even though he brought fewer galleys to the fleet than Venice, was the man who in Italy ruled the roost. By a royal order issued in Madrid on 26 March, the King had also given Don John one of those slaps in the face by means of which he reminded others who was master. Don John, everyone was informed, was entitled to be addressed as Excellency – but never Highness.

Old Don García de Toledo, nursing his rheumatism in Italian spas, and with a personal experience in Mediterranean warfare which went back over thirty years, had lately been kept busy answering Don John's many technical questions about how a fleet should be handled in action. With his own active career apparently in ruins, Don García had nothing to gain either by literal obedience to orders or by flattery. In his private letters he showed what must generally have been thought of that particular royal command, by always calling Don John 'Highness'. Even Don García's pulse was these days beating faster. 'I swear that if I had but a little better health,' he declared, 'I would ship myself as a soldier or a sailor under Don John.' To him Don John confided that his royal half-brother in Madrid was surrounded by 'a thousand persons, let us say, who use the excuse of my lack of years and experience to undermine me.' On the very day Don John sailed, a letter from the papal nuncio in Madrid was going by courier to Rome, to warn them that here came 'a young prince, and so desirous of glory that if the Council does not cool him down, he will think more of gaining glory than of saving his galleys.'

'Saving galleys' was one of King Philip's pet turns of phrase; he no doubt prompted the nuncio's warning. But aggression was never deflected – no great battle was ever won – by the type of mind which (like Gianandrea Doria's or the King's) thought instinctively in terms of 'saving galleys'. Yet King Philip though temperamentally cautious was highly intelligent. In taking all these precautions he had conventional wisdom on his side. Ruminating in the loneliness of the Escorial on the naval record since his father's day, it must have looked to him like a succession of lost causes and downright defeats – from the time when Charles V lost his fleet off Algiers to his own fiasco at Djerba. At sea the Turks always won. So why should King Philip break his ingrained habit of planning in terms of evading battle and avoiding defeat? Yet it was soon to be shown that in 1571 such customary ways of thought were an incipient betrayal. Nothing but real and undeniable victory at sea would check the Turk and deliver Christendom.

Don John's galley squadron called in at Genoa – where the sudden appearance offshore of such a powerful Spanish force made the Genoese nervous for their liberties. The Holy League had come into being to save Italy, but that did not mean that the Italians now loved Philip, or trusted him either.

The Venetian ambassador to Spain, Antonio Tiepolo, had been ordered by the Senate to Genoa, so as to observe Don John carefully, and report upon him. This young commander in chief, Tiepolo assured them, was 'most anxious to find the enemy'. On his way to Messina, Don John paused in Rome, and for the first and perhaps the last time in his life felt what it was to receive a full measure of approval and trust from a great man. Pius V took Don John to his heart, accepting him for all he was worth, with no equivocal side glances at his illegitimacy, his youth, or his reputed hot-headedness. Here – as the Pope saw it – was someone who in council would rise above pettiness and envy, who in battle would lead without flinching. The old Pope was as confident as Don John himself that the imminent naval battle could be won. 'I take it for certain,' he declared, 'that the Turks, swollen by their victories, will wish to take on our fleet, and God – I have the pious presentiment – will give us victory'.

The Pope went on to tell Don John what he must always have yearned to hear said. 'Charles V gave you life. I will give you honour and greatness.' But the Holy Father did Don John a bad turn when he hinted that his reward might well be an independent principality, perhaps even a throne – such a title and station in life as would wipe away all the implications of that deadly half compliment of 'Excellency'. The gist of this leaked back to King Philip, and provoked his suspicion. From then on Philip was clever enough to use the Pope's promise as bait. Whenever he wanted to lead Don John by the nose, there would be ever-louder whispers of a throne for him – in the Morea, in Tunis, perhaps, who knows, in Ireland or even England.

Ali, the Turkish admiral, was keeping up the pressure on Venice. In June he raided Crete. By attacking one Venetian island after another that summer, the Turks reasoned that they could compel Venice to

disperse her galleys, some here, some there, so that the entire Holy
League fleet would never arrive at Messina.

Ali in some ways resembled Don John. He too was young, ambitious, eager for glory, reputedly a hothead, and well-respected for his
decent treatment of the Christian captives among his galley slaves. His
strategy of obliging Venice to dissipate her war galleys made sense.
But his attempt to land Turkish troops on Crete was frustrated by
Marcantonio Quirini – the high-spirited Venetian commander who in
January had run the blockade of Famagusta. Quirini deployed his own
galley squadron so skilfully across Suva Bay, under the fortress guns,
that his ships were virtually untouchable, yet ready to pounce on any
Turkish galley which was beached to put men ashore. Ali sheered off,
edging his fleet along the Cretan coast, killing 3000 of the armed
peasants who put up a fight when he raided their coastal villages,
carrying off thousands more Cretans as galley slaves. In the mouth
of the Adriatic, from the islands of Zante and Cephallonia, Ali kidnapped yet more Venetian subjects to pull his oars – 7000 of them.

Ochiali's squadron of light and manoeuvrable Algerine corsair
galleys was supported by smaller galliots able to work close inshore.
With his eighty ships, Ochiali went right up the Dalmatian coast,
sowing havoc in Venetian colonies ashore, creating panic wherever he
appeared – all this to keep Sebastian Veniero and his galley fleet away
from the rendezvous at Messina. For as long as the fleets of Spain and
Venice remained disunited, the Turks had command of the sea.

With Kara Hodja cruising offshore – with all Venetian citizens
going about their business armed, and gangs of volunteers digging
defensive works in case of a Turkish landing – Doge and Senate took a
bold, severe and necessary decision: one marked by greatness. Quirini
was ordered to take his squadron away from Crete, and reinforce the
Holy League at Messina. Venice would gamble her island empire. She
would submit to the provocation of corsair raids on her own doorstep.
The only way to deal with Ali was to confront him with a fleet as large
as his own.

Sultan Selim II ordered Ali to Lepanto, nicknamed 'little Gallipoli',
the Turkish advanced naval base on the Adriatic, sited on a small and
well-protected bay within the Gulf of Patras. Ali's huge fleet could ride
safely at anchor under the protective crossfire from the guns of the
twin fortresses on the bay's enclosing headlands. Lepanto was not
only singularly difficult to attack, but could easily be supplied, since
the Gulf of Patras communicates directly with the Aegean through the

ancient, narrow Corinth Canal. At the eastern end of the canal was yet another Turkish naval base – at Negropont, modern Euboea – so that Ali's fleet could remain a close threat to Venice indefinitely, yet be continually fed and supplied.

Ali's sick and wounded were set ashore in Lepanto, the munitions he had so far expended were renewed. During this breathing space, Ali sent sixty of his galleys in a long procession one after the other down the narrow canal. Back they came from Negropont with 2000 spahis aboard and 10,000 janissaries. He had the armed force to land an expedition in Italy if he chose, a well-supplied battle fleet and an impregnable anchorage. By the late summer of 1571 the fact that Ali would winter at Lepanto had become plain to everyone. The threat was unmistakable. If not this year then next, not only Venice and Rome but the kingdom of Naples and the island of Sicily, Spain's breadbasket, would all lie within striking distance of this immense Turkish fleet and its army. The fine weather of the cruising season was slowly running out, and the galleys of the Holy League fleet were arriving only by slow degrees at their Messina rendezvous.

On his way down the coast to Messina, Don John went ashore in Naples. The Neapolitans were wild with enthusiasm for this young man who might be their deliverer. Riding through their bedecked and crowded streets came a young horseman splendidly mounted, so an eyewitness tells us, and dressed in white velvet with cloth of gold, wearing a crimson scarf and white plumes in his velvet hat. Of middle height, but with handsome and regular features, and bright, curling fair hair which fell backwards from his brow, Don John when hatless would unthinkingly lift both hands to ease the hair off his temples – and soon this typical gesture was a fashion being copied by young men everywhere.

When Don John reached Messina, on 23 August, his squadron of thirty-five galleys enlarged the League fleet there to eighty galleys and twenty-two supply ships. The Turks probably had 300 ships in their fleet, of which 200 would be war galleys. The Venetian squadron defending Crete had yet to come in, and there were not a few in Messina sceptical of Venetian good faith, who doubted if it would ever arrive.

Marcantonio Colonna, commanding the papal galleys, had reached Messina two days before Don John. Despite their difference in age,

Colonna had accepted the Pope's approval of Don John as supreme commander with his usual good nature. With him came three galleys manned by the Knights of Malta, and flying their distinctive cross as banner. Other Knights, including the famous Chevalier Romegas, were commanding papal galleys, and a Knight called Don Juan Vasquez Coronado had the responsibility of captaining Don John's flagship. Marcantonio Colonna's son Prospero was serving in his father's command. Though hardly out of his teens he too was a young fire-eater, who had volunteered for Malta and fought the Turks on Cyprus. The Colonnas had a long-standing family grudge against the Turks.

A generation earlier, in the summer of 1534, their kinswoman Julia, the young widow of Vespasian Colonna, count of Fundi, was thought to be the most beautiful woman in Europe. Helped by Neapolitan renegades, the Turkish admiral Barbarossa sent 2000 men ashore near Fundi, their orders being to capture Julia for Soleiman the Magnificent's harem. The intrepid young widow had escaped full tilt on horseback, clad in her nightclothes. Angered at losing her, the Turks sacked Fundi, killing the menfolk and carrying off women and boys to the slave market in Constantinople. For decades along the Italian coast, no one high or low had been safe.

Don John inspected the ships waiting in line for him at Messina, and what he saw was not encouraging. The best Spanish infantry had been sent away to the Duke of Alva, who was trying to crush the rebellion in the Low Countries. Far too many of those arriving to serve in the Holy League fleet were recent recruits, many of them ignorant as yet of their arquebus drill – and arquebus drill was a lot to get by heart. ('Take down your musket; blow, prove, shut; cast off pan; cast about musket; open cartridge; load; draw ramrod and ram; replace ramrod; lay musket on rest; blow match; cock and try; guard the pan; fire!') The arquebusiers of the League had one small technical advantage, however, over the Turks, who spilled gunpowder in the firearm anyhow, from the palm of the hand. Don Juan's men used that newfangled device, the powder horn. But could these raw recruits contend with janissaries?

The more galleys launched by that masterpiece of industrial organization, the Arsenal of Venice, the more thinly spread were their crews. Some of the Venetian galleys at Messina were suffering from having been laid up on the slipway too long. Venice was paying a price for her thirty years of bluff about her naval strength. King Philip's galleys, too, were short of rowers, but at least they were solid – newly built of Pyrenean pine, and heavily gunned. Don John found that the men waiting at the rendezvous were morose. He is reported as speaking boldly and looking confident. But on 30 August, after inspecting the Venetian galleys, he relieved his private feelings in another letter to Don García. 'You cannot believe in what bad order both soldiers and sailors were in – fighting is not to be done with such men – a certain spasm takes me when I see with what materials I am expected by the world to do something of importance.' Don García gave Don John the advice which the overcautious old seadog himself would probably have followed, had he been given the command: on no account to risk such a gimcrack fleet in a pitched battle, unless compelled to by a direct order. 'For the love of God,' wrote Don García, 'consider well the damage that may be caused by a mistake.'

But on the same day – 30 August – as he signed his letter to Don García, word came to Don John that the sixty galleys withdrawn from Crete had reached Syracuse in Sicily. The alliance was real. The Venetians were keeping their word. A year before, no one would have dreamed of expecting the Venetians to allow foreign soldiers – least of all Spanish soldiers – to serve aboard their galleys. But now that all the Venetian ships were in, and their weakness in manpower apparent, Don John managed to persuade fiery old Sebastian Veniero, for the good of the alliance, to accept a massive reinforcement of Spanish and Italian infantry. (The subtle, civilized Venetians found the Spaniards crude and arrogant, but nobly put up with them.)

On 16 September, after consulting his council of war, Don John wrote to tell Don García what he had decided. 'Taking into account that the [Turkish] fleet, even though more numerous than the forces of the League, according to the information I have, is not of the same quality, in ships or men, and confiding in our Lord God, whose cause this is, and who will aid us, the decision is taken to go and seek them out.'

Don John's cheerful readiness to fight was borne out, moreover, by the recently expressed opinion of the Duke of Alva, Spain's cleverest soldier. After brooding over the Turks' recent military performances, he had modified his former high opinion of them. 'Turks,' he wrote, 'know very well how to sap walls; they don't know how to cross a chalk line when they find on the other side troops determined to defend it.' But would this prove equally true at sea?

Don John's reply to Don García might sound like a young man's bravado, but was in fact the outcome of a singularly thoughtful appraisal. Ali would have by this time a comparable number of galleys under his command – perhaps a few more. Turkish galleys were sometimes built hurriedly, of unseasoned wood, but they were workmanlike copies of the standardized war galleys which rolled off the production line at Venice's Arsenal. They were built for the Sultan by highly paid runaways. Of the Sultan's seagoing captains, many were Greek or Venetian turncoats – some of them deserters – who could earn more in four months commanding a galley for Selim than in a year serving Venice. (There was a drawback to the Turkish service, however: no wine.) Though their mercenary captains were highly skilled, their crews were often inexperienced. The soldiers aboard Turkish galleys were likely to be better than the seamen, but their prowess was not often put to the test, since the Turks could usually trade on their reputation as winners.

The Turks, however, were not fighting inside the framework of a precarious alliance, but had the advantages of regular discipline and a single command. Ali was bound by orders sent him at intervals from Constantinople in the Sultan's name. But the men he commanded would be unhesitatingly prompt to do what they were told. Don John by his personality and tact had already done much to foster in the Holy League fleet a mood of unity which might transcend national pettiness. But he was well aware that between Genoese and Venetian, Venetian and Spaniard, Spaniard and Neapolitan, the old squabbles were latent, and at any moment might burst out.

The ninety or so galleys flying the Spanish flag were a mixed bunch. The contingent genuinely Spanish numbered only fifty-six, and, of the others, twenty-four had been hired – Gianandrea Doria was not the only Genoese plutocrat to hire out war galleys as a commercial speculation. Tuscany and Savoy had sent more than half a dozen galleys each. Twenty thousand soldiers were being paid for by King Philip, 5000 by Venice, 2000 by the Pope, and about 3000 were self-supporting volunteers who had arrived in Venice during that momentous summer from all over Christendom. Over a hundred Venetian galleys had by this time come in, but so badly manned that even after Don John had reinforced them with Spanish and Italian soldiers, the rule throughout the Holy League fleet had to be three men to an oar, with the more usual five men to an oar only in reconnaissance galleys and the flagships.

These ships' companies were a cross-section of Western European society as it then was. Most on board were Catholic, but a handful of Orthodox Christians would be fighting, and even some volunteers – soldiers of fortune or incorrigible romantics – from the countries of the north that in the last fifty years had turned Protestant. A poor man signed on from hunger, a debtor whose meagre pay as a galley slave was handed over to his creditor until the debt was extinct, a bandit who had been lucky enough to escape the gibbet – all three might be tugging at the same oar. Most whether chained or free were likely to have spent their lives near the Mediterranean under the perpetual threat of a Moslem raid which might lead them to slavery or death. Thus even the least fortunate among the galley slaves – unless they happened to be Moslem prisoners, of whom there were not many – had a personal interest in this fight. They would be contending, not in the first instance for pay or plunder, but for glory.

Among the commanders, financial and commercial magnates like Doria rubbed shoulders with territorial magnates like Colonna. In civil life Sebastian Veniero was a successful lawyer – for, like ancient Rome, the republic of Venice often sent its most accomplished civilians out as war leaders. From whatever class they came, most by the time they reached manhood had identified the Turks as a threat to their everyday lives. Latterly they had all been furnished with a common vocabulary of belief – rising sometimes to passionate conviction – in the words dinned eloquently into their ears by Pope and fleet chaplains alike. And the propaganda they heard coincided with experience. Everyday life with the Turks near enough to threaten cruelty, slavery or death had for too long been a nightmare.

This orchestrated religious revival tended to unify the fleet, even though questions of money and the sentiments of nationalism divided it. Spain, lording it all down Italy and responding to threats from Islam only when they occurred in the Western Mediterranean, was a nation-state and a world empire. Venice, almost the last considerable Italian power still independent of Spain, was a city state, past its prime. Venice's trade and empire, though diminishing, lay not in the Western Mediterranean but towards the East.

During the council of war which Don John reported on to Don García, these underlying differences had come to the surface. Since Don John owed fealty to King Philip, he was always under covert pressure from Madrid to work in the Spanish interest. But for the sake of the obvious needs of the Holy League itself, there were times when he would side with Venice, whatever the cost to his own future. At the council, the Venetians were advocates for boldness, and so, in his heart, was Don John. They wanted an attack on Turkish-held Morea, in southern Greece, where the Greek rebellion still smouldered. Or better yet, since Turkish lines of communication were by this time a thousand miles long, a devastating raid on Ali's supply base at Negropont. A convincing threat to Negropont might even fetch Ali's entire fleet away from Lepanto, down the Corinth Canal, and back into the Aegean.

This year as last, Gianandrea Doria believed himself to be reading King Philip's mind correctly when he preached caution. If cleverly aggressive gestures like a raid on Negropont might achieve the same result, why risk everything on a pitched battle? Was it not too late in the year for a serious campaign? Bear in mind that last year's fleet had lost more galleys from bad weather than from enemy action. As if to underline Doria's warning, between 11 and 14 September, the hot, calm Mediterranean off Messina broke up in the first autumnal storm.

Though he might sympathize with the Venetians' wish for some bold feat of arms, Don John knew that a consensus must first be reached among the council of war which would at least get the fleet out to sea. In summing up their discussion he gave a nod of recognition to particular national interests, but sought also to speak for the men he commanded.

Siding openly with Veniero and Colonna, he declared himself 'resolved to sail forthwith, and bring the Turk to battle, and with the help of God and the brave men around him he was confident of obtaining a splendid victory.' If he did not succeed, he added, in an enterprise to which the Holy Father, the Republic, and the King his master called him, he was at least ready to die in the attempt. In his last letter to Don García, just before putting to sea, he was more matter-of-fact and nearer the bone. 'He is stronger than we in the number of his vessels,' the young commander in chief admitted, 'but not, I believe, in quality, either of vessels or men.'

Doria, this time excessively cautious, found himself with the minority. The admirals accepted the minimal decision of putting to sea and at least confronting Ali with a challenge. In the very week the weather broke, the two hundred galleys at Messina, their oars rising and striking in cadence, moved ship by ship southward out of the narrow strait, towards the open sea. Whether free man or galley slave, each Christian aboard had been given a rosary. As the naked galley slaves, hauling on their huge oars, moved past the mole at the harbour mouth, they saw there the papal nuncio in his cardinal's robes, immobile, alone, holding up his arms to bless them until the last ship was gone.

Galleys may sound rather far-fetched and inconvenient nautical devices, but rivalries in the Mediterranean with its light winds and short seas had been settled by galley warfare ever since the siege of Troy. Oars meant you would never be becalmed; sail meant you would not always be tugging an oar. Odysseus and his men rowed what was virtually a galliot; Mark Antony led Cleopatra's galley fleet against Octavius at Actium, only a little to the north of Lepanto, and lost battle, mistress and empire there all at one blow.

Propulsion by oars as well as sail also meant that a galley in all but the roughest weather was splendidly controllable. War galleys could wheel or turn on the spot from file to line, or fight in echelon, as nimbly and precisely as the most highly trained cavalry. They could take rapid and unexpected evasive action, or suddenly change their point of attack. Galley manoeuvres in Don John's day, as a seagull looked down upon them, must have been as elegant as a ballet. 'The perfect galley,' wrote a contemporary, 'should resemble a graceful girl, whose every gesture reveals alertness, vivacity and agility, while at the same time preserving a seemly gravity.'

Once rival galleys had grappled one another, the seaman's job was done. The soldiers on board then swarmed from one deck to the next, and fought it out hand to hand. The galley fleet which Don John led out to sea in September 1571 – the last ever to fight a full-scale naval battle – was the most sophisticated the Mediterranean had seen for twenty centuries.

The West had certain substantial technical advantages. In the Turkish fleet, not even all the janissaries were yet armed with the arquebus. The Turkish leaders consoled themselves with the specious argument that a man trained in the use of a Turkish composite bow could loose off thirty arrows in the time it took an arquebusier to load and fire once. But many of their Christian opponents – and certainly all Don John's officers – would be wearing armour that was virtually arrow-proof, whereas an arquebus slug at 200 yards could put a hole right through a man wearing robes and turban, and perhaps through his neighbour as well. Massed arquebus fire could nowadays sweep decks which in Mark Antony's day could safely have been crammed with infantrymen. The heavy guns carried in the bows of a war galley could be traversed by skilful manipulation of the oars, and aimed with great precision, the whole length of the galley's hull serving as a waterborne gun carriage, so that the entire ship took the recoil as the great guns fired.

The League galleys were also fitted with boarding nets – then a novelty. And down from their Arsenal to join the fleet the Venetians were towing an unusual weapon which they hoped would disconcert the Turk – galliasses, six of them. In contriving their version of the galliass, the ingenious Venetians had taken a long stride towards making gunnery prevail in naval warfare. Though still propelled by oars and sail, the galliass was primarily intended to carry not soldiers but guns. The six Venetian galliasses carried forty heavy guns or more apiece, thirty-pounders on deck, fifty-pounders ranged down below, whereas Don John's flagship, *Real*, only carried five. To move the deadweight of these guns slowly through the water, at least seven men were put to each galliass oar, but they were kept below decks out of sight.

A galliass was a clumsy hybrid, so unhandy that as a rule she had to be towed into action by two consort galleys. The galliass was a technical compromise, but by the standards of the time, this monstrosity had enormous fire power.

There were sailing ships too, in the fleet Don John led out of Messina that gusty September day, but they were fat-bellied merchantmen, requisitioned to carry rations and munitions. The guns they mounted were only for defence. In the fickle winds of a Mediterranean autumn, these supply ships might straggle several days behind the galleys.

When sent into action, galleys kept to as strict an order of battle as troops in the field. Don John had already laid it down that the gap in line between one galley and the next must never be more than a hundred paces – enough room, that is, for one bank of oars not to clash with the next, yet never leaving a gap so wide that enemy galleys might pass through in line, like a column of horses, and turn to outflank or attack from the rear.

The usual Turkish battle formation was the crescent – which had for the Turks both a patriotic and a religious significance – with extending wings curved forwards to outflank, enfold and crush. Ali and his commanders would follow tradition. But in the Holy League fleet much thought had gone into devising a novel battle order, which would take full advantage of fire power.

In conduct as in battle tactics the fleet of the Holy League was to be different. Pius V had written asking Don John to make sure his men 'lived in virtuous and Christian fashion in the galleys, not playing or swearing.' Luis de Requeséns – the shadow placed at Don John's shoulder by Philip of Spain – signed a reply on the commander in chief's behalf with an almost visible shrug of the shoulder, saying 'We will do what we can'. But to make it clear to one and all that the Pope's injunction was to be taken seriously, Don John in the presence of the papal nuncio had two of his men hanged for blasphemy. That day the habitually foul-mouthed of his command must have been in a cold sweat. But Don John was clear in his own mind as to the terms on which Islamic aggression must be fought.

Here as in the Alpujarras, he had been given the task of fighting a total war against another system of ideas – historically, the hardest of all wars to win. For a man bred in Christendom to go over to the Moslem enemy had never been difficult – he need do no more than repeat the verbal formula which transferred his allegiance to Allah. The most prominent Turkish leaders had been Christian before being swept up in the *devşirme*. The Turkish fleet had largely been built and was captained by Christian renegades. It followed that in the ships of the Holy League blasphemy or any other kind of religious doubt, openly expressed, had to be treated as sedition. The impending battle could be won only by men who were unanimous.

For the next week or so, Ali and Don John alike were working in the dark, neither knowing quite where the other was to be found, or in what force, and each trying to mislead the other. Fleets in those days usually coasted from one port to the next and were seldom lost to sight. But if they decided to head away from shore, once their sails dropped below the line of the horizon they had vanished, unless someone on a masthead or a church tower caught a glimpse of them.

Gil d'Andrade, a veteran Knight of Malta who had fought Ochiali eleven years before at Djerba, was sent ahead of the Holy League fleet with four good galleys, each with a double force of rowers, to seek out the Turk and send back word. His first discovery was that the Turks only eight days before had landed on the Adriatic island of Zante – sailing down on it from the north. This set Don John a conundrum.

Was Ali's fleet really planning to winter at Lepanto, as everyone had supposed? Or might the Turks for some unknown reason be making their way back home to Constantinople, raiding as they went?

On 27 September, Don John's fleet entered the harbour of Corfu. They had logged 240 miles in ten days – tremendous going for a galley fleet. But, just before they arrived, Corfu – which lies to the north of Zante – had also been attacked. In his raid Ali had lost three galleys and had failed to take the fortress. In what looked like a petulant revenge, the Turks had gone on to make a mess of the place, pillaging houses, wrecking churches, kidnapping civilians. They had desecrated altars in various filthy ways, and lashed out with their scimitars at any Venetian paintings which impiously represented the human form, particularly in the shape of the Blessed Virgin or the Crucified. The anger of those in the fleet who had never yet seen Turkish handiwork was huge. No one, after Corfu, doubted that what all the chaplains had been telling them must be true.

Then on 28 September, a light, undecked pinnace called a *fregata*, which could move fast under both oars and sail, came in to Don John from Gil d'Andrade with firm news. After their raids on Zante and Corfu, the Turks had gone back to Lepanto. Every sign indicated that they would winter there. But the supplementary intelligence from d'Andrade about the size and condition of Ali's fleet was too good to be true. His informants had been local Greek Christians. They hated the Turks, and their plan was to tell encouraging lies to both sides, so that each would think the other weak, and therefore give battle. They told d'Andrade that the Turks were not only pitifully short of rowers (in fact, from their kidnapping raids they had plenty) but that plague had broken out at Lepanto. At the same time, the Greeks were telling similar tall stories to Ali about the weaknesses of his Christian enemy. Ali was more inclined to believe them than Don John, because last year's feeble performance by Doria and Colonna had given him a low opinion of the Christian alliance.

Ochiali had gone out himself to serve as the eyes of the Sultan's fleet. Personally, Ochiali had no thirst for glory to which profit was not attached. His private programme, after there had been enough small local victories to keep the Sultan happy – for instance, on Zante and Corfu – was to winter in North Africa. Ochiali led twenty-five of his corsair craft across to the Italian mainland, to discover what he could of Don John's intentions. He landed at Santa Maria, near the Calabrian village where he had been born and brought up. With a hideous scar across one forearm, gained at Scio when he suppressed a slave mutiny single-handed, his disfigured head, his well-known loathing of Christians, and his enormous reputation for cruelty, Ochiali when he came ashore must have been a figure to inspire mortal fear. Yet his *paisanos* though in fear and trembling managed to mislead him, telling him, characteristically, the lie they knew he would most want to hear. Ochiali reported back confidently to Ali that the crews of the Holy League fleet 'were still eating peaches in Messina' – that the Christians this autumn had given up any idea of putting to sea. He was soon proved wrong, and his reputation suffered accordingly.

An order had come in from Selim which put Ochiali in his place, since it forbade any corsair commander to return home this winter to North Africa on pain of death. Word of the fall of Famagusta had just arrived in Constantinople – though it had not reached Venice yet. With Cyprus added at long last to the Ottoman Empire, Selim had qualified like every sultan before him for the title of Extender of the Realm. In a wine haze that with Selim could be interspersed with moments of acute insight, or bursts of anger, or impulses of energy in which he exerted fully his supreme power, the Sultan was evidently toying with the dream of fulfilling another old prophecy – that true believers would one day say their prayers to Allah beneath the dome of St Peter's. The slipways in Constantinople were hard at work on fifty new galleys. When Selim ordered the corsairs to remain with the fleet at Lepanto, he intended that next year's campaign should start in good time.

Soldiers in Corfu sallying from their fortress had captured a valuable prisoner – Baffo, a famous Venetian renegade, who in the Turkish service had earned the high rank of Pasha. The Turks were offering a ransom of 10,000 crowns for Baffo – and the lives of two Venetian captains thrown in. But first the Venetians put him to the question. Baffo too spun a plausible but misleading tale. Ali according to Baffo had only 160 galleys, most of them badly manned. There was indeed much disease in the Turkish fleet. Ali had only 4500 janissaries – and they were unhappy at fighting a sea battle with the 50,000 infantry they had heard were serving with Don John.

More misleading information, though this time well-intentioned, had come in from friendly Adriatic fishermen, who caught a distant glimpse of Ochiali and his twenty-five sail when they headed across to Italy. The fishermen sent word to Don John that an entire corsair squadron was heading back to Africa. If true – and Baffo's lies made it sound probable – Ali's battle strength might have been reduced by as much as a third.

Thus, by the end of September, both Ali and Don John were in the dark about what they might encounter. Only one fact had been fixed beyond all reasonable doubt – that after attacking Zante and Corfu, the Turkish fleet had gone back to Lepanto, with every intention of wintering there. But none of the information true or false coming in to either commander was a positive discouragement to offering battle.

King Philip had laid a most strict command upon Don John that when battle might be imminent, he must take the advice of a council of war. The Prudent King was no doubt aware of the cynical military adage, 'a Council of War never fights'. And indeed, under a leader less single-minded than Don John, the confusing intelligence picture, and the habit of caution ingrained in all those who wanted to make a career for themselves under King Philip, might have led to some half-hearted decision. But by this time, the Pope had planted one clear conviction in all their minds: that the fate of Christendom rested with the 200 galleys of the Holy League, at present feeling their way blindly up the treacherous east coast of the Adriatic in bad weather. This solemn conviction, however, worked both ways. A single error of judgement one stormy night might leave Europe's Mediterranean coast stripped bare of war galleys, and wide open to future Turkish landings.

At Messina the overcautious had rejected the bolder strategic option – which Don John himself would have preferred – of striking hard at Negropont, and even going so far as to threaten Cyprus. This would certainly have fetched Ali out of Lepanto and down the canal into his home waters – the bolder choice was probably the safer. But now the question had become simple and terrible – whether or not to risk all on a battle. Yet between deciding in principle to fight if there should be no other choice, and actually seeking out the enemy with vigorous determination, there was a wide gap which, at the council of war, gave the less convinced plenty of scope to play it safe.

But there proved to be a resolute handful around the table who had made up their minds that if giving battle were a breathtaking risk, evading it for whatever good excuse was an even greater risk. Barbarigo the Venetian admiral, Colonna himself, and Santa Cruz, the best fighting seaman in the Spanish fleet, all backed up Don John. The less willing but more numerous were overawed. Their bland suggestion that, since it was so late in the year, the League fleet could save its face by an attack on some minor Turkish fortress or other was brushed aside. On 28 September, d'Andrade had confirmed that Ali's fleet was withdrawing to Lepanto. And there – the council of war decided – the galleys of the Holy League should seek him out.

Don John reviewed his fleet at Gomeniza – almost within striking distance of Lepanto. Kara Hodja – the corsair chief who that summer had raided into the Gulf of Venice – painted a twenty-two-oar galliot black, and in the small hours rowed it through the midst of the Christian fleet, noticing and counting. But the intrepid corsair got his sums wrong. He misjudged the weight and number of the bow guns in the fleet, and somehow failed to add in fifty war galleys. The Turks compounded their error when they pounced on three Spanish sailors taking a run ashore in Gomeniza. Even under torture the three of them, together and separately, had bravely confirmed Kara Hodja's false figures. They even told – and held to – a useful lie about the galliasses, as an extra flourish. This persuaded Ali to believe that there could be nothing much wrong with Kara Hodja's false appraisal. His own fleet must comfortably outnumber Don John's.

Venetian historians and the Turkish chronicler Hadji Khalifah give discordant and no doubt conjectural accounts of what passed at the council of war called by Ali in Lepanto. But though sometimes contradictory, the gist of what they say no doubt reflects the probable division of opinion among the Turkish leaders before the battle.

Pertev Pasha, a soldier of fortune promoted not long since to command the troops at Lepanto, was not greatly impressed by the reinforcements they had sent up to him by galley from Negropont. The best Turkish troops that year had been massed around the walls of Famagusta. The Pasha was a veteran who had uncomfortable memories of Malta – and apparently told the Turkish council of war that his men were too raw to give a good account of themselves. He was in the minority openly against offering battle.

The corsairs lived a long way from Constantinople – and though loyal to Selim in their fashion, it was always just as well for any Sultan not to be too emphatic with them. Ochiali was their leading spirit – but he had guessed wrong about the League fleet putting to sea, and then been ordered on pain of death to stay at Lepanto when he would rather have gone home. For the corsairs, the galleys were the source of their prosperity – why risk them for nothing very much? Ochiali himself, however, at fifty-two, was still ambitious, and had his reputation as a fighting man to maintain. A quick, cheap victory for the Sultan somewhere locally appealed to him more; a pitched battle was a disproportionate risk; shrewdly he advised caution before leaving the protected anchorage of Lepanto.

Mahomet nicknamed Scirocco, commanding the galleys from Egypt, was an elderly man of much seagoing experience. He too failed to see why it should be necessary to risk all on one throw, when with Castle Romelia on its high promontory to the north, and the Castle of Morea on its lower headland to the south, they were safe where they were, under the guns of Lepanto, with supplies coming up satisfactorily from Negropont, and in the best of postures for a triumphant campaign next spring.

The great Barbarossa's son, Hassan, had by this time become so corpulent that in a despairing effort to bring down his weight he was eating food only one day in five. As the astute son of a famous father, Hassan's reputation among the Turks was something like Gianandrea Doria's in the League. Hassan on this occasion expressed his own readiness to fight – though the opinion he is said to have given the council of war was clearly influenced less by naval considerations than what he surmised might be the pattern of intrigue going on behind all their backs in Constantinople.

Hassan's position was simple. If their moody but all-powerful Sultan now wanted most of all to hear of the destruction of the Christian fleet – if their young and singularly well patronized admiral Ali were so anxious for glory – then, why not? The Christian fleet – Hassan was reported to have said – might well be coming towards them in large numbers. But its ships were drawn from nations notoriously jealous of one another, and unaccustomed to serving, as did the Turks, under a single command. The League fleet, said Hassan sardonically, had been jumbled together and sent to sea to gratify the vanity of a young prince. Not only had the Turks already defeated such conglomerate fleets – in his own father's day, for instance, at the battle of Prevesa, not far from here, and in Ochiali's at Djerba. But only last year a very similar fleet under Colonna had actually sailed almost as far as Cyprus without plucking up courage to strike a blow against the Crescent. (And failing to attack Colonna, as everyone at the council of war must have been aware, was the reason given for dismissing a man better placed in his day than any of them – Piale Pasha.)

Hassan saw deeper than most, but he left out of account two factors.

One was the self-sacrificial mood generated in the Holy League fleet this year by priest and Pope. The other was the degree to which this burst of enthusiasm had been transformed to discipline and determination under the banner of Don John. The only Turkish leader who apparently had an inkling of this change was Hamet, in charge of the Turkish base at Negropont. He is said by some to have warned the council of war that successive Turkish victories, beginning at Cyprus and reaching ever closer to the heart of Christendom, might well in the past year have enlightened Christians to the need of fighting as one. The Turks themselves, said Hamet, should of course resist stoutly any attacks the League fleet might try to make on the Sultan's dominions (the proposition to attack a Turkish fortress had evidently reached the council of war). Apart from that, why not stay here in Lepanto, and wait for the Christian fleet to make its first mistake?

Ali, young, ambitious, impulsive, and enjoying the special patronage of Sultan Selim's wife (he had even named his flagship *Sultana*) had in fact just received from Sultan Selim an order impossible to disobey – that should Don John's fleet come close enough, it must be fought. Apparently, after the discussion Ali sprang this order on his commanders, as a surprise, and there was no more argument, though some may have regretted being quite so frank earlier.

What made this order from the Sultan so acceptable to Ali personally may well be made out. Take it that the composite fleet of the Holy League had been boldly engaged and – of course – destroyed outright. The unguarded islands of the Venetian empire would then fall to the Turks, one after another, like ripe fruit. And with Spain's galleys, too, out of the way, Ali could pick his next year's target along the entire coast of the Western Mediterranean. He might well go down in Ottoman history as one of its greatest conquerors. The Turkish intelligence picture was in fact overoptimistic – but adding his own galleys and galliots together, and taking into consideration what he thought he knew about the League fleet, there could have been little doubt in Ali's mind that he had a useful superiority in fighting ships. The 25,000 soldiers borne in his fleet included a higher proportion than usual of janissaries. The enemy might possibly have more and better guns – but what counted most was the man behind the gun, and warfare was the Turkish way of life. Christians were very apt to bicker; the Sultan's men obeyed.

A small and curious detail might give the Turks a slight advantage. Slaves at the oar of any Turkish galley were usually the property of her captain. If provoked, he might cut off the ears and nose of a recaptured runaway. But he had every personal motive for treating considerately those who did their duty. Ochiali had a name for cruelty towards his slaves – but he was an exception. Thus once battle was joined, galley slaves in Turkish ships – so their officers confidently believed – might be relied upon to stay neutral and passive, and be no hindrance. Ali himself was distinguished for his humanity towards his slaves – and in the crisis of any battle between fleets so closely matched, how the slaves performed might well make all the difference.

12

In Battle

When ships are locked and grappled together, the soldier has no
more space left him than two feet of plank on the beak-head . . .
though he knows that at his first careless step he will go down to
visit the deep bosom of Neptune, nevertheless with undaunted
heart, sustained by the honour which spurs him on, he exposes
himself as a mark for all their shot, and endeavours to pass along
that narrow causeway into the enemy's ship. And, most amazing
of all, no sooner does one man fall, never to rise again this side of
Doomsday, than another takes his place; and if he, in his turn, falls
into the sea, which lies in wait for him like an enemy, another, and
yet another, takes his place, without a moment passing between
their deaths: the greatest display of valour and daring
to be found in all the hazards of war.
MIGUEL CERVANTES: *Don Quixote*, Part I, Chapter 38

The battle fleet of the Holy League spent most of 5 October in harbour
at Viscando – not far from Mark Antony's Actium – kept there by fog
and foul winds. War galleys were a fair-weather weapon, and the
blustery Mediterranean winter was beginning to make itself felt.
Would the Turks move out of their snug anchorage? Coming close
enough to tweak their beards might provoke them.

Bad weather coming down like this had helped to hide the approach
of the battle fleet, and give it an advantage of surprise. When ebullient
with martial enthusiasm, or blundering about in their drill, Don
John's arquebusiers would sometimes loose off a live shot, so he
promulgated an order forbidding anyone whatever to fire a gun on
pain of death: in the shifting fog, the multitude of galleys was
uncannily quiet.

A brigantine coming up from Candia that day brought to Sebastian
Veniero and Agostino Barbarigo the belated news – despatched in
August but only just arrived – that Famagusta had been taken by the
Turks. For the first time they learned how Bragadino, their senator
governing Famagusta, had met his fate, on 17 August 1571, at the
hands of the Turkish treaty breakers: flayed alive.

The news ran from ship to ship, arousing all the Venetians in the
fleet – men who usually prided themselves on being calm and rational

– to a wild fury. Two of Bragadino's close kinsmen were in the fleet, commanding galliasses. There was no longer any doubt that the Venetians would fight. The Turks – with whom for so long they had done business – had shown themselves to be the enemies of God. Their policy of cruelty had created even in the calmest of men a zeal to destroy them.

Eight crack galleys of the Sicilian squadron, under Don Juan de Cardona, were sent on ahead. For a spell of twenty minutes such galleys could triple their speed, if the slaves rowed full out. They were to keep a sharp watch, and drop back at once to give word if the enemy were sighted, so that the fleet behind them could deploy in battle order. Tossing like corks in the wake of its little, briskly rowing vanguard, the League fleet moved slowly down the rock-bound coast, towards the Gulf of Patras.

In writing to Don John about what battle order to adopt, Don García reminded him that thirty-three years before, when Barbarossa had led the Turks to victory at the sea battle of Prevesa, the enemy admiral had found it easy to disrupt the most obvious battle formation: one long line. Don García advised three separate divisions, with gaps between them wide enough to allow for manoeuvre. By developing this hint, a cruciform formation had been worked out which would bring to bear the League's advantage in gunnery against the Turks' long crescent.

In battle, the division on the left would mostly be galleys from Venice, under the direct command of Agostino Barbarigo. Command of the war galley at the far end of the line – the flank which the Turks would fight their hardest to turn, and therefore the place of greatest danger – had been entrusted to the same Marcantonio Quirini who had broken the winter blockade of Famagusta, and bluffed Ali out of his landing at Candia. To the head of each division as the enemy came in sight would be towed a pair of heavily gunned galliasses, serving like massive breakwaters. Taking post ahead of the Venetian wing would be the two galliasses commanded by Antonio and Ambrosio Bragadino – waiting with sullen passion for their revenge. The division on the left wing numbered sixty-three war galleys, and flew a yellow pennant at the yard peak.

Included in the mixed division on Don John's right, flying a green pennant and commanded by Gianandrea Doria, were the galleys hired from Genoa. Also serving in Doria's division were some interesting volunteers. Don John's boyhood friend, Alexander Farnese, had brought 202 personal followers with him to the fight, including thirty-two noblemen and gentlemen, and 152 Italian soldiers in his pay. Despite their King's known disapproval, several individual Frenchmen of distinction had volunteered, including the celebrated Crillon – Henry IV's 'brave Crillon'. 'Commanding three galleys' was the English soldier of fortune and former pirate, Sir Thomas Stukeley. Having served every English monarch since the time of his reputed father – Henry VIII – whether they were Catholic or Protestant, and several foreign kings as well, Stukeley had now put his sword at the service of Philip of Spain against the Turk. Giacomo IV, whose dukedom of Naxos had been given by Sultan Selim to Joseph Micas as his recompense, was serving under the green pennant flown by Doria at the head of 500 men.

Aboard the galley *Marquesa*, in the ranks of Miguel de Moncada's regiment (most of them veterans of the fighting in the Alpujarras) was a well-read, high-spirited and chronically impoverished volunteer, a few months younger than Don John, called Miguel Cervantes. Later, in *Don Quixote* (where he dropped a hint that Don Quixote's real name might well have been Quixada) Cervantes was to mock and yet to immortalize the knight errant attitude – so incongruous in a sceptical, calculating, money-grubbing world. But this autumn morning, as he and his comrades moved uneasily in their tossing galley down the Adriatic coast, something of the spirit of chivalry could be sensed poignantly by anyone in their midst.

The rearguard, a reserve of thirty galleys, was to intervene in time of battle wherever Santa Cruz, their commander, might judge the fighting to be hottest. The rearguard flew a white pennant. Don John himself, from his flagship *Real* – three years old, built of Catalan pine, ornately gilded and carved, and even embellished with mural paintings – commanded the sixty-four galleys of the centre. Immediately to his left was the flagship of the Venetian commander in chief, white-bearded, cantankerous and combative Sebastian Veniero. Like the lawyer he was, Veniero would rather usurp the right of his commander in chief, Don John, than yield an inch of what he deemed should be his own. If Spanish soldiers serving aboard a Venetian galley misbehaved, he hanged them – and the fat was in the fire. On the very eve of battle, Don John had met Veniero's hot temper with a mingling of firmness and gallantry which quenched this last flare-up of the antagonism between Venice and Spain – a violent difference which could have lost the battle before it began.

In the papal flagship, at Don John's right hand, was that affable and well-intentioned aristocrat, Marcantonio Colonna. He too had helped pacify Veniero – it was difficult to quarrel with Colonna. As action came closer, Veniero and Colonna, as if to prove that the squabble was over, began signalling to each other jovial compliments. Veniero punned Colonna's name and well-fleshed figure to identify him as 'the stoutest column which supported the church'. Colonna answered in Vulgate Latin with St Peter's equivocal words, 'Yea, if I die I will not betray thee.' The spirit of the three leaders at the centre of the battle line, as danger approached, was becoming exuberant.

Gianandrea Doria, astute and ugly, did not share their mood. Doria was probably the cleverest tactician in the fleet – but his intimates were inclined to wonder if he had ever got his nerve back after his defeat at the age of twenty-one, when up against Ochiali. Though Doria had managed to keep the good opinion of King Philip, his capacity as a fighting admiral had never been tested since. But whether or not he lacked stomach for the coming fight, Gianandrea Doria brought about two tactical innovations that were to prove of great – perhaps of decisive – value in the course of the battle.

Since the galliasses had boarding nets, and anyway stood too high out of the water to be boarded easily, was the usual defensive force of pikemen and swordsmen necessary? Why not stuff their decks tight with arquebusiers? Knowing what havoc might be wreaked by such massed fire across the deck of each advancing Turkish galley as it passed in range, Don John at once ordered 500 arquebusiers to go on board each of the six galliasses.

Doria's second recommendation had been even more of a surprise – unship the rams. Ever since the days of Mark Antony, a Mediterranean war galley had always carried a ram jutting from its bows – in Venetian ships they were gilded – to smash into the enemy's hull at the moment of collision. But Doria saw that the ram was an unconsidered survival from the past. Nowadays the bows of a war galley carried a weapon much more effective: guns. Heavy guns fired point blank would do much more damage to a hull than the single impact of a ram driven home by sail and oar. But with the ram in their line of sight, the gunners in the bows of a galley tended to fire high – into the enemy's rigging – rather than below the waterline. Let the Turks use their own rams if they chose – and thus waste shots.

On the night of 6 October 1571, with a fair wind in their sails, the Turkish battle fleet under Ali was preparing to move from Lepanto into the Gulf of Patras, though neither Gianandrea Doria nor Don John yet knew this. Having clinched his value as a tactician, Doria dropped the mask. He asked Don John to remember that, late though it was, a pitched battle could still be avoided. Were the Christian fleet to be defeated so far from base, Doria pointed out, disaster was certain. Then why not turn back? Over Doria's shoulder the circumspect Ascanio de la Cognia voiced a similar opinion in other words. 'Gentlemen,' Don John told them, courteously but bluntly, 'the time for counsel has passed; the time for fighting has come.'

7 October 1571 was a Sunday. Mass that day was celebrated throughout the fleet with particular solemnity, since all were well aware that the testing time of battle might be close. The galleys of the Holy League had edged around the northerly shore where the Gulf of Patras begins to narrow. The naked slaves on their benches were obliged to pull against the wind, standing up to thrust against the huge and heavy oars as they dipped in the sea, sinking back to the bench with all their weight for the long tug that kept the galley in motion. Back and forth on the catwalk, observant, went a bosun with a silver whistle round his neck and a bull's pizzle in his hand, to lash at the man he saw not pulling his weight. Then from galley to galley ran a sudden buzz: the Turks were in sight.

Ali's fleet, about fifteen miles further into the Gulf, and just visible, numbered 274 ships of war, of which 208 were galleys. It stretched across from shore to shore, in one vast crescent. The Turks had left their safe refuge at Lepanto, and were sailing out to sea with a following wind. When Ochiali, as the fleets came in sight, had urged on Ali the possibility of a feigned retreat, to draw the Christian enemy deeper into the narrowing Gulf until their complex battle order became confused, the Turkish commander in chief had replied loftily, 'I will never allow the Sultan's ships even to appear to be taking flight.'

Fluttering from Ali's flagship could be seen a green Islamic pennant, identical in shape with the banner carried before the Prophet Mahomet during his career of conquest, but bearing the name of Allah repeated in gold calligraphy 28,900 times. The flag was one of the treasures of Mecca. Over the centuries, when Moslems had carried its green and gold into battle, they invariably gained the day. From each approaching Turkish ship of war fluttered streamers and pennants in abundance, and over the sea moved strange music. Turkish soldiers in joyous anticipation of battle were belly-dancing on the deck, to the sound of tambour, cymbals and flute.

Across the League fleet, according to a man who was there, fell by contrast an unwonted Sunday quiet, as men went urgently yet with no unnecessary noise about their duty – rigging boarding nets, sharpening pike or sword on a whetstone, greasing the deck so that an enemy might miss his footing.

Armourers were knocking the fetters off Christian galley slaves, and passing them out weapons. Even the hardened criminals among them took up sword or half-pike with a cheerful will. While this was being done, each Moslem galley slave was handcuffed to his oar – if the ship went down, so would he. Officers put on casque and cuirass, arquebusiers made sure their powder was still dry, and Don John's order all this time was strictly obeyed: from the League fleet, not a shot was fired. The eight reconnaissance galleys were falling back to their place in the line. The six bulky, cumbersome galliasses were being towed and rowed slowly to their designated places, in pairs, over half a mile ahead of the three divisions of the fleet.

Crucifix in hand, Don John proceeded in a *fregata* along one wing, to rectify order in the line of battle and hearten the men. Luis de Requeséns did the same duty on the other wing. To one ship's company after another, Don John's clear and almost boyish voice pealed out with the same assurance: 'My children, we are here to conquer or die. In death or in victory, you will win immortality.' Tactics, technique, equipment, all had their importance. But as all the leaders knew, today's battle would be won or lost in the hand-to-hand fighting. What counted that morning above all else was the spirit of the men.

Observing that the Christian fleet was coming down upon him in an unusual formation, Ali advanced his crescent at the centre by bringing up his flagship, *Sultana*; at the same time he let his own wings fall back. Ali's battle line, thus extended, was a thousand metres longer than Don John's, reaching without a break from the shoal water, northwards, on the mountainous Albanian shore, to the shallows southward, along the coast of the Morea. His fleet therefore blocked entirely the entrance to the Gulf; his tactics now were to advance, outflank and surround. Along the decks of approaching Turkish galley and galliot, goose-winged, borne forward by the pressure of their sails, the high plumes and splendid weapons of his janissaries were by this time conspicuous. Turkish bowmen crowded along decks, and hung in the rigging. Ali himself was going into battle with a short but powerful Turkish bow as his chosen weapon.

Christian slaves at the oar in Turkish warships were customarily shackled by the foot. With the following wind doing their work for them, they had been forced this morning to duck below the benches, and told that any man among them lifting his head would be killed. In Ali's fleet there were upwards of 14,000 galley slaves owing Christian allegiance. The risk of death for all of them, and yet the chance of freedom, was coming at every moment closer. Ali had always treated them better than most others. To gain at least their obedient neutrality, he spoke to the slaves aboard *Sultana* in Spanish: 'Friends, I expect you today to do your duty by me, in return for what I have done for you. If I win the battle I promise you your liberty; if the day is yours, Allah had given it to you.'

Ali himself was in direct command of the ninety-six warships at the Turkish centre, facing Don John. Against the Venetians Mahomet Scirocco led fifty-six galleys, mostly from Egypt. Already he was inching his shallow-draught galliots close to the Albanian shore, so as to outflank Marcantonio Quirini, in the post of honour on the Venetians' extreme left wing. That cunning and disfigured old man of the sea, Ochiali, led the sixty-three galleys and galliots on Ali's left wing, most of them manned by corsairs. He would be up against his old acquaintance, that other wily seaman Gianandrea Doria – who as a young man had run from him, at Tripoli. A mass of smaller craft crowded the Turkish rear, acting as a reserve.

Towed out in pairs ahead of his enemy's battle line, the huge galliasses were evidently a surprise to Ali. From the crescent of Turkish ships as under sail they moved closer to their Christian enemy came yells, random shots, religious ululations of defiance. Gongs and huge cymbals clashed, conches blared: the Turkish uproar was meant to shake the nerves. From the ships of the Holy League, not a shot had yet been fired – this prolonged and deliberate silence was ominous. As the ships of the Holy League laboured onwards, their oars dipping and lifting, the Turks could see priests like dark-robed insects, scurrying across decks, crucifix in hand, often scrambling high into the rigging, the better to exhort that crowd of armed men waiting on deck.

All at once, the wind that morning turned right around.

The triangular Turkish sails came down to deck with a rush. Ordered up peremptorily from under their benches, Turkish galley slaves grasped oars and were whipped into activity. While Ali's ships visibly lost momentum, all along Don John's battle line, lateen sails were being shaken out along spars. They filled as if from a mighty and confident breath. As they heard or half heard the chaplains' insistent voices, there were few in the League fleet who doubted that God had intervened.

Only a short while before, the decks of Don John's galleys had been crowded with kneeling men, as chaplains served Mass and repeated the general absolution – indulgence in this life and a pardon in the next to steadfast soldiers. The theme that Sunday of all their sermons had been, 'No Heaven for cowards.' Men hitherto in their lives no more than vaguely religious waited for the onset now, rosary in one hand, weapon in the other, as if the meaning of life had mysteriously deepened. One chaplain – a Capuchin from Rome – worked himself up to such a pitch that he lashed his crucifix to a boathook, and joined the first boarding party. With his gift for the dramatic moment, Don John broke out the banner bearing the giant cross of the Holy League from the jackstaff of *Real*. An immense cheer rose up and spread down the line left and right, from one ship to the next, like a reiterating echo. At a signal from the flagship, every vessel in the fleet raised up a crucifix.

An accepted convention of sea warfare in those days laid down that flagships do not engage. But Ali and Don John, as if their minds were set on a duel, were seen to be heading directly towards one another. The first gunshot of the battle from the Christian side – breaking the imposed silence – was fired by Don John at extravagantly long range, straight at Ali, like a personal challenge. Don John ordered the Maltese Knight who served as his sailing master to lay him alongside Ali's *Sultana*.

Ali meanwhile was beginning to discover what the firepower of those clumsy galliasses could signify. A war galley rowing past would now and then stagger off at a tangent as the man at the tiller was hit when huge arquebus volleys tore holes through the turbanned soldiers massed on deck, or would shudder as heavy shot splintered into the hull. The perfect advancing crescent was marred; the Turkish line opened up. And the main concussion was yet to come.

On Don García's advice, bow gunners in the League galleys were holding their fire until they could see the actual faces of their Turkish opposite numbers. Then at the word of command, the bow guns fired, and so systematic had the drill been that Don John's gunners got off three shots or more to the Turks' one. Firing simultaneously from a line of galleys which looked oddly naked – gelded – without the projecting rams, his gunners were landing shot after shot below the enemy's waterline, while at that close range Turkish shot flew high, into sail and spar.

The two flagships had steered towards one another implacably, at the pace of a trotting horse. Visible to all in his gilded breastplate, Don John walked slowly, very calmly, to give his men encouragement, from the forecastle where he had said prayers, down the catwalk between the naked rowers, to the poop. As the instant of collision with Ali's *Sultana* approached, he and two of his gentlemen, said an eyewitness, 'inspired by youthful ardour danced a galliard on the gun-platform to the music of the fifes.' A galliard was a sexy dance and Don John a famous dancer: the tautness of his religious sobriety had been broken in upon at last by physical eagerness.

Aboard a galley there was little privacy. Don John may well have known already – and chosen to ignore – that one of the soldiers in *Real* now crowding toward the bows, sword in hand, was a woman. María la Bailadora – *the dancer* – was dressed as an arquebusier. She had come aboard in this disguise, and served in Lope de Figuera's command, rather than be parted from her soldier lover. At the moment that the ram in *Sultana*'s prow crushed into the forecastle of *Real*, the peak of Don John's flagship – says our eyewitness – thrust its way through Ali's rigging. Grappling lines quickly flung held the two ships fast. Arquebus volleys and flights of arrows swept both decks. The Turks came up in a mass to board *Real*, but were baulked there by an unfamiliar obstacle: boarding nets. María la Bailadora was nimbly over the side – some asserted afterwards that she was the first – and on the deck of *Sultana* was seen to kill her Turkish antagonist with one sword thrust. Women had been the Turks' victims; she was there for love, but also for revenge.

As soldiers of the crack Sardinian Regiment hewed their way ahead, it became clearly evident that Ali's deck and not Don John's was to be the place where the contest would be fought out. Ali's flagship 'was like a battlefield'. Eight hundred men, weapon in hand, cut and thrust one way and then another up and down *Sultana*'s slippery deck. Twice the Turks were driven to the mast, twice they fought the Sardinians back to the bows. By this time the masts and spars of *Real* were bristling like elongated pincushions with Turkish arrows. Prayer, dance, apprehension had given way to an insane hilarity of combat.

Even Don John's pet marmoset was seen to join the fight – running across the deck to pick up a live grenade, and drop it in the sea. When fighting sword in hand near the jackstaff in the bows of *Real*, to hurl back Turks trying to scramble aboard, Don John was wounded in the leg – but made light, then and later, of the wound, so as not to upset his morbidly apprehensive half-brother, King Philip.

A third rush had carried the Sardinian boarding party from *Real*, with María la Bailadora well to the fore, all the way to Ali's poop. Bow in hand, firing arrow after arrow with rapid expertise at the ring of men closing in upon him, Ali at last was struck in the forehead by an arquebus bullet. An armed galley slave from Malaga ran forward to hack off the Turkish admiral's head in a frenzy. The galley slave stuck Ali's head on his half-pike and carried it to *Real*'s quarter-deck at a run, like a dog with a bone. The grisly piece of evidence was lifted on high. The sudden apparition – the proof that their commander in chief was dead – demoralized the Turks, and *Sultana* was quickly overrun.

The green flag from Mecca with its gilded Allah repeated 28,900 times came down from the peak at a run, and up in its place went the papal banner, to the blare of trumpets. Without a pause, Don John's victorious soldiers and their avid galley-slave helpers began to plunder *Sultana*. In the hold of the Turkish flagship they discovered an incredible treasure – which they kept for themselves. Ali had brought his entire personal fortune to sea with him – 150,000 gold sequins – rather than leave it behind in Constantinople, and risk having it confiscated should he happen to displease Sultan Selim. By two in the afternoon, with the Turkish admiral killed and his flagship taken and gutted, Don John could afford to wipe the bloody sweat from his eyes, and consider the fight elsewhere.

Mahomet Scirocco's ships on the wing near the northern shore of the gulf outnumbered the Venetians'. He clearly intended first to encircle then to overwhelm them. The fighting around Quirini's galley, at the extreme end of the line, was therefore ferocious. The Turks managed to turn the flank, and the flagship of the Venetian admiral, Agostino Barbarigo, was attacked by eight Turkish galleys at once. Wounded in the eye by an arrow, Barbarigo was forced early on to hand over his command to Federigo Nani. Word that their commander was hors de combat spread quickly, yet the individualistic Venetians apparently did not so much as hesitate, as if for them this day's fight were a matter of personal honour that must go to a finish. What they had done at Famagusta was being paid for by the Turks in their own blood.

Half a dozen Venetian galleys had already been sunk, and a number of the Turkish galleys, crippled earlier by gunfire, were becoming waterlogged. The outcome was uncertain – tilting slightly, perhaps, in Mahomet Scirocco's favour – when in the Turkish ships a mass of the Christian galley slaves, having filed away at their fetters in readiness, broke free at a signal from the leaders of their conspiracy. Blindly defiant they joined the fray, swinging broken chains, leaping on Turks from behind to grab their weapons, taking their oppressors by the throat. This intervention of mutinous oarsmen from the Turkish galleys – some of them Greeks or Italians kidnapped on Ali's recent raids – tipped the balance. From Don John's flagship the Venetians could be seen, slowly gaining the upper hand.

Mahomet Scirocco himself was killed in the hand-to-hand fighting. His body, floating face downwards in a sea running red with blood, was recognized by his gorgeous apparel. Venetian soldiers promptly chopped off his head and raised it on high – the dismal sight took the heart out of the Turks. Though prolonged and hard fought, the battle over there on the Venetian wing had evidently been won.

The Venetians too – it was their custom – had freed and armed their own galley slaves, and promised that every man who fought could expect to be given his freedom. But where property was concerned – and galley slaves were property – Venetians after making such a promise were apt to finesse as to exactly what it meant. As battle ebbed, a great crowd of debtors, Jews, overtaxed peasants, heretics, perverts and petty thieves, turning their backs on their oars and their fetters, and taking with them the weapons they had been lent, jumped over the side before they could be ordered to their places again. Wading through shallow water to the marsh fringing the mountainous Albanian shore, they disappeared into the hills, to begin a new career, as bandits.

In Veniero's flagship at the very centre of battle, the white-bearded, hot-blooded veteran – he was seventy-five – fought that day in carpet slippers, explaining to anyone who enquired that they gave him a better grip on the deck. He had fired the first shot from the bows of his own ship with a blunderbuss, which he had aimed almost point blank into the faces of the Turkish bow gunners in the enemy galley bearing down on him. Back on his own quarterdeck, Sebastian Veniero took up the crossbow – a weapon he had known all about in his own youth, when the arquebus was newfangled. A seaman had been told off to stand at Veniero's side and wind the crank for him – a task beyond his strength. But the old man could still aim. He stood coolly amid the hail of arrows and gunshot, concentrated upon him as admiral by the enemy's sharpshooters, picking off one Turk after another, and exclaiming, we are told, that he would count himself 'not unfortunate, if his days should end in such a battle, if God so pleased.'

On the right wing, where Gianandrea Doria and his old antagonist Ochiali manoeuvred for advantage, many brave men took their chances. Alexander Farnese stormed out of the Genoese flagship at the head of his 200 followers, and went aboard the nearest Turkish galley with such headlong impetus that the galley was captured almost intact. The duty for which his captain, Diego de Urbino, picked out Miguel Cervantes shows that though serving in the ranks, the bookish and poetical young man was esteemed as a soldier. A not uncommon diversionary tactic after an enemy's galley had been grappled and boarded was to send a dozen picked men in the ship's longboat to her far side, from whence they could clamber on deck and surprise the enemy in the rear. Every small detail of Cervantes' life has been debated and disputed – not least his exact place of duty at Lepanto – but the overwhelming probability is that he commanded the men in *Marquesa*'s longboat; he was certainly wounded twice, in breast and hand. ('Wounds in the face or chest,' he wrote long afterwards, 'are the stars which guide one through honour to the skies.') He described the battle, succinctly, as *la mayor jornada que vieron los siglos* – the greatest day's work seen for centuries.

Apart from such individual feats by men clear in their own minds what they were fighting for, the battle on Doria's wing went as might have been guessed. Doria had tried on the very eve of battle to discourage Don John. Ochiali too had appealed to Ali not to risk his fleet, but to be satisfied with some less costly feat of arms. When Don John's fleet came in sight, he had urged on Ali a feigned withdrawal; Ali, overconfident, had refused.

Ochiali had more ships than Doria, but he had, as well, an invisible and more valuable advantage: the moral ascendancy. Ochiali had beaten Doria once already. He was prepared, today as always, to risk his ships and sacrifice his men for any great personal advantage. But for Gianandrea Doria, even a battle was a matter of profit and loss.

Nearly half the galleys in his command were a private speculation made by rich Genoese. Prizes and plunder signified profit; losing galleys was money thrown away.

Doria, clever and calculating, had managed to persuade himself that this time he could outmanoeuvre Ochiali. He would avoid the need of a fight to the death; he would fight a battle of position and surprise. But Ochiali read his mind.

As their ships came closer, Ochiali continually extended his own line towards the low shores of the Morea. This tactic was to be anticipated – in his efforts to outflank the Venetians, Mahomet Scirocco at the far end of the line was doing much the same. To avoid being outflanked, Doria was obliged to follow suit, easing the ships of his own command slowly and ably towards the Morea, so that the Turks could not get inshore of him. But he had fewer ships than Ochiali, and they would not stretch so far.

Perceiving what might soon go amiss, Don John sent a quick *fregata* to Doria, ordering him not to overextend his line. But Doria – like Ochiali – was seldom prompt to obey the orders of those he thought less clever than himself. As the Genoese admiral met Ochiali's outflanking manoeuvre by groping towards the shore, a wide gap of clear water – a hole in the line – had opened up between Doria's command and the centre. Ochiali's outflanking move had been a cunning feint. Doria had been tricked.

Ochiali put over the helm, and went as fast as his slaves could row towards the 1000 yard gap that this clever bluff of his had temporarily opened up in the Christian line. Close behind him came a file of corsair galleys, their captains in the secret and only waiting for Ochiali's signal to break away. Before the neighbouring galleys of the League could close the gap between them, Ochiali and his dozen or so closest followers were through. The corsair galleys turned about in the rear of Don John's battle line. They now had the wind behind them. They could pick out their prey.

The manoeuvre was brilliant, but Ochiali, always more corsair than admiral, had abandoned to their fate the slower ships in his command – and Doria now outnumbered them, though he did not appear anxious to close with them. Ochiali had never wished to fight this battle – he lacked Ali's taste for death or glory. He could already see that the day had gone against the Turks, but for Ochiali, personally, that was not altogether a bad thing. With every other Turkish admiral dead or discredited, a glittering promotion might be within his grasp.

Ochiali knew that all he needed to redeem his own good name was some token of victory which would impress Constantinople.

What Sultan and harem detested most of all were the Knights of Malta. Their religious commitment – the huge and strange cross they flew when sending their piratical galleys deep into the Levant – was an affront the Turks could never digest. Today three Maltese galleys with ninety armoured Knights aboard were serving under Santa Cruz in the rearguard, while others of the 'chivalry of the religion' manned the papal flotilla. Ochiali at the head of seven galleys went straight for *Capitana*, the Knights' flagship, commanded by Pietro Giustiniani, who happened also to be his personal enemy.

Meanwhile, sixteen of the galleys abandoned by Ochiali inshore of the Morea were doing their best to turn and get away. But they were held fast there and compelled to engage by eight League galleys, under Don Juan de Cardona. Each League galley had to fight it out with two Turkish galleys – cruel odds. Of the 500 Sicilian soldiers aboard Cardona's own galley, only fifty were to survive unwounded. In two of his ships – the papal galley *San Giovanni*, and *Piamontesa* from Savoy – every officer and every soldier aboard was either killed fighting or died afterwards from his wounds. With the Turkish centre overcome, Don John himself was moving down to tackle the leaderless Turkish left wing, and relieve Cardona. His arrival there broke what was left of the line Ochiali should have led into battle. Rather than fight it out, some of the Turkish captains beached their galleys. Their men swam ashore, and ran away on foot into the hostile Morea.

In the rear of the Christian line, Ochiali when he laid those seven galleys alongside *Capitana* knew what he was after, and was willing to pay a price for it: the fight was fierce. Thirty armoured Knights together with their entourage of men-at-arms died fighting on the deck of *Capitana*. Pietro Giustiniani with five arrow wounds in him was to every appearance the sole survivor aboard his own flagship. (Two other Knights, though taken for dead, were in fact later to recover from their wounds.) Ochiali ran down the Knights' huge ensign – the Maltese Cross – and with Giustiniani, Prior of the Order, as his prisoner, took *Capitana* in tow. He had a prize and a prisoner, he had a trophy; he had all the proof he needed.

But as Ochiali sought to sheer off from the battle and make his escape, Santa Cruz bore down on him with the rearguard. Captain Ojeda with the galley *Guzmana* laid himself alongside *Capitana* and managed to board her. Ochiali intended to survive the battle – he cut the disputed prize loose and made off. When the Knights' galley was retaken from its Turkish prize crew, Ojeda found that the thirty dead or dying Knights littering her deck had accounted between them for three hundred Turks. (In gratitude for Ojeda's feat of rescue, the Maltese Order awarded him a pension for life.)

Ochiali had lost his prize – the Maltese flagship – but not his presence of mind. He cut and ran from the battle, carrying with him *Capitana*'s ensign. Thirteen Turkish galleys and galliots – mostly corsairs – managed to follow in Ochiali's wake, the only naval force obedient to the Sultan still at large in the Adriatic. For the next day or two, Ochiali dodged in and out of the islands, until he had managed to pounce on a lagging Venetian galley, *Bua*. With a prize in tow once more, he led his little squadron east, to Constantinople – the battle's only notable survivor. Every other admiral in the Turkish battle fleet was dead at Lepanto, amid the wreckage of his command.

As a sop to the people – since almost every Moslem family in the city had lost a relative – Sokolli the Grand Vizier ordered the ensign of *Capitana*, with its Maltese Cross, to be displayed on the dome of the mosque which, in Byzantine days, had been the cathedral of Santa Sophia, and the principal shrine of Orthodox Christianity. When Sultan Selim was told about Lepanto, he is reputed in his blind rage to have ordered a massacre: of every Christian slave in his dominions? – of every Spaniard and Venetian? – some accounts say, of every Christian. Since there were then about 40,000 Christians earning a living in Constantinople alone, that would have been a memorable massacre, even for Turks.

Sokolli was still doing his best with French help to negotiate a separate peace with Venice behind the scenes, as a way of destroying the Holy League without striking a blow. Any such blind slaughter of Christians living under Turkish rule could hardly be forgiven. In political terms, a far too high price had already been paid for the wanton torture of Bragadino. A cry for revenge would go up; the war would drag on. By pointing out to Selim that the Christians by this time had thousands of Turkish captives, if they chose to take reprisals, Sokolli managed to change Selim's mind.

During the war so far, Sokolli can hardly have regretted seeing his personal rivals go down one after another to defeat or disgrace. Of those who had hoisted Selim to the throne, he was the survivor; for the rest of his life, he would have more power than any grand vizier before him. He must have been well aware, as a former admiral, that

Ochiali's little triumph, of which so much was being made, had no real substance. But the fiction was convenient for his purpose – which was to end the war by diplomacy. He agreed to appoint Ochiali admiral of the fleet – even though, except for fifty partially built galleys now on the stocks, there was no fleet. The tall, thin, grave, impassive Grand Vizier even nodded his straight-faced approval when the Sultan announced his intention of giving Ochiali a complimentary new surname: Kiliç, meaning Sword. The Ottoman Turks, once invincible, had come by this time to the impasse where all imperial peoples apparently arrive – when victories are won with words, and let those disbelieve who dare.

By four on that Sunday afternoon, 7 October 1571, the battle of Lepanto was over. The specific menace which had brought the Holy League fleet into being – the Turkish battle fleet – had been destroyed. Though Gianandrea Doria looked spectacularly gory – one of his men, killed nearby, had bled profusely over his fine clothes – he had never once exchanged a shot with Ochiali. In the confusion of battle he had managed, however, to cut out for himself several fine prizes. His was the only flagship undamaged, so the surviving commanders met there that evening in council. Don John with gentle irony paused as he came aboard, to admire the splendid condition of Doria's ship – the only sign of disapproval he was ever to allow himself. Luis de Requeséns, when asked later, privately, by King Philip, how the Genoese had conducted himself at Lepanto, replied diplomatically that he had been 'unable to see'. The Pope, though, when he got to hear, was furious, snatching a phrase from the air to condemn Doria for acting 'more like a corsair than a Christian admiral', and sending him a fierce hint that for the time being he would do well to keep out of Rome.

As the light faded on that hectic October afternoon, all the admirals on the poop of Doria's flagship – except Barbarigo, pierced in the eye and at death's door – as they sat at their deliberations amid floating wreckage and floating corpses, must have been astonished at the completeness of their own victory. More than 12,000 Christian galley slaves, of whom over 2000 were Spanish – all victims of kidnapping raids in past years around the Mediterranean – were now free men. Thousands of Turkish prisoners were morosely taking their place at the oar, thus guaranteeing to the allies in time to come the muscle power they needed to propel their war galleys – and, for the present anyway, leaving the Turks hamstrung.

Both sides claimed to have had over 80,000 men at Lepanto, but such large numerical claims do not bear examination; perhaps 50,000 on each side actually fought. The League lost about 7000 men, of whom 4800 were Venetians, and lost twelve galleys from their battle line. Of the English volunteers, ten were killed in action. The names of four are known: Neville, Clabourne, Beaumont, Brooke. The Turks at the most moderate estimate lost 25,000 men. A hundred and eighty of their galleys ended up in the hands of the allies, though many had been badly knocked about. The Pope got some of his own back, since one of the prizes – the Turkish paymaster's galley – turned out to be the flagship of the papal squadron, lost at Djerba in the days of Pius IV. One hundred and seventeen large guns and 274 small were taken. Only about 10,000 Turks scrambled back to their nearby base at Lepanto – most of them in the small ships of the rearguard. Sultan Selim's war fleet, and the army it would have carried for him when and where he chose, had been knocked out of existence.

With pay so irregular, plunder in those days was the soldier's or seaman's perquisite. They and the freed oarsmen had already laid hands on the best of the portable loot – including the 150,000 gold sequins found in Ali's ornate flagship *Sultana*, with its poop gilded and carved and hung with gold-embroidered green silk awnings; as well as the 40,000 gold sequins accumulated in his piratical raids that summer by the corsair Kara Hodja. Among the allies, the inevitable squabble broke out over prizes and enslaved prisoners and captured guns: the instinctive brotherhood which held them together on the day of glory was not going to last for ever. But Marcantonio Colonna, that man of generous and impartial mind, worked out a compromise. Though by far the poorest among the leaders, Don John gave his own share of prize-money – his tenth as commander in chief – to unlucky men in the ranks, particularly the wounded, who had failed in their own chance of plunder. The city of Messina made him a gift of 30,000 ducats, which he also gave to the wounded.

That night it turned blustery and rainy. The supply ships had not turned up. For several days afterwards, the victors had nothing to eat but Turkish rations of rice and beans. Don John himself, as he began his despatch to King Philip in his cabin on the evening of Lepanto, was dining on a dry ship's biscuit. He wrote generous praise of all his comrades, and made nothing of the wound in his leg ('the cut which I received on the ankle, I hardly know how, having turned out a mere nothing.') He glided lightly over Doria's conduct, and inserted in his despatch a characteristic marginal plea that provision be made by the King for a youngster in the fleet now without legal right, but who had been the acknowledged bastard son of Don Bernadino de Cárdenas, killed in action. He sent to King Philip as souvenir the famous green banner from Mecca, with the name of Allah multitudinously reiterated – and for the next hundred years, until destroyed in a fire, it was a prize piece in the royal collection at the Escorial. The Sultan's imperial banner went to the Pope.

When the lagging supply ships finally caught up with the hungry fleet – at Corfu, on 24 October – there was feasting and three days of fireworks. As reminiscent jokes, boastful anecdotes and pious exaggerations came like a solace to the lips of those who had fought (since few can face in their own minds the bloody reality of a battle), Lepanto like every other such action before or since began imperceptibly to turn into a legend. Don John had given orders – so everyone said, and for once it was true – that María la Bailadora, for her exploit in dressing as a soldier and killing her man, should be borne on the books of her regiment and draw pay. Pius V's ne'er-do-well nephew, Paolo Ghislieri, ransomed by the Pope from captivity only to be driven from Rome for misdemeanour, had been the first man from his ship aboard a Turkish galley. There he had found himself face to face with one Karabaivel, well known to him, said Ghislieri, when he was 'dragging a chain in Algiers'. With a certain regret, so Ghislieri said, since in Algiers the Turk had treated him well, when Karabaivel lunged he was obliged to shoot him in the chest. A bastard son of the marqués de Canete, nicknamed El Marquesillo, condemned for his previous misdeeds to pull an oar in the King of Spain's galleys, had shown such bravery that after the battle was over his officers had a whip-round, and gave him 200 ducats along with his freedom. El Marquesillo gambled the money away and when it was gone went back to his oar as a volunteer. Sir Thomas Stukeley – yet another illegitimate son – furbished up a new reputation for himself in the fight, and another who added lustre to his name that day was young Prospero, Colonna's heir. And there were the antiheroes – the skulkers – crafty old sweats who hid under mattresses when the fighting was on, only to come out and swagger when it was all over.

When news of the victory reached old Don García de Toledo, he shouted with delight, 'Now we must take Jerusalem!' But at Lepanto Don John's fleet had already achieved everything of which it was technically capable. Turbulent winter seas, in which a war galley could be broken into matchwood, were the imminent danger. Veterans of Lepanto ashore in the streets of Naples were to hear themselves reproached not long afterwards – they should have sailed away full tilt and taken Constantinople. That was a landsman's way of looking at the matter – though Sokolli was making much of the threat to the city, and sending out 30,000 men with pick and shovel to fortify Gallipoli within twenty-five days. But with the Grand Vizier you never could tell – he may have set that particular panic going for a political motive many layers deep.

While waiting after battle for the supply ships to arrive, Don John would have liked to sail his more serviceable galleys down the Gulf of Patras and lay hands on Lepanto itself, so as to deprive the Turks entirely of this naval base of theirs in the Adriatic. But so late in the year, even this enterprise had its grave risks. The council of war compromised, giving Doria a chance to redeem himself by leading an attack with 3000 men on nearby Turkish-held Santa Maura. But army engineers reported that the fortifications of Santa Maura would take fifteen days to reduce. Winter storms were approaching, and the project petered out.

In Venice, citizens who not long before had been digging ditches to repel a Turkish landing saw an ominous galley approach, Venetian by her rig, yet with armed men on deck, wearing turbans. Panic spread through the city.

But these 'Turks' were soldiers of the League, larking about with some of the souvenir turbans which after the battle had floated in thousands across the bay. Venetians crowding the waterfront as the galley came closer could see blood-coloured Turkish banners trailing from her deck into the sea, as an emblem of victory. Panic turned to a delirium of joy. All Venice crowded into St Mark's for a *Te Deum*; Venetian festivities went on for days. The victory at Lepanto had been almost too complete. Not once for the next seventy years did the Turks dare attack the Venetian Republic, strung out and vulnerable though her empire might be. In losing her fear, Venice had also lost her need for allies.

In Rome, celebrations were more theatrical, yet more decorous.

'We think we shall all die with joy,' wrote Cardinal Pacheco, who had helped negotiate the League, when the good news spread through the city. The Pope had not slept for three days. He was in secret agony with stones in his bladder. But now the Pope and all about him, said Pacheco, were *locos de placer* – crazy with pleasure. Remembering that Don John had been – as he saw it – the answer to his own prayers for a leader, Pius V quoted to them triumphantly from the Gospel: *fuit homo missus a Deo, cui nomen erat Joannes* – there was a man sent from God, whose name was John.

On 4 December 1571, a bright, dry winter's day, Marcantonio Colonna, dressed against the cold in fur-lined black silk mantle, white boots, crimson breeches, and displaying the Order of the Golden Fleece on his breast – the aristocratic Order of men devoted to the fight against the Turk – entered Rome astride a white jennet. Behind him, chained in pairs and wearing red and yellow liveries like an operatic chorus, marched 120 Turkish prisoners. The Rome Pius V had reformed would allow a procession, but there was to be no costly banquet – the money would be set aside instead to give dowries to orphan girls. The streets were crowded, and the watching Romans knew that had the battle of Lepanto been lost by Colonna and his brother admirals – and very few expected him to win – then those captive Turks might have been marching through the streets of the Red Apple as conquerors.

King Philip's news of the victory came to him by an overland courier from Venice, some time before Don John's despatch arrived. Their father Charles V had been well known for never changing his expression whether told good news or bad, and Philip tried to emulate him in everything. Impassively after glancing at the despatch he told the priests to go on with vespers. Afterwards he announced the news with stolid calmness and asked them to sing a *Te Deum*.

For 'the victory' as King Philip described it 'which Our Lord has seen fit to give our fleet', a Mass has been said every year since in Toledo Cathedral – as it has in Santa Maria Maggiore, the parish church of Rome – and Don John's pennant is there in Toledo on show. King Philip's first response to Don John's despatch had been fulsome: 'I cannot express the joy it has given me to learn the particulars of your conduct in the battle. Happy am I that it has been reserved for one so near and dear to me to perform this great work.' But to the papal nuncio at his court, the Spanish King remarked frigidly, 'Don John risked much and came out victorious. But he might have lost the battle.' Apart from the King's usual morbid suspiciousness, fed by hints from ill-intentioned courtiers, there was henceforth in King Philip's attitude to his immensely popular half-brother a whiff of the secret envy felt for the active hero by the man who governs with the pen.

With the Turkish fleet destroyed, Spain for the time was without a rival in the Mediterranean large enough to challenge her or check her. The response of the nominally Catholic King of France to the great victory was secretly to offer Sokolli a firm alliance against Spain. ('They would be happy to lose one eye,' Alva had said sarcastically, of the French, 'if we lost two.') In besieged Leyden, Dutch Calvinists there who followed the Prince of Orange wore little brass crescents in their caps. But though excommunicated by the old Pope as a heretic and treated by him as a usurper, Elizabeth of England showed greater political penetration. For her, Lepanto was not so much a victory for Spain or the Pope as a triumph for all Christendom – a guarantee that the values upon which Western Europe had been established would survive. To show exactly what she thought, the Church of England which she had established by law was ordered to hold services of thanksgiving.

In 1572, a new star blazed for seventeen lunar months in the heavens – the first such star, men whispered, since Bethlehem. But religion and statecraft, in so many ways incompatible, had been brought together at Lepanto for only a brief alliance. Already, tensions of national interest were pulling the League this way and that. The afterglow of its mood of exultation lingered on elsewhere, among men not chiefly interested in national advantage or political power, and found expression in painting and literature.

The Venetians had made their city itself a work of art. For them a question of very great importance was how best the victory could be celebrated in painting. The Doge wanted a large mural in the Hall of Scrutiny of the Ducal Palace – but the greatest living painter, Titian, who was ninety, declined the task as being too much for him. His other important patron, King Philip, would no doubt be willing to accept a more manageable work. A coming man, Jacopo Robusti – called Tintoretto – offered to complete a large wall painting on the theme of Lepanto in a year, and for no fee, and to take it down again if a better painting should turn up within the next two years. The commission made Tintoretto's name. Titian later sent to King Philip, for his private collection, a less immense canvas, which skilfully celebrates at one and the same time both the sea victory and the birth of a royal heir. Philip of Spain, with a prostrate and turbanned Turk at his feet, holds up his little son, while an angel swoops down on him, and in the middle distance the Sultan's fleet is afire. The elements would seem to be rather incompatible, but Titian brings them together, and in the Prado the casual observer may be perplexed as he goes by, but he is also touched.

The Spanish poet, Fernando de Herrera, celebrated the battle with his resonant *Canción de Lepanto*, still a standard anthology piece, but the deeper literary echoes of Lepanto come later on. The penetrating irony of *Don Quixote* clearly has its origin on 7 October 1571, when as two young men of the same age, Cervantes and Don John alike attained in terms of action the high point of their lives. Action, intention, belief, illusion – for thirty years Cervantes meditated the profounder significances of that one day, before distilling them in *Don Quixote*.

At twelve, a lonely, bookish little prince was given 'Lepanto' as a theme for a poem. He was the future King James I of England, son of Mary Queen of Scots. His mother was heir to Elizabeth's throne, but imprisoned – and, eventually, decapitated – for her Catholic belief. The little boy was kept strictly apart from his mother, and as a precaution had been handed over by the Scots nobility to the scholar George Buchanan, so as to have Calvinism drummed into his head. (Years later, when he was King of England, the mere thought of George Buchanan would give James I nightmares.) But Lepanto had been a cause near to his mother's heart – she had once even expressed her willingness to marry Don John. Swept away by boyish enthusiasm, little James produced 11,000 lines in ballad metre. But when in 1591 his juvenilia were published, in Edinburgh, the Kirk felt obliged to add this apologetic note: 'it was far contrary to his degree and religion, like a mercenary poet, to pen a work in praise of a foreign Papist bastard.'

Another intelligent and receptive boy of seven had almost certainly begun his first term at Stratford Grammar School in Lepanto year. For the next five years his master there was an Oxford man called Simon Hunt, secretly a Catholic, and so single-minded that in 1576 he went into exile, joining the 'poor English' at the newly founded English College at Douai – he was to become an eminent Jesuit. In many of Shakespeare's plays, buried reminiscences of Lepanto re-echo. Othello goes to serve the Venetians in Cyprus; there are kings in

Tunis; there are dukes called Prospero, and the diffused tone of magnanimity characterizing what was best at Lepanto is found all through both Shakespeare and Cervantes, in the masterpieces of two great literary languages. The ripples of waves go enormous distances.

13
Honour and Necessity

Liberty . . . an infectious disease which goes on
infecting one neighbour after another, if the
cure be not properly applied.
DON JOHN to the Emperor Rudolph, 14 January 1578

Faith must be the result of conviction and should
not be imposed by force. Heretics are to be
overcome by arguments, and not by arms.
ST BERNARD OF CLAIRVAUX

In Constantinople that winter there was a frenzy for building galleys.
Even in the Sultan's pleasure gardens along the Bosphorus there were
temporary slipways. The launching of this new fleet was overseen by
Ochiali, and by 8 May 1572 the French ambassador was reporting to
his King that the Turks had built 150 galleys in five months.

They were manoeuvrable, on the model of Algerine corsair galleys,
but lightly gunned, and the guns were badly cast. These new galleys
were not meant for fighting pitched battles – most of them were
cheaply knocked together, from unseasoned wood – but for making
their presence felt, as a high card in the diplomatic game.

Ochiali bought up 20,000 arquebuses, to re-equip his bowmen, and
energetically rounded up substitutes for the oarsmen lost at Lepanto.
Rebellious Greeks in the Morea who had nursed hopes of seeing Don
John as their king were enslaved wholesale. Muscle power for the new
galleys was marched to Constantinople from imperial possessions as
remote as Basra on the Persian Gulf: many dropped down dead on the
road. The French sold Ochiali sails; the Dutch rebels traded him oars,
spars and cordage. One day, when he happened to be at his wits' end
to find 500 anchors, Ochiali was told by Sokolli, 'Pasha, the wealth
and power of this empire can supply you, if needful, with anchors of
silver, cordage of silk and sails of satin: whatever you need for your
ships, you have only to come and ask.'

Despite the Grand Vizier's high-flown encouragement, naval warfare on the Lepanto scale was costly, and was soon accentuating in
both the Ottoman and Spanish empires the baffling economic ailment

of inflation. By 1574 the Turks had so devalued their currency that the janissaries were complaining of being paid in coins 'light as the leaves of the almond and worthless as drops of dew.' In 1575, the Spanish state formally declared itself bankrupt. Worse still, both Sultan Selim and King Philip had been at the prolonged expense of putting down revolts. The Arab uprising in the Yemen – source of coffee, incense and spices – was said to have cost the Ottoman Empire two million ducats a year, at a time when the Venetians were estimating the total annual Ottoman revenue as between seven and eight million ducats. Spain had been financing an army perhaps as large as 60,000 men, under the Duke of Alva, to crush the revolt in the Netherlands. And the cost every year of sending out the Holy League fleet was 4,000,000 ducats, of which Spain had to find half. Plunder was splendid, but the men in the ranks were not working productively, the requisitioned supply ships were not trading. The war was invisibly burdensome.

In the Holy League alliance, Venice was the weakest link. Venice paid for her daily bread by trade and banking – and the war, now in its third year, had brought her trade almost to a standstill. Sokolli's plan, therefore, was to shadow-box with his new galleys – without ever risking them in combat – until he had broken the Venetians' will to fight. Sultan Selim in a typical flight of fancy put the case thus: 'When the Venetians sank my fleet they only singed my beard. But when I captured Cyprus I cut off one of their arms.' In fact, supreme power had no more charms for Selim. By adding Cyprus to the Empire he had satisfied tradition. Selim now withdrew to the harem – leaving government to Sokolli his Grand Vizier – and so wholeheartedly did he indulge his private pleasure that in December 1574 at the age of fifty he died, worn out.

His successor was Murat III – Shakespeare's Amurath. Joseph Micas delivered to the new Sultan his customary weekly hamper of safe food and choice wine, only to have it contemptuously refused. Micas's vast political influence – and his health, too, he suffered from gall-stones – declined rapidly. He was lucky to die with his fortune more or less intact.

Sultan Murat III had inherited the throne after killing off his five younger brothers – the usual procedure. He was avaricious to the point of mania. His bed in the harem was placed above a pit filled with treasure – he fathered 100 sons. In 1579 he is alleged to have intended killing all the Jews in his dominions, and to have changed his mind only because of the enormous backsheesh offered him by the Jewish community. The allegation has been denied – but Murat's plan is consistent with his own reputation, and with the mood of the times. The genial Turkish tolerance of People of the Book, Jew or Christian, had worn thin.

The Jews were able for a while to count on the good offices of Joseph Micas's old ally Esther Kyra – once the most beautiful woman in the harem, though now grown fat. She used her great influence in the harem to deflect Murat III from harming her people; then came the day of reckoning. Esther Kyra was stabbed to death in the Vizier's Yard, dragged by ropes downhill to the centre of the city, and left in the streets to be eaten by stray dogs. Next day her son was killed, and dragged to the same place, but by then (says the chronicler) the dogs were surfeited.

With King Philip it was often hard to know whether he delayed a vital decision from neurotic procrastination or deep policy. Pope Pius V had died of his malady on 1 May 1572, so there was no one at the heart of things to shame King Philip into a summer of effective action, which this year would in fact have been in Venice's interest rather than his own. Philip sent no orders for Spanish galleys to play their proper part in the fleet the Holy League sent out in 1572, until the campaigning season was half over. The chance of following up quickly the stunning victory at Lepanto was lost. Don John hung about on shore with mounting impatience, while the odds and ends of his fleet – Venetian, Papal, Maltese, Florentine – were taken out to sea by Marcantonio Colonna. Any hope there might have been of striking quickly and recovering Cyprus was let slip. King Philip did not really care about Cyprus.

All that summer the Turks went on avoiding the risk of another Lepanto. They outnumbered Colonna by 200 ships to 126, yet he could never bring them to battle. But one bizarre incident showed that the passionate popular hatred of the Turks, which had contributed so much to the great victory, was still latent.

Hamet Bey, a nephew of the great Barbarossa's, was a Turkish commander notorious for his cruelty. The adroit Santa Cruz cut out Hamet Bey's war galley from the rest of the Turkish fleet, and brought up his own flagship to engage. Along the Turkish galley slave benches, the hope of revenge and escape again blazed up. Hamet Bey's stroke oarsman felled him with one blow. Heedless of whip or

scimitar, the manacled slaves passed the body of the Turkish captain
they so detested along the benches from one rower to the next. Their
teeth – their only weapons – had been sharpened by hunger. Each man
took a bite from the living flesh – and after a hundred such bites from
his galley slaves, and before Santa Cruz could board his prize, Hamet
Bey was dead.

The Venetians knew that if the war dragged on, they had nothing to
look forward to except bankruptcy – and for them, bankruptcy meant
starvation. Publicly, however, the Venetians dissimulated, as was
their way, asserting in confident voices that next year, 1573, they
would like to see 300 galleys sent out, and 60,000 men. Blandly they
asked the Pope if he would let them pay their share of next year's
hypothetical fleet by taking over church property in Venice. The Pope
was astute enough to limit his help to a money grant of 100,000 ducats
This was just as well, for on 7 March 1573 the news broke that Venice
had signed a separate peace.

From the terms of this peace, as Voltaire was later to remark, one
might well suppose that at Lepanto the Venetians had lost. Sokolli had
driven the hardest of bargains. Yes, Venice might have back her old
privileges in the Levantine spice trade. But Venetian prisoners of war
must all be ransomed – though Turkish prisoners were to be sent
home gratis. Venice was to pay 2500 sequins of tribute annually for
Zante and Cephallonia, as well as war reparations of 300,000 sequins
by instalments over three years. In any one year, Venice could send
out only sixty of her galleys – whereas the Sultan might send out 300.
As a rebuff to King Philip – the unpopular overlord of so much of Italy
– the Turks solemnly undertook to protect the integrity of Venice
against any future attack by Spain. The treaty was that classic diplomatic turnabout, the Reversal of Alliances.

The new Pope, Gregory XIII – remembered nowadays for his
reform of the calendar – went into a towering rage when he heard all
this. Don John, however, then in Naples, took it more calmly. He
walked alone to the end of the mole, hauled down the crucifix banner
of the League with his own hand, and ran up in its place the flag of
Spain. He at once cancelled the licence granted to Venetians to buy
corn in Sicily – but men noticed that he carefully avoided language
calculated to exasperate Venice. By this time in his life, Don John
identified himself so closely with the Holy League and its objectives as

no longer to form his political judgements exclusively as a Spaniard. About some of the policies emanating from Madrid he had misgivings. The romantically chivalrous boy had become a man profoundly at odds with the trend of his time. He had begun to think and act in terms of European Christendom and its unity on the eve of an age of violent nationalism, which in its dying convulsions was to leave the Europe we know almost destroyed.

Venice had struck a better bargain with the Turks than might appear. An indemnity of 300,000 sequins, though it sounded enormous, was in fact no more than the cost of keeping the Venetian fleet at sea for about four months. The Republic got back in exchange her Levantine trade and all her empire, minus Cyprus. Sokolli was a man surviving from a past age – his brilliance masked the Ottoman Empire's weakness. The Venetians had guessed correctly that Constantinople was hollow at the heart. With the decay of the Sultanate and the exemplary defeat at Lepanto, the tide of Turkish aggression was on the ebb. Their bargain with Sokolli bought the Venetians seventy years of peace – and during that long interim, the gimcrack galleys of Ochiali's rapidly built fleet rotted to tinder at their berths.

With Venice out of the game, the allied fleet was predominantly Spanish – and hardly large enough to fight a pitched battle with the Turks, even were Ochiali rash enough to offer one. But in the summer of 1573, King Philip could have made use of it to strike a blow on his own account. Spain had a long-established right to Tunis – seized by Ochiali only a few years before, when he turned his back on the plight of the Moriscos. Recapturing the city where in years gone by his father Charles V had won his great crusading victory had a certain appeal to King Philip's sense of what was right.

Spain still maintained a useful foothold nearby, at La Goletta – the fort commanding the entrance to the channel which runs from the shallow bay of Tunis, vivid with flamingoes and stinking with sewage, out to the open sea. The Spaniards had at their beck and call another puppet king – Muley Mahomet, brother of the unpopular King of Tunis whom Ochiali had so unceremoniously turned out, and a man descended, according to legend, from Melchior, the third Wise Man at Bethlehem. Taking Tunis with the Holy League fleet should be straightforward – though holding the city afterwards might well be less easy.

King Philip's order to go ahead and capture Tunis arrived almost disastrously late – but by a combination of dash and skill Don John brought it off. The allied fleet did not leave Sicily for Tunis until 7 October 1573 – the second anniversary of Lepanto. But next day Don John was off La Goletta with 104 galleys, forty-four supply ships, and 19,280 infantry, Spanish, Italian and German. The Turkish garrison retreated inland from Tunis itself to the holy city of Kairouan, and bided its time. Muley Mahomet was installed on his brother's throne. Overdue repairs to the decrepit fortifications of both Tunis and La Goletta were put in hand. But 1 November 1573, with the city once again a Spanish protectorate, Don John was on his way back to Sicily. The conquest had been deceptively sudden and complete.

After his brief campaign, Don John had this time kept for himself a piece of the plunder – a lion cub from the ruins of Carthage 'which lived and slept in his room'. Back in Sicily he found waiting for him an intelligence report which gave warning that next year the Turks had in mind to send out a fleet bigger than ever. When a Greek who had been caught spying for the Sultan was delivered up to him, Don John not only reprieved him from the gallows, but showed him all over his naval base at Messina. He then sent the Greek back to his Turkish paymasters in Constantinople with this message: 'although I could have put him to death, not only did I save his life, but afforded him every leisure to see my provisions and plans – which are to wage perpetual war against you.'

The Turks were more in awe than perhaps they need have been of Spain's worldwide empire – and they had by this time a considerable respect for Don John. Some of his more expansive gestures – like heaping captured children of the harem with presents, and sending them home without exacting ransom – had struck the Turkish imagination. Don John was well aware of all this, and played his hand accordingly. But even the largest of his gestures would hardly save Tunis, if King Philip should lack the will to defend his new possession.

King Philip had begun to fear that their loss of Tunis might provoke the Turks into carrying on indefinitely this expensive naval war. Sokolli the Grand Vizier now held the high cards. He had already made known his terms for a treaty, and they were severe. ('If the King of Spain wants peace he will have to pay tribute, and sacrifice some castles in Sicily.') The fleet the Sultan was sending out in 1574, though still too gimcrack to risk battle, would in mere numbers be larger than the Turkish fleet Don John had destroyed at Lepanto. In both Tunis and La Goletta fortification had been scamped. As Ochiali and Sinan, the Sultan's admiral, arrived offshore, the former Turkish governor of Tunis marched on the city's feebly held landward side with several thousand Bedouin irregulars. By 23 August, after a five-week siege, the stronghold of La Goletta fell. Tunis was lost almost as quickly as it had been won.

And what was the Holy League fleet doing all this time? Swinging at anchor off Sicily, only a day distant by fast galley. And the orders received by Don John that summer from King Philip had been almost past belief. He was forbidden to risk his galleys to save Tunis. If for some reason the fleet did put to sea, Don John was to hand over his command to that stiff-jointed and cautious veteran, Don Garcia de Toledo — or, still worse, to Gianandrea Doria. Finally, should the galleys ever be obliged to leave port, Don John was to go into hiding ashore, but have it put about on his behalf that he was actually at sea, with the fleet. Since an abject secret of this kind can never be kept, its intention was clearly to undermine Don John's good name among his own men — to make him out a liar and a coward. Don John returned to Madrid, where these intrigues against him had their origin, telling his half-brother in advance, with his usual candour, 'I have left my post and incurred the guilt of disobedience rather than the certainty of dishonour.'

After Tunis, someone behind the scenes began systematically making trouble for Don John, though he was never to discover who or why. King Philip might sometimes be afflicted by moods of envious mistrust but he tried always to render strict justice to his more popular half-brother. These days, however, his morbid fears were being played upon by a master hand.

Ruy Gomez, to whom Don John had written letters during the Morisco campaign 'as to a father', had headed the Peace Party at court — those who had believed, rightly, that Alva's policy of terror in the Low Countries would end in disastrous failure. In 1573 Ruy Gomez died, and his place as minister was taken by Antonio Perez — a man outwardly serene and omnicompetent, but secretly walking a tight-rope like any Turkish vizier, where one small lapse of judgement might mean his ruin.

Perez was only a few years older than Don John, and he too was illegitimate — his father had been Charles V's secretary, and he had been legitimated, as a favour, by imperial diploma. King Philip relied on Antonio Perez to an unprecedented extent. The new minister proved to have an almost uncanny knack of anticipating what the King would want to do next. Perez could disentangle the King's secret thoughts with such precision because he had seduced the King's mistress.

Though by force of will and with the help of prayer King Philip did all he could to repress his aberrations, he was the grandson of Juana la Loca, he even looked like her, and this sad physical heritage betrayed itself in astounding lapses. While engaged impassively in some rigid court ceremonial or other, the Spanish king would lose control of himself and start babbling lewd scandal, or he might break into the screaming giggles. In his amours, Philip was furtive. The handiest congenial woman after Ruy Gomez's death had happened to be his widow, the Princess of Eboli – a fascinating creature, with the piquant slight disfigurement of a drooping eyelid. Her marriage with Ruy Gomez had left the Princess with a grasp of high politics, so the King had at last someone to confide in. The liaison suited him, giving him from time to time a pause in his life of endless toil. But the Princess passed on all the King's political secrets to her no doubt more sprightly lover.

Perez had reason to fear that one man at court might have penetrated his secret – Don John's secretary, Juan de Escovedo. Perez clearly envied Don John. As usual in such cases, he credited the man he disliked with more malice and cunning than Don John in fact possessed. He snatched at the obvious expedient: to discredit Don John, so that should Escovedo ever confide in him, and Don John pass it on, whatever the King's half-brother could reveal might not be taken at its face value. Small and morbid doubts about Don John – as about almost everybody else – were already fermenting in King Philip's mind. Antonio Perez set himself to exaggerate them.

His ascendancy over the King was of course a wasting asset. Perez fell off his giddy tightrope at last. On 28 July 1579 King Philip, having stumbled upon the facts of the case, at once ordered the arrest of his hitherto all-powerful minister-traitor. But the years between were bad ones for Don John. The King went on giving him difficult tasks, but met all his pleas for support with pathological mistrust.

The reward Don John had asked for himself as a return for his great services to the Spanish crown betrays how King Philip's pinpricks over the years had left him scarified. Don John asked to be accepted as an Infante – an authentic child of the royal house – even though the least important and the lowest in rank, yet with a clear right at last to the title of Highness. But such a promotion would in theory bring Don John a small step closer to the throne; it could be twisted so as to confirm some of the suspicions that Antonio Perez had been planting in King Philip's mind. The King gave his half-brother an inexplicably frigid refusal.

Pope Gregory XIII made matters worse by reiterating the opinion first ventured by Pope Pius V, that for his great services Don John deserved a throne. The Pope suggested the throne of Tunis, a proposal King Philip found it easy to counter with sarcasm. Then the Pope nominated Don John for, in his own words, 'the Enterprise of England, it being much desired, as has already been shown by the English Catholics, that he should become their King, by marriage to Mary Queen of Scots.' The Enterprise of England had a flavour of knight errantry – the rescue of an imprisoned queen – and was baited with the half promise of a throne. The intrigue was well advanced – Mary Queen of Scots expressed her willingness to marry Don John, when the question was put by her secret agent, an intrepid Jesuit called Nicolas Sander. King Philip assured Don John that for his own part, 'if all goes well with this Enterprise of England it will please me to see you settled there.' But the attractively baited hook proved to be more than Don John could swallow.

Girolamo Lippomano, Venice's ambassador in Naples, was asked in the summer of 1575 to send home to the Senate one of those confidential but coldly accurate delineations of a political figure which the Republic found of use in its diplomacy. Lippomano describes Don John as being a man of middle stature, well made, of beautiful countenance and admirable grace. He dressed sumptuously and had no rival in the management of horses. Nor was he at all ashamed – reported Lippomano – of being a natural son, though he was regretful that the Emperor had not provided for him otherwise than by dependence on the Council of Spain. For relaxation, Don John would play tennis for hours at a time, putting his whole heart into the game. He was, moreover, 'wise and very prudent, eloquent, wary, dexterous in business,' and 'careful to seek his pleasure with those women who are in the habit of intriguing with princes'. He spoke French 'excellently well' and understood German and Flemish. Clearly this was someone older and wiser than the eager boy who had earned his spurs fighting for King Philip in the Alpujarras.

The Enterprise of England – the papal scheme for toppling from her throne the heretic Queen of England, Elizabeth, and putting in her place her Catholic rival and legal heir, the imprisoned Mary Queen of Scots – had one gross defect. It was based on false information, provided by men who had been losing touch with reality. The English Catholic exiles upon whose advice the Pope was obliged to depend were still living in the past – in the brief reign of Mary Tudor – and hoping against hope for a chance to turn the clock back and restore the preeminence of their own faith. They were yearning for miracles. Among them, however, was one experienced military man, Sir Thomas Stukeley, Henry VIII's presumptive son and Don John's comrade in arms at Lepanto. Stukeley was already neck-deep in the rescue plot. When cross-questioned carefully by Don John, he spoke of a plan so simple as to be slapdash. He would put a detachment of men ashore somewhere handy on the English coast, and gallop them hell for leather across country to Sheffield Castle, hoping to set Mary free by taking her guardians there by surprise. Stukeley went on to boast confidently that with 3000 men he could conquer England (though to crush the ineffectual Catholic rising of 1569, Elizabeth had needed to call out an army 14,000 strong).

Don John gently pointed out that a landing such as Stukeley had in mind could hardly pass unnoticed. When Elizabeth got to hear even a rumour of it – and Sir Francis Walsingham's spies were everywhere – she had merely to remove Mary Queen of Scots to some other prison, and the galloping rescuers would not know where to look. Any landing in England, even a small one, would rally the realm around Queen Elizabeth. 'To all which objections,' Don John reported to King Philip, 'he answered by making light of them, as is the way with men driven from home, and longing to return.'

After serving as Don John's right-hand man at Lepanto, Luis de Requeséns had been sent by King Philip to the Low Countries, as governor, in the vain hope that the damage caused there by Alva's brutality could be patched up by making a few small concessions to the rebels. There were in fact only two measures which might have given confidence to Catholic and Protestant alike: toleration of unorthodox religious beliefs, and the giving back to the seventeen provinces of all their ancient liberties. But these were what King Philip would never willingly grant. In the midst of his impossible task, Luis de Requeséns unexpectedly died.

King Philip could usually see clearly in any such crisis of government, though he might act slowly. The revolt in the Netherlands against royal authority was led by William Prince of Orange, Charles V's one-time favourite, and someone Philip had intensely disliked for his charm and supple intelligence and obstinate deviousness even as a youngster. William since then had made a great name for himself in the world, as spokesman for Protestantism and rebellion. As his governor, King Philip needed a spokesman of equal prominence and authority on the Catholic side of the question. There was no one to match Don John.

Whatever the King's secret misgivings – and Perez was sedulously fostering them – Philip deferred to this obvious political necessity. Don John was ordered north to the Low Countries, in Luis de Requeséns' place. The last great confrontation of Don John's career was to be with a worthy antagonist – a man well aware that he represented the future.

William of Orange – Holland's national hero – is better known abroad as William the Silent. But though confidence inspiring, the nickname does not give a true picture of the man. 'Silent' is a tactful mistranslation of *shluwe*, meaning wily or sly. William's use of language to animate his followers, mislead his opponents or hide his own thoughts was masterly. Nor was he a puritan – though by the age of forty, having been once a Lutheran and twice a Catholic, he was taking the sacrament in the Calvinist manner with his hat on. That was no more than a clever gesture, meant to reassure the Calvinist militants who were his best soldiers.

In 1558, William had shocked the Diet of Princes out of their wits by informing them that in his opinion adultery was no sin. His annual income when a young man had been enormous – over 170,000 florins. But he lived so extravagantly that he was soon a million in debt to the moneyed merchants of Antwerp, many of them Protestant sympathizers. William first became well acquainted with the burgher class, which later was to sustain him politically, by going to them for money.

His radical supporters were even better reassured when for his third wife William married a runaway nun, Charlotte de Bourbon, who had turned Calvinist from bitter personal conviction. Her highborn family had forced her into a convent at the age of twelve, to save money on her dowry; she eventually became abbess. When she came across Calvin's *Institutes*, Charlotte adopted the new and persuasively argued religious standpoint as her own, escaped over the convent wall, and went to the limit by falling in love with the middle-aged widower, William of Orange, who was the hero of the Calvinist cause. Charlotte in fact made William a splendid wife, even winning praises from her mother-in-law, who described her as 'distinguished by her virtue, her piety, her great intelligence, in sum, as perfect as he could desire her.' Their happy marriage also won the approval of William's extremist followers – who differed from their leader in being intolerant of any other view than their own.

As a public man who had shifted his ground several times with little inner difficulty, William was unlikely to have developed – as they had – the tastes of a persecutor. 'To see a man burned for doing as he thought right,' William once said, 'harms the people, for this is a matter of conscience.' Though he might shift his own religious allegiance for a political advantage, William's private conviction was that every variety of belief should be tolerated. Catholics and Jews were Netherlanders too: how better than by sinking their doctrinal differences could they be united against the Spanish oppression, which threatened both? Toleration with William of Orange was not an expedient but a principle – a view highly original in his own day, and one which marks him off as a great man of a different stamp from Don John.

Although Don John usually exercised the power allowed him by the King in ways that for the time he lived in were generous and humane, the mere idea of religious toleration would have been too much for him to swallow. He had come to manhood inside a ruling class which regarded liberty as an infectious complaint – something inexplicable which made hitherto loyal people ungovernable. Was it not obvious that only when all the people under a government were of one mind in their profounder values of conduct and belief – their religion – could a nation be brought into being and held together? How could any government long survive that tolerated heretics? Spain in the course of her long war with Islam had proved all this up to the hilt.

When at the age of twenty-eight he took over the Netherlands – chief source of the imperial revenue – from his father Charles V, King

Philip had been disgusted by what he found there. He spoke no
Flemish and hardly any French, but he could see that the Catholics of
the great trading towns were dangerously easy-going. They did business freely with Lutherans, Anabaptists, Calvinists and Jews; they
connived at their differences in belief. And revenue would be more
plentiful if each of the seventeen provinces did not have its distinct and
jealously guarded laws, traditions, local government and taxation. To
wipe out all these discrepancies and impose on the Netherlanders
equal laws worked out by their monarch for their own good was
justifiable in Philip's eyes both politically and morally. He had no
intention of ruling over heretics. The Netherlands – prosperous,
various, turbulent, civilized – were to be brought to heel by army and
Inquisition, and governed at the centre, by Philip himself, with a slip
of paper, as was Spain and her vast overseas empire. Having put this
doctrinaire plan in motion, Philip of Spain left the Low Countries,
never to return. There had been trouble ever since.

Defiance of his authority always brought out the worst in King
Philip, and he was never a man to find cruelty repugnant. Against the
advice of better-natured and more discerning men like Ruy Gomez,
the King had sent the Duke of Alva to the Low Countries with a large
army and orders to sow terror. The method employed by Alva's
'Council of Blood' is still being used by oppressive governments in
our own day: they went for the potential ringleaders. The Council
began by compiling a list of all who had publicly shown any independence of mind – men of learning, men of property, courageous
officials, religious dissidents, personalities who might be capable of
heading a local resistance. Those on the list were arrested, tortured to
yield up yet more names, sent peremptorily to the block, and had their
property confiscated to pay Alva's army. The mood of systematic
horror at the time is given expression in Pieter Breughel's *Massacre of
the Innocents*, painted in Antwerp towards the end of his life. Flemish
women in a snow-covered landscape clutch their murdered babies.
The deed was done by soldiers, Herod's men, led by someone with
Alva's face.

This time of terror made a different man of William. The high-living
aristocrat, since boyhood a servant of the crown, became a tribune of
the people. He used the printing press skilfully to organize opinion
against Spain. He raised little armies in Germany, and marched them
over the border to take on the huge Spanish occupation forces. His
men were nearly always beaten in the field, but their mere audacity

kept hope alive. William himself was lucky enough to survive Alva's terror – at Nassau-Dillenburg he had a base beyond Alva's reach – though it killed off many of his friends. His immense Netherlands estates were confiscated. His eldest son, a student at Louvain, was kidnapped and shipped off to a Spanish prison. William himself tasted poverty and exile. But his sublime, almost arrogant persistence won through; the tide turned.

Some of the Channel pirates, calling themselves the Beggars of the Sea, had adopted a patriotic and Calvinistic stance. They were difficult men to handle, ready to plunder both foe and friends alike. But when they captured the port of Brill in the estuary of the Rhine, they acknowledged William of Orange as their chief. In the name of his own little principality, William gave the pirates regular commissions: the rebels now had a navy. By stiffening the local militia with Calvinistic volunteers from abroad – Scots, English, French, German, Swiss – he put together a little army which at least was disciplined if not yet capable of fighting a pitched battle.

Since the King of Spain had recently acknowledged himself bankrupt, he had no credit just at present to call upon in the European money market. Were he to try sending bullion by sea to pay his soldiers, the Channel pirates lay in wait. Spanish troops had once been frugal, loyal and proud. Even though long unpaid, they would probably have kept their discipline – most European armies of the time were irregularly paid. But under Alva they had been used for too long as armed bullies. Terrorism as a system of government reacts upon the morale of those who use it.

On 8 November 1576, King Philip's army marched mutinously into Antwerp, and the 'Spanish Fury' began. The city was the centre of gravity of the European financial system, and immensely rich. Guicciardini, an Italian merchant trading there, had declared in 1560 that more business was done in Antwerp in a fortnight than in Venice in a year. Though Antwerp's official creed was Roman Catholic, almost every belief was represented there, from Anabaptism to Islam. The Spanish soldiers had prided themselves on being Catholic, but once inside the walls of Antwerp, the constraints and loyalties of their religion meant less than nothing to them. The city was sheer plunder. The infection of a pernicious kind of freedom was upon them: they were mad for money. From unpaid soldiers they became greedy bandits overnight.

The English poet, George Gascoigne, an eyewitness, wrote thus of the Spanish soldiers in his *The Spoyle of Antwerp*: 'They spared neither friend nor foe, Portingale or Turk: the Jesuits must give their ready coin and all other religious houses both coin and plate. Within three days Antwerp which was one of the richest towns in Europe had no money or treasure to be found therein, but only in the hands of murderers and strumpets.' The Spanish soldiers indiscriminately killed off 7000 citizens, and burned down a third of the city. By seeking to make religious loyalty the tool of power politics – as did caesars, sultans, tsars, kaisers and commissars before him and since – King Philip ended not only by disrupting the armed force upon which his authority ultimately depended, but in wrecking the very civil society his government was in existence to preserve.

This was William's chance. In the entire Netherlands, only William's little rebel army was capable of maintaining everyday law and order. Netherlanders were willing to identify William of Orange, at least for the time being, as their one guarantee against state-sanctioned cruelty. The war was not over by a long way – in a desultory fashion it would last for eighty years. But for Philip of Spain, the crisis had come – his moral right to govern in the Netherlands, inherited from his father, was almost extinct. The decision had already been taken in Madrid to send the victor of Lepanto to the Low Countries, as the new governor.

King Philip had ordered Don John to save time by riding across France – the direct way to the Netherlands, but a route the French would have liked to bar to Spanish officials. He was to go on horseback, in a cavalcade of not more than twelve riders, carrying not more than 20,000 ducats with him for the expenses of his government – taken from the fleet's treasure chest. Nor was he to tell the Pope what route he would be taking (though the Pope, who by this time tended to think of Don John as his own man rather than King Philip's, found out soon enough).

Don John had tried to lay down conditions. He had been brought up as a boy by a Flemish musician, and knew the language. He already understood something of the people he would have to deal with. His father the Emperor Charles V had at the outset of his life been a popular Duke of Burgundy. His mother, Barbara, was still an uproarious figure in the nightlife of Antwerp and Brussels. And his years in the service of the Holy League had by this time given Don

John a clear insight into the shortcomings of Spanish policy: it could be both dilatory and bigoted. Don John wanted King Philip to give up his plan of centralizing the administration in the Netherlands – soon to be pointless, since after the shock of the Spanish Fury the King's writ ran in only two of the seventeen provinces. As a new governor from whom better things might be hoped, Don John could then gain support by offering the rebel provinces some of their ancient liberties back. Vengeance was no part of Don John's nature – he asked for the right to pardon. He tried also to extract a guarantee that the money needed to carry on his government would be regularly forthcoming – but with the King's credit at such a low ebb, that would be asking too much.

Don John made an irregular detour to kiss goodbye to Magdalena de Ulloa, his widowed foster mother. He then stained his face with walnut juice, and went over the Pyrenees, disguised as his friend Octavio Gonzaga's Moorish groom. He knew enough about horseflesh – and everyday village life – to pass muster as a groom in a wayside inn. Gonzaga passed through France almost unnoticed, as a private gentleman travelling with three servants.

In Paris Gonzaga put up at an inn across the street from the Spanish embassy, and let the ambassador, Don Diego de Cuniga, know that they had arrived. The same night in the palace of the Louvre there was to be a royal ball. The dark-faced, well-attired and self-possessed young stranger – such a good dancer – drew attention to himself that night by falling helplessly in love. Everyone watched him partner the notorious Marguerite de Valois, La Reine Margot, sister to the effeminate King Henri III – the *femme fatale* among Catherine de' Medici's four degenerate sons – and drew their own conclusions. Margot was witty, intelligent, unprincipled, freethinking and free-living. Her literary talent would have kept her name alive had she been born a nobody.

Not long since, and for reasons of state, Margot had gone through a form of marriage with the Protestant leader, Henry of Navarre. But rumour went that she had at the same time been the mistress of the duc de Guise, who led the militant Catholic party. La Reine Margot was apt to take lovers at random, for their looks and stamina, but she also relished an explosive mixture of passion and power. That evening at the Louvre, Don John's personal fascination alone, quite apart from his rank and fame, would have been enough to flutter her. But Margot also knew that a liaison with Don John might lead to pickings for the

French royal family. He could win back the southern provinces of the Netherlands – modern Belgium – only with French goodwill. Why should those provinces not one day be ruled over by her royal brother, Anjou, at present unemployed?

Don John had never fallen in love with a woman so clever and so decadent as La Reine Margot: she bowled him over. 'Her beauty,' he confided to a friend, 'is more divine than human – fitter to destroy men's souls than save them.' At their passionate parting the two of them agreed, whatever the obstacles, that they must somehow meet again. From then on for the remainder of his life, every step Don John took led him downhill.

In Paris Don John evidently found himself emotionally as well as politically in another world. Religion here in the contentious north was no longer what it had been for the best of them at Lepanto – the very centre of a man's life. Often it was a mere party label, to be changed at will; it might even become a badge of shame. Guise's extreme Catholic party had invited all the best-known Huguenots to a conference in Paris, only to slay them on St Bartholomew's Day in cold blood – such a deed of perfidy as would have disgraced a Turkish Sultan. The massacre had been prompted by the Queen Mother, Catherine de' Medici, who notoriously 'did not believe in God'. It had been approved of by her depraved son the King. But it had been carried through by solid and hard-working citizens, the fervently Catholic members of the Paris guilds.

The significance was draining from the code of chivalry which had meant so much to the heroes of Lepanto. And Don John's European rivals – not entirely tongue in cheek, either – were already beginning to expropriate the values of chivalry much as they had expropriated the lands of the church, the patrimony of the poor. Instead of adoring the Blessed Virgin, as they had done with such fervour in the medieval past, Englishmen were making a public cult of their Virgin Queen. The first great English poet openly to attach himself to the Protestant cause, Edmund Spenser, was about to elaborate all this in his *The Faerie Queene* – written in a beleaguered castle in the violent, romantic and tormented Irish countryside. His poem showed how the rhetoric of knight errantry could be used just as easily to embellish the Protestant side of the question. In the Low Countries, Sir Philip Sidney, that pattern of the English gentleman, was to fight and die on the side of William of Orange. The virtues of the gentleman were perfectly acceptable as guise or mask to the acquisitive governing class of

Protestant England, which would be unremittingly engaged for centuries to come in foreign conquest. In Paris, the myth that had sustained Don John's life of action and given it a moral content began no longer to ring true for him. The crisis of his life was approaching.

On 3 November 1576 Don John reached Luxembourg, the nearer of the two provinces still loyal to King Philip. He had gone there to carry out a difficult preliminary duty imposed on him by the King.

Don John's mother, the once fascinating Barbara, had become a wild and extravagant middle-aged woman. The pension of 200 ducats allowed her by Charles V on his deathbed had since been increased to 3000 ducats, yet she always overspent. 'To send her money,' the Duke of Alva had warned Madrid, 'is to throw it into the sea.' In years gone by she had been irresistible; now, at fifty, she was impossible.

In Lepanto year, King Philip and the Duke of Alva together had quietly agreed that this dissipated and unmanageable woman should be removed from public view. Alva sweetened Barbara's disposition towards him by paying her debts, then in September 1571 he almost managed to trick her aboard a ship 'going to Antwerp' – but in point of fact heading for Spain, with orders to shut her up there in a convent. Barbara outwitted her would-be kidnappers – and from then on she made herself a thorn in their flesh.

According to the Venetian ambassador, the scandal caused in the Low Countries by his mother's presence had been used against Don John by his enemies at court, when the need to send him there as governor was being argued. Barbara was already being used as a backstairs means of getting at the new governor. For instance, Mary Queen of Scots had recently interceded with the Countess of Northumberland, a Catholic noblewoman exiled to Liège, to procure the release from prison of another exile called Stanton. Instead of waiting for Don John's arrival and asking him directly, the countess tried to make sure by first winning over his mother. This kind of thing was more than King Philip proposed to allow.

In Luxembourg, Don John saw his mother face to face for the first time since he had been taken away from her by force, as a small boy. But this meeting of mother and son could hardly be a spontaneous outpouring of emotion. Don John was there to make his mother yield to the King's will. He was to persuade her to go away, voluntarily and without fuss, on board a warship in a convoy soon leaving for Spain.

He got his way with Barbara – for her son's sake she would go to the
Spanish convent. He was her own flesh and blood – brave, handsome,
and irresistible. He overcame her much as other men had done, but
Barbara had always known a way to get her own back. Her triumphant parting shot left Don John with a poisoned and rankling wound
for the rest of his life. 'It was a mistake,' she is said to have remarked,
loud enough for others to hear, 'to call him the son of the Emperor.'
While Barbara was sharing the Emperor's couch and nursing his gout,
a handsome artilleryman had also taken her fancy.

The climate was detestable; the heavy drinking and coarse debauch
which in the Low Countries were everyone else's solace did not appeal
to him in the slightest; the people here were 'walking wineskins'. Don
John soon found himself plunged, as he put it, into a 'Babylon of
disgust', and, worse still, 'without a single person in whom I can
confide.' He saw very clearly what he was up against as governor,
writing to King Philip with uncourtierlike directness to warn him that
'in the Netherlands, the name of Your Majesty is as much abhorred
and despised as that of the Prince of Orange is loved and feared.' He
advised Philip to prepare for 'a rude and terrible war' because the
money-minded Dutch were by this time sure that Spain must be at the
end of her financial resources. (They were wrong. Silver from the
apparently inexhaustible mine of Potosí in Bolivia was soon to give
the Spaniards a second wind.)

In the gloomy situation there was one glimmer of light. When
William of Orange preached tolerance to his followers he was seldom
listened to. The zealous Calvinists who served as the backbone of his
little army and fleet were convinced, as such men usually are, that
none but themselves could possibly be in the right. Unless William
kept his hand firmly upon them, they tried to have everything their
own way.

In the wake of William's army, embittered exiles were returning to
the cities in the south where Calvinism had maintained a clandestine
presence even under Alva. Some began using force to make their own
minority creed preponderant. Calvinist militants would seize a
Roman Catholic church, gut out the art, whitewash the walls, break
down the altar, and use the shell of the building to propound their own
sombre services. A propaganda trick they were fond of was to discredit the Franciscans – men well regarded even by non-Catholics for

their simplicity of life and their work among the poor – by hauling them up in front of some magistrate of the revolutionary persuasion on a charge of sodomy. This doctrinaire aggression, by alarming the peaceable Catholic majority in the south, played into Don John's hands. Everyone hated Philip of Spain, but some began to have better hopes of Don John.

William of Orange was alive to the danger of identifying his own cause with that of the unpopular Calvinist fringe, good soldiers though they might be. The more friends won by Don John, the greater the risk that at least in the south, William of Orange himself might be isolated. The Prince of Orange underestimated Don John at first, assuring his followers that the new governor was no different from Alva except in being 'younger and more foolish, less capable of concealing his spite and his plans, and more impatient to imbrue his hands in our blood.' Yet it had begun to dawn on people that this new governor was no persecuting torturer.

Don John presided with a fixed smile at convivial burgher banquets where most of the guests were liable to end the festive evening on their faces under the table. At Louvain, at a fête held by the five guilds entrusted with the university city's defence, he borrowed a crossbow and was the first man to knock down the popinjay, winning the gold badge for marksmanship against all comers and the title 'King of the Year'. In the spring of 1578, an English spy called Fenton sent in a report, describing what had begun to happen in the neighbourhood of Don John's camp at Hainault, in the Catholic south. Don John paid for all supplies, and had put down pillage. He treated the peasants fairly. 'By these humanities,' wrote the spy, 'he maketh deep impression in the heart of the people, and so changeth the course of the war that he beginneth to make less, in the popular sort, the hatred universally borne to the nature of the Spaniard.' Not only did Don John restore where he could the Netherlanders' traditional privileges. He would, in matters of religion, have been glad to return to the good old days of Charles V, when appearances were saved by maintaining Catholicism as the official creed, but a blind eye was turned to the more respectable forms of Protestantism.

This kind of tacit toleration in religion would also have suited Queen Elizabeth of England, by easing the pressure exerted on her by those extremists on her Council who wanted her to make war against Spain on behalf of the Dutch. In politics Elizabeth could see a long way ahead. An endless proxy war in the Netherlands, led by disrespectful

plebeian revolutionaries, might in the long run threaten the monarchi-
cal system itself. (In point of fact only a few months after the frontiers
of Holland were settled and the war finally ended by the Treaty of
Westphalia, English puritans were cutting off the head of her royal
successor, Charles I.)

As Don John's quiet effectiveness began to gain him ground, there
were plots to kidnap or even kill him. To these plots William of
Orange was usually privy – a measure of his fear of what might
happen if Don John kept the initiative. Suppose Don John disarmed
the Netherlanders' vigilance, so that their hatred of the Spaniards
waned. What was to stop King Philip sending in yet another Duke of
Alva?

Another Spanish army – though much smaller than Alva's – was
already on the march. On 15 December 1577, Alexander Farnese,
small, fine-drawn, dark, intelligent, Don John's close friend since
boyhood and his comrade at Lepanto, reached the Netherlands with
10,000 reinforcements, 4000 of them being Frenchmen obligingly sent
by the duc de Guise in expectation of favours to come.

In the tradition begun at Malta and Lepanto, a company of English
volunteers served with Alexander Farnese. They were recognizably
the predecessors both in style and demeanour of the next century's
Cavaliers (or *caballeros*). A larger force of Englishmen of the opposite
conviction, perhaps six times as many, was already serving under the
banner of William of Orange. They were the unmistakable precursors
of the Roundheads, so many of whom gained their first military
experience in the prolonged Netherlands war. Oliver Cromwell –
with a nice sense of historical symmetry – was eventually to turn a
profit by selling off some of his Cavalier prisoners of war to the
Venetians – as galley slaves.

On 31 January 1578, on the field of Gemblours, Alexander Farnese's
army, under a crucifix banner harking back to Lepanto – *In hoc signo
vici Turcos in hoc Hieraticos vincam* – scattered William's Dutch zealots
and foreign volunteers with disconcerting ease. Most of the Scots
Presbyterian volunteers were taken prisoner, and they expected harsh
treatment for meddling in a quarrel not their own: Don John let them
all go free.

Alexander Farnese like others who had known Don John in the past
could not help noticing when he met him again in the Netherlands

that his physical radiance was gone. He looked pale and thin, and in these aguish lowlands had already suffered three bouts of fever. Though by patient sagacity he had won a breathing space, all his work so far had been done in the midst of cloud and drizzle, treachery and drunkenness, fear and mistrust. Some in Don John's household noticing the change in him even suspected slow poison. The choice put to him in early manhood by the terms of the Emperor's will had begun to appear to him unfortunate. He regretted now not having devoted his life to religion. He 'could think of nothing save to turn hermit, a condition in which a man's labours, being spiritual, could not be entirely in vain.'

Sir Francis Walsingham, the lawyer who ran Queen Elizabeth's astoundingly efficient secret service, was also spokesman on her Council for those extreme Protestants who wanted to help William of Orange by going to war. Walsingham was yet another prepared to contemplate simplifying his problems by assassinating Don John. Locked up in the Tower of London he had at his disposal a man called Radcliffe – said to be an earl's bastard, another of these natural sons who flicker through the political half world of the time. Sir Francis Walsingham saw to it that Radcliffe understood clearly what was expected of him. He was then released from the Tower and crossed the Channel in the guise of an English Catholic going surreptitiously into exile. Using religion as a pretext he was to gain an interview with Don John, then stab him with a poisoned dagger.

But in London the Queen's master spy was himself spied upon by the King of Spain's ambassador, Don Bernadino Mendoza. Warning came in time, and Radcliffe was seized when an arm's length from Don John in his audience chamber. As soon as Don John got to know of the ugly pressure put upon Radcliffe by Walsingham he characteristically, though the man had been caught red-handed, used his 'power of pardon' to save him from the gallows.

Only a few days later, Don John found himself conferring face to face with the man who had planned to have him stabbed. Sir Francis Walsingham happened to be visiting Don John on a diplomatic mission from Queen Elizabeth: murderer and victim looked one another in the eye, and spoke courtesies. Since that Sunday morning in 1571, when Don John, with *Real* heading straight at the Turkish flagship, had danced a galliard on the poop from sheer joy, he had come to inhabit a different moral world. Walsingham made a private note of their encounter. Don John had impressed him. 'I never saw a gentle-

man,' he wrote, 'for personage, speech, wit and entertainment comparable.' But he claimed to have observed, as well he might, 'a great
conflict in himself between honour and necessity.'

To make sure of the southern Netherlands, Alexander Farnese needed
there a base to work from which had good communications with his
Catholic allies in France – the equivalent in the south of the Prince of
Orange's Brill.

Namur, where the rivers Sambre and Meuse came together, was
guarded by a fortress on a rock five hundred feet above the river. Don
John moved to Namur, partly to escape for a while the ever-present
risk of assassination. He also had his eye on the fortress. But there was
a private motive too. La Reine Margot – 'fitter to destroy men's souls
than save them' – was on her way to Spa to take the waters. From
Liège she would make a detour, and meet Don John at Namur.

During those few days, the grey and humdrum little town was as
lively as had been the courts of Italy, when young Don John was the
hero of the Holy League, with every woman's eye upon him. Queen
Margot – tall, dark-haired, high-complexioned, and with a foot, so
they said, as small as a child's – approached along the Liège road,
looking out for him through the glass windows of a litter with gilt
pillars, the inside lined with scarlet velvet. Ten ladies of honour rode
side-saddle behind her, then came six chariots with servants and her
guards.

Don John had gone to meet her at the head of an escort of splendidly
equipped horsemen. Springing from the saddle he kissed Queen Margot on the cheek, and conducted her into Namur. Now that the sun
had gone down, all the shops and streets there were brilliantly illumi-
nated with candles in her honour. The apartments he had prepared for
her were magnificent. The bed hangings in her chamber were
embroidered with heroic scenes from the battle of Lepanto – the last
thing she would see before his kisses closed her eyes.

Next day began with a high Mass to the sound of trumpets. There
was a picnic on an island in the river. As they rowed across in a gilded
barge, they were saluted with music by waterborne musicians. After
dark, by torchlight, there was dancing on the grass. The citizens and
garrison were all so bemused by this organized enchantment that Don
John's men found it easy to climb the rock not long after, and seize the
citadel.

Hardly had Don John provided Alexander Farnese with the impregnable base he would need for his long-term plans when he was dead. Typhoid fever came down upon him so unexpectedly that afterwards there were those who spoke of poison. Don John died at Namur under the low roof of a pigeon cote, hurriedly scrubbed out when he fell ill, so as to shelter him from the weather. But there was this time to be no dangerous interregnum. In a lucid interval, Don John signed over all his powers to Alexander Farnese. The appointment was irregular – a defiance of Madrid and its dilatory ways – but it held because there was no other choice. Don John left all he possessed in the world to the King his master – the man who, wrongfully mistrusting him, had harassed him with impossible orders, 'as if war could be waged by words alone'. To his lifelong friend Alexander Farnese he once again confided, privately, his regret at not having gone into religion.

On 1 October 1578 Don John received the last sacraments, and died soon after, delirious, shouting orders in an imaginary battle. His heart was buried at Namur. His carcass, embalmed and cut up in three pieces, was galloped at the saddlebow across unfriendly France by three of his troopers. Once in Madrid the corpse was fitted together again, dressed up in state, and taken to the large chamber in the Escorial designed for the tombs of all the royal family. The mortal remains of Don John are interred alongside the tomb of his father Charles V – if Charles V was indeed his father.

Selected Bibliography

(All titles published in London unless otherwise stated)

ALVAREZ, M. F., *Charles V*, 1976.

ARMSTRONG, E., *The Emperor Charles V*, 2 vols., 1902.

ATIYAH, E., *The Arabs*, 1955.

BOXER, C. R., *The Dutch Seaborne Empire 1600–1800*, 1973.

BRADFORD, E., *The Great Siege: Malta 1565*, 1970.

BRADFORD, E., *The Sultan's Admiral: The Life of Barbarossa*, 1969.

BRANDI, K., *The Emperor Charles V*, 1939.

BRANTÔME, P. DE B. DE, *Vie des hommes illustres et grands capitaines étrangers de son temps*, Paris, 1594.

BRAUDEL, F., *The Mediterranean and the Mediterranean World in the Age of Philip II*, 2 vols., 1978.

BRENAN, G., *The Literature of the Spanish People*, 1962.

BYRON, W., *Cervantes*, New York, 1978.

CAMBON, H., *Don Juan d'Autriche, Le Vainqueur de Lepanto*, Paris, 1952.

CERVANTES, M. DE, *The Adventures of Don Quixote*, trans. J. M. Cohen, 1950.

CURREY, CDR E. H., *Seawolves of the Mediterranean: The Grand Period of the Moslem Corsairs*, 1910.

DISRAELI, I., *Literary Character of Men of Genius*, n.d.

ELLIOT, J. H., *Imperial Spain 1469–1716*, 1972.

FISHER, SIR G., *Barbary Legend: War, Trade and Piracy in North Africa*, Oxford, 1957.

GIBB, E. J. W., *A History of Ottoman Poetry*, 6 vols., 1900–1909.

GRAVIÈRE, J. DE LA, *La guerre de Chypre et la bataille de Lepanto*, Paris, 1888.

GUGLIELMOTTI, A., *Storia della Marina Pontifica*, 10 vols., Florence, 1856.

GUGLIELMOTTI, A., *Marcantonio Colonna*, Florence, 1862.

HABSBURG, O. VAN, *Charles V*, 1970.

(HADJI KHALIFAH), *Histoire des guerres maritimes des Ottomanes*, Constantinople, 1728.

HAMMER, J. VON, *Histoire de l'empire Ottomane*, trans. J. J. Hellert, 18 vols., Paris, 1835–43.

HERRE, P., *Barbara Blomberg*, Leipzig, 1909.

HUIZINGA, J., *The Waning of the Middle Ages*, 1924.

THE KORAN, ed. G. Sale, n.d.

LEA, H. C., *History of the Inquisition of Spain*, 2 vols., New York, 1905–8.

LYBYER, A. H., *The Government of the Ottoman Empire in the Time of Suleiman the Magnificent*, Harvard, 1913.

MARCH, J. M., *La batalla de Lepanto y Don Luis de Requeséns*, Madrid, 1944.

MARGOLIOUTH, D. M., *Mohammedanism*, 1911.

MARMOL, L. DE, *Historia de rebelión y castigo de los Moriscos del reino de Granada,* Granada, 1600.

MATTINGLEY, G., *The Defeat of the Spanish Armada*, 1962.

MAXWELL, SIR W. S., *Don John of Austria*, 2 vols., 1883.

MENAVINO, G. A., *Trattato de costumi et vita de Turchi*, Florence, 1548.

MENDHAM, REV. J., *The Life and Pontificate of Saint Pius V*, 1882.

MENDOZA, D. H. DE, *La guerra de Granada*, Valencia, 1776.

MERRIMAN, R. B., *The Rise of the Spanish Empire*, 1934.

MEYER, A. O., *England and the Catholic Church under Elizabeth*, 1916.

MORE, T., *The Dialogue concerning Heretics*, 1528.

MOTLEY, J. L., *The Rise of the Dutch Republic*, 3 vols., 1856.

PARRY, J. H., *The Spanish Seaborne Empire*, 1973.

PASTOR, L. F. A. VON, *The History of the Popes from the End of the Middle Ages*, 10 vols., 1891.

PIRENNE, H., *Histoire de la Belgique*, 7 vols., Brussels, 1906–26.

RODGERS, VICE-ADMIRAL W. L., *Naval Warfare under Oars (4–16 C)*, Annapolis, 1939.

ROTH, C., *The Duke of Naxos*, Philadelphia, 1948.

SIMPSON, R., *The School of Shakespeare*, 1878.

SLOCOMBE, G., *Don John of Austria: Victor of Lepanto*, 1935.

SUAU, P., *Histoire de St Francis de Borgia*, Paris, 1910.

UNAMUNO, M. DE, *Vida de Don Quijote y Sancho*, Madrid, 1966.

WEDGWOOD, C. V., *William the Silent*, 1944.

WILLIAM OF MALMESBURY, *Gesta Regum*, ed. W. Stubbs, 1887–9.

YEO, M., *The Greatest of the Borgias*, 1936.

Index